GLOBAL STRATEGIES
AND LOCAL REALITIES

Global Strategies and Local Realities

The Auto Industry in Emerging Markets

Edited by

John Humphrey
Institute of Development Studies, University of Sussex

Yveline Lecler
Institute of East Asian Studies, University of Lyon

and

Mario Sergio Salerno
Production Engineering Department, Polytechnic School
University of São Paulo

in association with

GERPISA

Réseau International
International Network

Groupe d'Etudes et de Recherches Permanent sur l'Industrie et les Salariés de l'Automobile
Permanent Group for the Study of the Automobile Industry and its Employees
Université d'Evry-Val d'Essonne - Centre de Recherches Historiques (EHESS-CNRS)

First published in Great Britain 2000 by
MACMILLAN PRESS LTD
Houndmills, Basingstoke, Hampshire RG21 6XS and London
Companies and representatives throughout the world

A catalogue record for this book is available from the British
Library.

ISBN 0–333–80485–6

First published in the United States of America 2000 by
ST. MARTIN'S PRESS, LLC
Scholarly and Reference Division,
175 Fifth Avenue, New York, N.Y. 10010

ISBN 0–312–23307–8

Library of Congress Cataloging-in-Publication Data
Humphrey, John, 1950–
Global strategies and local realities: the auto industry in
emerging markets/by John Humphrey.
p.   cm.
Includes bibliographical references and index.
ISBN 0–312–23307–8 (cloth)
1. Automobile industry and trade.   2. International trade.
I. Title.
HD9710.A2 H85 2000
382′.456292 – dc21
99-086557

This book is printed on paper suitable for recycling and made from fully
managed and sustained forest sources.

10   9   8   7   6   5   4   3   2   1
09   08   07   06   05   04   03   02   01   00

Printed in Great Britain by Antony Rowe Ltd, Chippenham, Wiltshire

Contents

v

List of Tables

List of Figures

List of Abbreviations

ACMA	Automotive Component Manufacturers' Association (India)
ADEFA	Asociación de Fábricas de Automotores de Argentina
AFTA	ASEAN Free Trade Area
AIC	ASEAN Industrial Co-operation
AICO	ASEAN Industrial Co-operation Organization
AMIA	Asociación Mexicana de la Industria Automotriz
ANFAVEA	Associação Nacional dos Fabricantes de Veículos Automotores (Brazil)
ASEAN	Association of South East Asian Nations
BBC	Brand-to-Brand Complementation
BU	Built-up
CBU	Completely Built-up
CEPT	Common External Preferential Tariff
CIS	Commonwealth of Independent States
CKD	Completely Knocked Down
CMEA	Council for Mutual Economic Assistance
ERMs	Emerging Regional Markets
EU	European Union
FDI	Foreign Direct Investment
FSO	Fabryka Samochodow Osobowyh
GATT	General Agreement on Tariffs and Trade
GDP	Gross Domestic Product
GERPISA	Groupe d'Etude et de Recherche Permanent sur l'Industrie et les Salariés de l'Automobile
GNP	Gross National Product
IMF	International Monetary Fund
IMVP	International Motor Vehicle Program
IPMs	Integrated Peripheral Markets
JIT	Just in Time
MPV	Multi Purpose Vehicle
NAFTA	North American Free Trade Area
NATO	North Atlantic Treaty Organisation
NCAER	National Council of Applied Economic Research
NMT	Non-motorised transport
OECD	Organisation for Economic Co-operation and Development

OICA	Organisation Internationale des Constructeurs d'Automobiles
PAMs	Protected Autonomous Markets
PLEMA	Periphery of Large Existing Market Areas
SKD	Semi Knocked Down
SMMT	Society of Motor Manufacturers and Traders
TRIMs	Trade-Related Investment Measures
UNECLA	United Nations Economic Commission for Latin America
UNEP	United Nations Environmental Programme
VRDL	Vertical Regional Division of Labour
VOCs	Volatile Organic Compounds
WHO	World Health Organisation
WTO	World Trade Organisation

Foreword

Over the next few decades, will 'lean production' and a generalised deregulation of trade have become the norms for the international environment in which firms and political and economic spaces will be operating?

The GERPISA Group (Groupe d'Etude et de Recherche Permanent sur l'Industrie et les Salariés de l'Automobile), a French-based research network devoted to the study of the automobile industry and its labour force, has been transformed into an international network of researchers whose backgrounds cover a wide range of social sciences (economics, business, history, sociology, geography and political science). From 1993 to 1996, the Group carried out an initial international programme entitled, 'The Emergence of New Industrial Models'. This examined whether existing industrial models were effectively starting to converge towards the principles of 'lean production' – as had been theorised by MIT's International Motor Vehicle Program (IMVP) team. By focusing on what was happening in the automobile industry, the GERPISA group's work was able to demonstrate the great diversity and divergence in the trajectories that firms have been following in recent times. Examples have been the wide spectrum of product policies; of productive organisations and labour relations; and the hybridisation of production systems in the new spaces towards which firms have been expanding. There is no 'one best way' today – there never has been, and there probably never will be. In fact, the first GERPISA research project identified not one, but three industrial models, all of which have been in operation since the 1970s: the Toyotaist model, the Honda model and the Sloanist model (epitomised today by Volkswagen, not GM). This made it possible to construct theories that can explain the processes which had led to this multiplicity of models. Companies follow different profit strategies. In other words, their attempts to increase their profitability cause them to favour certain policy combinations rather than others (for example, volume and diversity, quality and specialisation, innovation and flexibility, the ongoing reduction of costs in a zero growth environment, volume, etc.). However, in order to be efficient, all of these strategies have to fit in with the environments in which they are to be applied – especially with respect to the modes of income growth and distribution that are being practiced in the spaces under consideration. Moreover, to form an 'industrial model', made of an 'enterprise–government compromise' between the main parties (that is, shareholders, management, unions, workforce and suppliers), the strategies need to be implemented coherently.

Since 1997, GERPISA has been running a second international programme, entitled 'Globalisation or Regionalisation?'. This project, due to last until the year 2000, has been testing the thesis that globalisation is an imperative for corporate profitability, and that it is the inevitable consequence of the deregulation of trade in the 'new' automobile spaces. This is the logical extension of the first programme, given that 'lean production' is often presented today as the most suitable model for markets which are variable and diversified, and which are ostensibly moving towards a single global standard. Firms are establishing themselves across the four corners of the planet; new industrialised nations are emerging, as a result of their having opened up to international trade; and more recently, certain vehicle makers have been at the heart of some mega-mergers. All of these events have supported the thesis of globalisation, a process which is supposedly driven by the fact that companies, in their efforts to benefit from economies of scale, and from improved costs structures, are forever increasing their organisational integration, and are doing this on an ever greater geographical scale. The opening of the new spaces to more extensive trade, which some expect to create a homogenisation of demand, is also deemed to contribute to this process.

The present study constitutes a first attempt to put this hypothesis to the test, and it does so by focusing on the situation in the emerging countries. The main objective here is to scrutinise a concept that is being presented nowadays as if it were self-explanatory: economic globalisation. Are we in fact witnessing the total convergence of world-wide automobile policies, of markets, and of the job conditions in the emerging countries? How are the automobile manufacturers' subsidiaries organised in these areas, and what types of relationships do they maintain with their home office? How much hope should the companies be placing in the development of these countries? Will they be able to find the volumes which they can no longer hope to achieve in the industrialised countries' markets? The authors contributing to the present volume have all emphasised the diversity of the productive and spatial configurations which can be observed in the emerging countries.

As a result, GERPISA's upcoming publications will aim to carry out a systematic description and analysis of the trajectories of internationalisation that are being followed by the various types of firms which are involved in the automobile industry (manufacturers, suppliers and dealers). They will also focus on the trajectories that are being followed in the different spaces (in the industrialised and emerging countries, in the regional groupings), and they will test the hypothesis that these spaces are diverse and divergent. If these studies succeed in validating this hypothesis, they will then attempt to identify and characterise the different processes of periodic re-heterogenisation, and the conditions that are necessary if firms, and spaces, are to be successful. Moreover, within this perspective, they will be particularly keen to analyse the steps that are being taken in order that the trajectories of firms and spaces can be adjusted and hybridised – actions which in all probability will require considerable strategic and organisational inventiveness.

GERPISA's books are not only the result of the work done by their authors, and by the co-ordinators who have assembled and edited them. Through their participation in the international meetings, and in the annual symposiums, the members of the programme's international steering committee, and the other members of the network, have contributed to various degrees to the discussions, and to the general thought process. In addition, the books would have never seen the light of day had it not been for GERPISA's administrative staff, who take care of the tasks that are part of the daily life of an international network. We thank them all.

MICHEL FREYSSENET
YANNICK LUNG
Scientific coordinators of the GERPISA programme
'Globalisation or Regionalisation?'

The Steering Committee of the Gerpisa Programme 'Globalisation or Regionalisation?' is made up as follows:

Annie Beretti (PSA Peugeot Citroën), Robert Boyer (*CEPREMAP, CNRS, EHESS*, Paris), Juan José Castillo (Complutense University, Madrid), Jean-Jacques Chanaron (CNRS, Lyon), Elsie Charron (CNRS, Paris), Jean-Pierre Durand (University of Evry), Michel

Freyssenet (CNRS, Paris), Patrick Fridenson (EHESS Paris), Takahiro Fujimoto (University of Tokyo), John Humphrey (IDS, University of Sussex), Bruno Jetin (University of Paris XIII), Ulrich Jurgens (WZB, Berlin), Lydie Laigle (CSTB Paris), Yveline Lecler (IAO, Lyon), Yannick Lung (IERSO, University of Bordeaux IV), Andrew Mair (University of London), Jean-Claude Monnet (Renault), Daniel Raff (University of Pennsylvania), Mario Sergio Salerno (University of São Paulo), Koichi Shimizu (University of Okayama), Koichi Shimokawa (Hosei University), Giuseppe Volpato (Ca Foscari University, Venice).

PARTICIPANTS IN THE GERPISA PROGRAMME 'GLOBALISATION OR REGIONALISATION?'

Argentina

Julio Cesar Neffa (PIETTE, Buenos Aires), Marta Novick (General Sarmiento University, San Miguel), Martha Roldán (FLACSO University, Buenos Aires), Jorge Souto (INDEC, Capital Federal), Julia Vera (INDEC, Capital Federal), Miguel Zanabria (Ministerio de Industria, Buenos Aires).

Australia

Greg Bamber, (Griffith University, Brisbane), Russel Lansbury (University of Sydney).

Belgium

Michel Albertijn (Tempera, Antwerpen), Leen Baisier (Stichting Technologie Vlaanderen, Bruxelles), Rik Huys (University of Leuven), Geert Van Hootegem (Universiteit Leuven), Johan Vanbuylen (European Centre for Work and Society, Bruxelles), André Vandorpe (Stichting Technologie Vlaanderen, Bruxelles), Isabel Yepez del Castillo (University of Leuven).

Brazil

Ricardo Alves de Carvalho (University of Belo Horizonte), Glauco Arbix University São Paulo), Luis Paulo Bresciani (DIEESE,

UNICAMP, Campinas), Luis Antonio Cardoso (University of Rio de Janeiro), Nadya Araujo Castro (Federal University of São Lazaro), Jussara Cruz de Brito (Cesteh, Rio), Edna Castro (Federal University of Belem), Afonso Fleury (University of São Paulo), Cândido Guerra Ferreira (Federal University of Minas Gerais), Gerson Koch (Curitiba), Mariano Laplane (UNICAMP, Campinas), Michel Marie Le Ven (Federal University of Minas Gerais), Roberto Marx (University of São Paulo), Magda Neves de Almeida (Federal University of Minas Gerais), Ruy de Quadros Carvalho (UNICAMP, Campinas), Sergio Queiroz (UNICAMP, Campinas), Mario Sergio Salerno (University of São Paulo), Rosa Maria Sales de Melo Soares (Brasilia), Fernando Sarti (UNICAMP, Campinas), Leila Maria da Silva Blass (University of São Paulo), Mauro Zilbovicius (University of São Paulo).

Canada

Wayne Lewchuk (McMaster University), Charlotte Yates (McMaster University).

Colombia

Anita Weiss de Belalcazar (Universidad Nacional, Bogotá).

France

Annie Amar (IREP-D, Grenoble), Kamel Amazouz (University of Paris XIII), Béatrice Appay (CNRS, Paris), Michel Aribart (Ministry of Industry, Paris), Denis Audet (OECD, Paris), Etienne de Banville (CNRS, Saint-Etienne), Laurence Baraldi (IREP-D, Grenoble), François Beaujeu (University of Paris IX), Kémal Bécirspahic dit Bécir, (University of Evry), Marie-Claude Bélis-Bergouignan (University of Bordeaux IV), Ben Bensaou (INSEAD, Fontainebleau), Annie Beretti (PSA Peugeot–Citroën), Anca Boboc (LATTS, Paris), Gérard Bordenave (Université Bordeaux IV), François Bost (University of Paris X) Norman Bower (OCDE), Frédéric Bourassa (Paris), Robert Boyer (CEPREMAP, CNRS, EHESS Paris), Joël Broustail (University of Pau), Christophe Carrincazeaux (University of Bordeaux IV), Béatrice de Castelnau (CCFA, Comité des constructeurs français d'automobile, Paris), Didier Chabaud (University of Cergy Pontoise), Jean-Jacques Chanaron (CNRS, Lyon), Elsie

Charron (CNRS, Paris), Pierre Chastanier (University of Nice), Thomas Chieux (ICDP Paris), Bertrand Ciavaldini (PSA Peugeot-Citroën), Yves Cohen (EHESS Paris), Philippe Colin (Renault), Christophe Collard (EDHEC, Lille), Gabriel Colletis (Commissariat général du Plan, Paris), Guy Cornette (University of Evry), Emmanuel Couvreur, (Renault), Isabel Da Costa (IRES, Paris), Frédéric Decoster (Renault), Yves Doz (INSEAD, Fontainebleau), Michel Dupaquier (Nantes), Gabriel Dupuy (CNRS, Paris), Jean-Pierre Durand (University of Evry), Joyce Durand-Sebag (University of Evry), Saïd El Mankouch (INRETS, Arcueil), Béatrice Faguet-Picq (INTEC, Evry), Simone Feitler (Renault), Michel Freyssenet (CNRS, Paris), Patrick Fridenson, (EHESS, Paris), João Furtado (University of Paris XIII), Eric Gabison (ISMEA, Paris), Christophe Gallet (University of Lyon II), Philippe Gambier (University of Paris XIII), François Gardès (Paris), Gilles Garel, (CRG, Paris), Isabel Georges (CSU, Paris), Xavier Godard (INRETS, Arcueil), Armelle Gorgeu (CEE, Paris), Nicholas Grant (Institut de gestion sociale, Paris), Nathalie Greenan (INSEE, Paris), Françoise Guelle (IAO-MRASH Lyon), Dominique Guellec (OCDE), Pierre Guenebaut (Automobiles Peugeot), Gilles Guiheux (Université d'Artois, Arras), Armand Hatchuel (Ecole des Mines, Paris), Nicolas Hatzfeld (University of Evry), Helena Sumiko Hirata (CNRS, Paris), Raphaël Houillon (University of Paris XII), Jean-Paul Hubert (University of Paris XIII), Marie-Noëlle Hume (University of Evry), Hee-Young Hwang (University of Paris X), Didier Idjadi (University of Paris XIII) Bruno Jetin (University of Paris XIII), Maojing Jin (CRH, Paris), Bernard Jullien (University of Bordeaux IV), Young-Cheol Kang (University of Paris I), Alex Kesseler (CRG Paris), Maria Kostopoulou (CIREP, Paris), Hadjila Krifa (IFRESI, Lille), Daniel Labbé (Renault), Andrea Lago da Silva (ESSEC, Paris), Lydie Laigle (LATTS, Paris), Pascal Larbaoui (University of Paris XIII), Xavier Larralde (University of Bayonne), Marc Lautier (Paris), Jean-Bernard Layan (University of Bordeaux IV), Christophe Le Guehennec (University of Paris XIII), Yveline Lecler (IAO-MRASH, Lyon), Xavier Legrand (IEP, Aix-en-Provence), Cédric Lomba, (CSU, Paris), Jean-Louis Loubet (University of Evry), Yannick Lung (University of Bordeaux IV), Jean-Loup Madre (INRETS), Alain MARTIN (Renault), Claire Martin (Renault), Fausto Mascia (University of Bordeaux II), René Mathieu (CEE, Paris), Valérie Mazeau (CSU Paris), Séverin Menard (Paris), Alain Michel (CRH Paris), Christophe Midler (CNRS, Paris), Jean-

Claude Monnet (Renault), Christian Mory (CCFA, Paris), Aimée Moutet (University of Paris X), Jean-Philippe Neuville (CSO, Paris), Anne Nippert (Paris), Jean-Pierre Orfeuil (INRETS, Paris), Claude Parthenay (University of Cergy-Pontoise), Udo Rehfeldt (IRES, Paris), Jean-Philippe Rennard (Paris), Xavier Richet (University of Marne-la-Vallée), Gwenaële Rot (CSO, Paris), Luiz Rothier Bautzer (Paris), Frédérique Sachwald (IFRI, Paris), Laurence Saglietto (University of Nice), Jean-Claude Sardas (Ecole des Mines, Paris), Raphaël Savalle (PSA Peugeot-Citroën), Anne-Marie Schlosser (EAP, Paris), Michel Sonzogni (IREP-D, Grenoble), Jean-Fabrice Traversaz (IRESCO-LSCI, Paris), Jean-François Troussier (IREPD, Grenoble), Graham Vickery (OECD, Paris), Benoît Weil (Ecole des Mines, Paris).

Germany

Peter Auer (WZB, Berlin), Ulrich Bochum (FAST, Berlin), Gerhard Bosch (Institut Arbeit und Technik, Gelsenkirchen), Steven Casper (WZB, Berlin), Rainer Dombois (University of Bremen), Andrea Eckardt (University of Erlangen-Nürnberg), Egon Endres (Technische Universität Hamburg-Harburg), Detlef Gerst (University of Göttingen), Rainer Greca (University of Eichstätt), Bob Hancké (WZB, Berlin), Mike Hoffmeister (ICDP, International Car Distribution Programme, Wolfsburg), Jörg Hofmann (IG Metall), Peter Jansen (WZB, Berlin), Ulrich Jürgens (WZB, Berlin), Holm-Detlev Köhler (University of Erlangen-Nürnberg), Katharina Kohn (Daimler–Benz), Martin Kuhlmann (University of Göttingen), Steffen Lehndorff (Institut Arbeit und Technik, Gelsenkirchen), Peter Lessmann-Faust (University of Dortmund), Ludger Pries (Institut Arbeit und Technik, Gelsenkirchen), Christian Sandig (University of Erlangen-Nürnberg), Eike W. Schamp (Goethe University, Frankfurt-am-Main), Michael Schumann (University of Göttingen), Stefan Speckesser (WZB, Berlin), Roland Springer (Daimler-Benz), Jay Tate (WZB, Berlin), Torsten Vogt (University of Kaiserslautern), Theo Wehner (Technische Universität Hamburg-Harburg), Frank Wehrmann (Volkswagen).

Hungary

Attila Havas (University of Budapest), Csaba Mako (University of Budapest).

India

Avinandan Mukherjee (Indian Institute of Management, Calcutta).

Italy

Franco Amatori (Luigi Boconi University, Milano), Giovanni Balcet (University of Torino), Arnaldo Camuffo (Ca'Foscari University Venezia), Aldo Enrietti (University of Torino), Massimo Follis (University of Torino), Francesco Garibaldo (IRES, Roma), Stefano Micelli (Ca'Foscari University, Venezia), Giuseppe Volpato (Ca'Foscari University, Venezia).

Japan

Tetsuo Abo (Teikyo University), Hisao Arai (Shiga University), Alexandre Beaudet (University of Tokyo), Koshi Endo (Kanagawa University), Takahiro Fujimoto (Tokyo University), Masanori Hanada (University Kumamoto Gakuen), Masayoshi Ikeda (Chuo University), Yasuo Inoue (Nagoya University), Osamu Koyama, (Sapporo University), Hiroshi Kumon (Hosei University), Kazuhiro Mishina (JAIST, Tokyo), Yoichiro Nakagawa (Chuo University,), Hikari Nohara (Hiroshima University), Masami Nomura (Sendai University), Ichiro Saga, (Kumamoto Gakuen University), Shoichiro Sei (Kanto-Gakuen University), Koïchi Shimizu (Okayama University), Koïchi Shimokawa (Hosei University), Takeshi Shinoda (Ritsumeikan University), Kazuo Wada (Tokyo University).

Korea

Myeong-Kee Chung (Han Nam University), Young-suk Hyun (Han Nam University), Hyun-Joong Jun (Séoul University), Byoung-Hoon Lee (Korea Labor Institute, Seoul), Sung-Soon Lee (Sung Kyun Kwan University), Chang-Yeul Park (Sung Kyun Kwan University).

Mexico

Ilan Bizberg (El Colegio de México), Jorge Carrillo (El Colegio de la Frontera Norte), Patricia García-Gutierrez (University of México),

Sergio González López (Universidad Autonoma de México), Fernando Herrera-Lima (University of México), Yolanda Montiel (CIESAS, Mexico City), Selene Villa Méndez (University of México).

Netherlands

Jos Benders (University of Nijmegen), Ben Dankbaar, (University of Nijmegen), Frank Den Hond (Vrije Universiteit, Amsterdam), Job de Haan (Kath. Universiteit Brabant), Arnoud Lagendijk (University of Nijmegen), Anne Sey (University of Nijmegen), Rob Van Tulder (Erasmus University, Rotterdam), Harm Weken (Erasmus University, Rotterdam).

Portugal

Paulo Alves (University of Lisbon), Antonio Brandao-Moniz (University of Lisbon), Oliveira Paula (UNINOVA, Lisbona), Maria Leonor Pires (University of Lisbon), Marinùs Pires de Lima (University of Lisbon), Pedro Pires de Lima (University of Lisbon), Manuel Secca Ruivo (University of Aveiro), Mario Vale (University of Lisbon).

Russia

Léonid Sintserov (Institute of Geography, Moscow).

South Africa

Anthony Black (University of Cape Town).

Spain

Ricardo Aláez (University of País Vasco, Bilbao), Javier Bilbao (University of País Vasco, Bilbao), Vicente Camino (University of País Vasco, Bilbao), Juan José Castillo (Complutense University, Madrid), Jordi Giro (Reus), Juan Carlos Longás (University of Navarra), Javier Méndez (Complutense University, Madrid), Miguel Perez Sancho (University of Valencia), Manuel Rapun (University of Navarra).

Sweden

Christian Berggren (Linköping University), Per Olav Bergström (Metallförbundet, Stockholm), Anders Boglind (Volvo Car), Göran Brulin (Institutet för arbetslivsforskning, Stockholm), Kajsa Ellegård (University of Göteborg), Tomas Engström (Chalmers University of Technology, Göteborg), Henrik Glimstedt (University of Göteborg), Nils Kinch (University of Uppsala), Anders Anders Larsson (University of Göteborg), Lars Medbo (Chalmers University of Technology, Göteborgion), Tommy Nilsson (Arbetslivsinstitutet, Stockholm), Lennart Nilsson (University of Gothenburg), Åke Sandberg (Arbetslivsinstitutet, Stockholm).

Switzerland

Ronny Bianchi (Bellinzona), Winfried Ruigrok (University of St Gall).

Turkey

Lale Duruiz (University of Marmara), Cem Kubat (Eskisehir), Nurhan Yentürk (Istanbul Technical University), Gamze Yücesan (Abant Izzet Basal University).

United Kingdom

Ken-Ichi Ando (University of Reading), Rick Delbridge (University of Wales, Cardiff), Ismail Hakki Eraslan, (University of London), Julie Froud (University of Manchester), Philip Garrahan (University of Northumbria), Colin Haslam (East London University), John Humphrey (University of Sussex), Sukhdev Johal (Royal Holloway University, London), Kevin Maccormick (University of Sussex), Andrew Mair (University of London), Miguel Martinez Lucio (University of Leeds), Andy Pike (University of Newcastle), Daniele Principato (University of Bath), Valeria Pulignano (University of Warwick), David Sadler (University of Durham), Mari Sako, (Oxford University), Paul Stewart (University of Wales, Cardiff), Joseph Tidd, (Imperial College, London), Steven Tolliday (University of Leeds), Karel Williams (University of Manchester), Jérôme Zamblera (Windsor).

United States

Paul Adler (University of Southern California, School of Business Administration), Steve Babson (Labor Studies, Detroit), Bruce Belzowski (University of Michigan, Office Automotive Transportation), Christoph Büchtemann (CRIS International, Santa Barbara), Charles Fine (MIT, Sloan School of Management), Richard Florida (Harvard University, Kennedy School), Michael Flynn (University of Michigan, Office Automotive Transportation), Carol Haddad (Eastern Michigan University, Ypsilanti), Susan Helper (Case Western Reserve University), Ruth Milkman (UCLA), Frits Pil (Pennsylvania University, The Wharton School), Daniel Raff (Pennsylvania University, The Wharton School), Saul Rubinstein (School Management and Labor Relations, New Brunswick), Harley Shaiken (University of California, Graduate School of Education).

Notes on the Contributors

Michel Freyssenet is a Research Director at the National Scientific Research Centre in Paris. He is working on division of labour, industrial models, employment relations and the concept of work. He is a co-director of the GERPISA international network and programmes. His latest book, which was co-authored by Andrew Mair, Koichi Shimizu and Giuseppe Volpato, is entitled *One Best Way? Trajectories and Industrial Models of the World's Automobile Producers*, and his latest article is entitled 'Emergence, centrality and end of work'.

Takahiro (Taka) Fujimoto is a professor in the faculty of economics, Tokyo University, and Senior Research Associate of the Harvard Business School. His main publications in English include: *Product Development Performance: Strategy, Organizatione* and *Management in the World Auto Industry* (1991) with Kim B. Clark, and *The Evolution of a Manufacturing System at Toyota* (1999).

Gilles Guiheux is a graduate in Social Sciences from the Ecole Normale Supérieure de Cachan (France) and has a Doctorate from the Ecole des Hautes Etudes en Sciences Sociales (Paris). He is presently Senior Lecturer in Chinese contemporary history at Université d'Artois (Arras, France) and a researcher at the Institut d'Asie Orientale (Lyon, France), specialising in Chinese, and especially Taiwanese, business history.

Attila Havas is a Research fellow at IKU, Innovation Research Centre, Budapest University of Economic Sciences, working on economics of innovation, impacts of privatisation and FDI on innovation in various industries in Hungary and Central European countries (automotive, electronics, telecommunications equipment manufacturing, instruments, laser technology, etc.) as well as on science and technology policy. Since 1997 he has been on leave from IKU, working as the programme director for the OMFB TEP, Technology Foresight Programme.

John Humphrey is a Professorial Fellow at the Institute of Development ment Studies, University of Sussex. He has researched extensively on global value chains and linkages between developed and developing countries, publishing widely on this topic. He is co-author of a recent book on production organisation and supplier development in India, entitled *Industrial Restructuring: Crompton Greaves and the Challenge of Globalization*, Sage: New Delhi.

Jean-Bernard Layan is a lecturer in economics at Université Montesquieu, Bordeaux. He teaches economic geography and industrial economy. He has published various papers on the automotive industry in emerging countries. He is preparing his PhD thesis on 'Industrial dynamics in the auto industry: a comparison between Mexico and Spain'.

Yveline Lecler, doctor in social sciences (Ecole des Hautes Etudes en Sciences Sociales, Paris), is an associate professor in the Faculty of Economics and Management at the University of Lyon 2 and a Senior Research Fellow at the Institute of East Asian Studies. She has written numerous articles on the Japanese economy, focusing on small- and medium-sized enterprises, subcontracting, purchasing networks, and the globalization issue. She is the author of *Industrial Partnership: Japan as a Reference*, published by L'Interdisciplinaire.

Yannick Lung is Professor of Economics at Université Montesquieu, Bordeaux and Director of the Institut Fédératif de Recherches Dynamiques Economiques (IFREDE). He has published various papers and books on the car industry, recently editing *Coping with Variety* (1999). He is co-director of the GERPISA international programme, 'Between Globalization and Regionalization: What Future for the International Auto Industry?'

Shobhana Madhavan is Principal Lecturer and Director of the Centre for Business and the Environment at the University of Westminster and a member of the Chartered Institute of Transport. Her research interests in the context of developing countries include technology transfer, the motor vehicle industry and rural transport. She is the author of numerous publications in these areas.

Antje Oeter is a graduate in economics with special reference to Latin America from the University of London (QMW/ILAS). She has worked a researcher at the Institute of Development Studies at the University of Sussex focusing on the impact of globalisation on the automotive industry in developing countries, and she is now re-searching in Brazil on the car industry.

Mario Sergio Salerno is an Associate Professor in the Production Engineering Department, Polytechnic School, University of São Paulo, Brazil. He has researched on production and work organisation and published various papers on new forms of production organisation and assembler-supplier relationships, mainly on modular consortium and industrial condominiums. He has written chapters in three previous GERPISA books: *Between Imitation and Innovation, Teamwork in the Autombile Industry* and *Coping with Variety: Flexible Productive Systems for Product Variety in the Auto Industry.*

Yasuo Sugiyama is a doctoral candidate in the Graduate School of Economics, University of Tokyo, and a Research Fellow of the Japan Society for Promotion of Science. He is working on strategy and organisation of product development and impacts of globalisation on them in various industries, as well as on knowledge management within and across organisations. Since 1998 he has stayed at the Wharton School, University of Pennsylvania, as a visiting doctoral fellow.

1 Introduction

John Humphrey, Yveline Lecler and
Mario Sergio Salerno

In the 1980s, debates on the restructuring of the automotive industry focused on the impact of lean production and the restructuring of supplier relations in Europe and North America, largely in response to the success of Japanese companies. In the 1990s, attention shifted towards the globalisation of the automotive industry. The stagnation of vehicle production and sales in the Triad regions (North America, Western Europe and Japan), together with the startling performance of the automotive industry in wide range of emerging markets, put the issue of globalisation and relations between Triad and emerging markets at the centre of debates.

This volume focuses particularly on the more dynamic emerging markets, including the Association of South East Asian Nations (ASEAN) region, Central Europe, China, India, Mercosur (Argentina and Brazil) and Mexico. It analyses the prospects for these markets following the successive crises that have affected them since 1995, the different spatial and productive configurations seen across them and the relationships between the emerging markets and the Triad economies. The chapters in this book do not provide a general, descriptive account of each of these markets. Rather, they are thematic and comparative in perspective, raising issues of general relevance to emerging markets and comparing developments in different emerging markets.

The 'new automobile spaces', or emerging markets, were heralded as the major sources of growth in the automotive industry during the early part of the 21st century. Compared to the mature markets of the Triad countries, where growth perspectives seemed to be very limited, the emerging markets appeared to offer a combination of continuing rapid growth in sales, low-cost production and opportunities for experimentation with new approaches to production and work. Even following the peso crisis in Mexico, and the consequent collapse of vehicle sales in 1995,[1] analysts remain optimistic about growth prospects, forecasting continued growth in sales, as can be seen in

Table 1.1. Growth was expected to increase in double figures in all emerging market areas in the period 1996–98.

Following the crisis in East Asia, however, optimism about the prospects for emerging markets dampened considerably. In mid-1997, the ASEAN region succumbed to a major crisis in banking and in investor confidence. Rising interest rates, recession and collapsing consumer confidence led to a 70 per cent decline in vehicle sales across the region. The East Asian crisis also had a direct impact on Brazil, where interest rates were doubled to defend the currency and vehicle sales fell by one-third. Not all emerging markets were affected directly by international financial instability, but even those markets insulated by exchange and investment controls showed lacklustre performance in 1997 and 1998. Short-term sales forecasts for both markets proved to be wildly optimistic, as can be seen in Table 1.1.

The only emerging markets to show positive sales growth in the period 1996–98 were Argentina and the peripheral regions of the

Table 1.1   Forecasts and outcomes of growth in vehicle sales in selected emerging market regions, 1996–98

Region	Economist Intelligence Unit, 1996	Outcome[a]
ASEAN[b]	+10	−68.5
Argentina	+10	+21.0
Brazil	+14	−11.4
China	+22	+9.1
India	+38	−19.2
Central Europe[c]	+29	+23.6
Mexico	+75	+93.5

Notes: [a] Outcomes based on 1996–97 growth figures from Fourin (1998) and latest available data for Argentina (*ADEFA*, 1999), Brazil (*ANFAVEA*, 1998; 1999), ASEAN, China and India (*Auto Asia*, March/April 1999), Central Europe (Automotive Emerging Markets, 20 April 1999) and Mexico (*AMIA*, 1999).
[b] Indonesia, Malaysia, Philippines and Thailand.
[c] Czech Republic, Hungary and Poland.
Sources: EIU (1996a,b) and Fourin (1998).

Triad economies, Mexico and Central Europe. Even these growth figures are deceptive. In both Argentina and Mexico rising vehicle sales were merely recuperating losses suffered in 1994–95. Argentine vehicle sales in 1998 were still below the level recorded in 1994, and in Mexico, domestic sales for 1998 were only 8 per cent above the 1994 level.

The bubble had burst. Nevertheless, in spite of these setbacks, it is important not to replace unbridled optimism about the prospects for the emerging markets with equally deep pessimism. This book addresses three questions about the emerging markets and their role within the global automotive industry. First, what are the production and sales prospects for these markets? Secondly, what spatial configurations are likely to emerge within these markets and within the global automotive industry more generally? Thirdly, what division of activities is likely to develop between the emerging markets and the Triad regions, and what impact will the emerging markets have on Triad regions?

THE PROSPECTS FOR EMERGING MARKETS

The shift of the emerging markets from being backwaters of the global automotive industry to being at the centre of new developments occurred in part because the growth prospects for the Triad economies looked poor. Markets for vehicles appeared to be saturated. In contrast, the emerging markets looked increasingly attractive. The long-term potential of these markets had never been in doubt. Eventually, levels of motorisation would increase in the developing world. In the early 1990s, it seemed that the widespread introduction of economic reform packages, combined with new policies to encourage the auto industry, would both accelerate the advance of motorisation and provide better conditions for the transnational auto companies to take advantage of it. Both assemblers and component manufacturers began to make major investments in emerging markets. They sought access to growing markets for vehicles and low-cost production sites.

These developments appeared to satisfy the interests of both transnational vehicle companies and national governments. In the ideal scenario, rapidly growing vehicle markets in developing countries would provide overall scale to spread vehicle development costs, cheap production sites for the production of selected vehicles and components and new markets for higher-end vehicles, which would still be produced in the Triad economies. At the same time, the motor industry's growth would provide income and employment in the host countries. Governments also expected motor industry investment to promote technological capabilities within their countries and to improve the balance of trade through reduced imports and increased exports.

The prospects for the emerging markets are addressed directly in four chapters in this book. In Chapter 2, Lung analyses the growth and crisis of the emerging markets, identifying a number of obstacles to their development. First, he notes that the level and nature of demand is more problematic than anticipated. The very processes of liberalisation and foreign direct investment (FDI) which opened up the emerging markets have also led to market instability and crisis. The clearest examples of crisis have been seen in Mexico (1995), the ASEAN region (1997 onwards) and Brazil (1998–99). Demand in India has not lived up to initial expectations, and China may yet succumb to the same problems. Secondly, most emerging markets remain characterised by excessive fragmentation of demand across products and producers, and by overcapacity. Lung argues that both features are endemic to emerging markets and that vehicle producers must adapt their strategies accordingly.

Similar issues are addressed in Chapter 3 by Humphrey and Oeter, which considers the policies adopted by governments in emerging markets. Governments have intervened actively in order to promote local motor industries. While the use of quantitative restrictions on imports of vehicles and components has declined, there is continuing use of local content requirements, high tariffs on imported vehicles, foreign exchange balancing requirements and duty drawback schemes.[2] Continuing protection, combined with investment liberalisation and incentives for motor industry investment tended to create overcapacity and uneconomic scales of production even before the falls in demand seen in 1997–98. Among the emerging markets, only Brazil has managed to attain large-volume production in a range of models. Protection has not created motor industries that could easily survive the phasing out of such measures as local content requirements and foreign exchange balancing, as required by the Uruguay Round agreement on Trade-Related Investment Measures.

Chapter 5 by Madhavan raises a more fundamental issue about the viability of the vehicle in emerging markets. Anyone who has visited Bangkok, Bombay (now called Mumbai) or Mexico City will have witnessed the declining returns to car ownership in cities that lack the necessary infrastructure for both public and private transport. Despite low levels of car ownership, high rates of growth of traffic in cities have led to congestion on roads and environmental damage from atmospheric pollution. The rapid growth in the ownership and use of motor cars (the purchase of larger and/or more powerful cars following liberalisation of economic policies) have resulted in considerably increased congestion and pollution.

Chapter 5 discusses both transport policy measures (policies to restrain car use, traffic management) and environmental policy measures which aim to counteract the consequences of the use of private motor vehicles (incentives to use unleaded petrol, installation of catalytic converters, and so on). It discusses the complexities of the formulation and implementation of these two types of policies, and the extent to which these two policies may, in turn, be constrained by other policies, such as urban development, and/or land use policies.

Freyssenet and Lung, in Chapter 4, place the development of the automotive industry in emerging markets in the broader context of the competitive strategies of transnational vehicle producers at the global and regional levels. Internationalisation is one element of the competitive strategies of vehicle companies, and it interacts with many other elements of company strategy, including product simplification, platform reduction, supplier relations and relations with labour. While the automotive industry is much more internationalised than in the past, significant and persistent differences between regions and between companies will remain, and a scenario of regional segmentation of the global vehicle industry seems more likely than global homogeneity.

EMERGING MARKET CONFIGURATIONS

The vehicle industry in emerging markets was transformed in the 1990s. The industry in Central Europe was completely restructured following the collapse of the Soviet bloc, becoming more closely tied to the European Union (EU). The Mexican vehicle industry became much more integrated into the North American market. The Chinese and Indian governments began to promote production of passenger cars and liberalised investment rules, allowing the entry of transnational companies. Car sales and production in Argentina and Brazil were given new life by a combination of new policy regimes, economic stabilisation and regional integration. The vehicle industries of the ASEAN region continued to grow and develop, attracting new investments.

These various regions are commonly referred to as emerging markets, but this should not be taken to mean that they are homogeneous. The dynamics of development in Mexico and Central Europe, for example, are clearly quite different from those of such regions as ASEAN or Mercosur, and also from the underdeveloped continental markets of Indian and China. No single classification of the emerging markets does justice to the variations seen between them, partly because these markets are still evolving, and partly because it is not clear which configurations will remain viable within a changing global automotive industry. Therefore, it is more important to discuss the factors that define the different configurations. The future configuration of emerging markets will be defined by the interplay of three different tendencies:[3]

1. continuing protection of domestic markets;
2. increased liberalisation of automotive trade within regions, but possibly combined with continuing, or even increasing, barriers to inter-regional trade;
3. increased liberalisation of trade in vehicles and components between countries and regions in a global economy which progressively limits tariff levels and those Trade-Related Investment Measures (TRIMs) such as local content requirements and foreign exchange balancing obligations that contravene the General Agreement on Tariffs and Trade (GATT) agreements on national treatment and quantitative restrictions.[4]

A variety of configurations can be seen within the emerging markets. One clear group of countries is those that retain an ambition to develop a locally based industry and use a variety of protective measures to restrict access to the domestic market. We refer to these markets as *Protected Autonomous Markets* (PAMs). The clearest examples of the strategy are found in India, China and Malaysia. The policies used in these three countries are discussed in Chapter 3 by Humphrey and Oeter. While each of these countries protected the domestic market from external competition, their approach to the question of ownership differed significantly. Malaysia opted for the promotion of locally owned companies, establishing first Proton and later Perodua. Chapter 9 by Guiheux and Lecler shows the limitations of the strategy in the context of the East Asian crisis and regional integration policies. In contrast, China looked to modernise its car industry through joint ventures between Chinese car producers and transnational firms. The attractiveness of the Chinese market (at least up to the late 1990s) allowed the government to attract foreign auto companies while regulating ownership and technology transfer. The Indian government, on the other hand, largely abstained from regulating ownership in the car industry. Between 1996 and 1999, 10 new ventures for passenger car production were established, and companies in both the assembly and components sectors became almost entirely free from ownership restrictions.

Nationally oriented strategies may be possible in very large markets. In small markets, regional integration is one option for gaining greater scale in production and sales. Regional groupings facilitate trade within the region at the expense of trade with countries outside. The nature of regional integration can vary from the creation of regional governments and largely homogeneous markets to limited forms of free trade. Within the emerging markets, the trends towards regional integration take two distinct forms.

The first type of integration is seen in the *Integrated Peripheral Markets* (IPMs), Mexico and Central Europe, which are discussed in Chapter 6 by Layan and Chapter 10 by Havas.[5] In Chapter 6 Layan discusses the case of Mexico's integration into the North American Free Trade Area (NAFTA) and compares it with an earlier example of regional integration, Spain's integration to the EU. The IPMs tend to specialise in the production of products in which they have a comparative advantage – particularly assembly and labour-intensive manufacture of parts and components. Eventually, the spaces should be totally integrated into their respective regional production/consumption systems. Layan's comparison between Spain and Mexico illustrates this point. In the late 1970s, Spain made a transition from an import substitution economy with a protected local motor industry, to a producer of low-end vehicles directed predominantly towards the broader European market. However, Layan also points to differences between Spain and Mexico. The immaturity and volatility of the Mexican market for vehicles has meant that its production is becoming increasingly specialised in vehicles for the North American market.[6]

The transformation of the motor industry in Central Europe (the Czech Republic, Hungary and Poland) is discussed in Chapter 10 by Havas. Many automotive companies have invested in Central Europe. Existing companies and facilities have been bought up and rebuilt, and new greenfield sites have been established. While part of this investment has been made with a view to capturing markets in Central and Eastern Europe, the largest investors in the region, such as the VW group, Fiat, Daewoo and Suzuki, view their Central European operations as part of a broader, European-wide strategy, predicated on the increasing integration of markets. Central Europe attracted significant investments, not only for plants producing low-end, mass market vehicles for markets right across Europe (typified by the Fiat Seicento in Poland), but also for the assembly of low-volume niche vehicles (for example, the Audi TT and the VW Bora), engine assembly and production of an increasing range of components. This transition appears to be more similar to that of Spain, but it remains to be seen just what role Central Europe eventually plays in the European motor industry. In part, this will depend upon the broader economic transformation of Central Europe itself.

A second pattern of regional integration is also evident in the emerging markets. The clearest examples are ASEAN and Mercosur, where some attempts have been made to liberalise trade between member countries.[7] These cases are discussed in Chapter 9 by Guiheux and Lecler and Chapter 7 by Humphrey and Salerno. We refer to this group as *Emerging Regional Markets* (ERMs). It is possible that other ERMs will develop, particular in cases where the PAM strategy runs into difficulty. For example, the Russian motor industry might integrate with other parts of the Former Soviet Union in order to gain scale through the division of labour and access to a broader customer base. Similarly, Turkey might form the focal point of a Middle East vehicle region. Politics aside, it might make sense for South Asia to offset the problems of limited market scale through a closer integration of the markets of Bangladesh, India, Pakistan and Sri Lanka.

The future of the ERMs is unclear. If they are to work, then regional preference must win over preferences for national automotive industries or closer integration into the global automotive industry. In the case of Mercosur, such a tendency was clearly visible in the period 1995–98. Each country was by far the largest vehicle and component trading partner of the other, and some incipient division of labour was developing. Should these trends continue, then Mercosur would become a well-defined regional space within the global automotive industry. Such a regional space would not be completely cut off from the global industry. It would retain linkages with the Triad economies, particularly in terms of technological, managerial and capital flows, but trade linkages would be limited to niche market vehicles and high-value components.

The case of regional integration in ASEAN, discussed by Guiheux and Lecler (Chapter 9), is rather different. Up until 1998, the four vehicle producers in the region developed largely separate motor industries, with limited trade in vehicles and components between them. The dominant vehicle producers in the region, the leading Japanese companies, were happy to develop small-scale production in each market, and various schemes to encourage intra-ASEAN trade had little effect. However, the regional strategies of Japanese car manufacturers changed dramatically following the East Asian crisis. It remains to be seen whether this creates a stronger market within the ASEAN or orientates production towards broader regional markets, such as Australia and New Zealand, or even to Europe and North America.

The development of national and regional markets will take place within the overall context of increasing internationalisation. An extreme globalisation hypothesis might predict the total de-linking of production and consumption of vehicles and components. These would be produced at whatever site was deemed cost-effective and then shipped to where they were needed. World Trade Organisation (WTO) agreements and regulations which would eventually reduce tariffs and outlaw local content regulations and incentives for local producers might lead in this direction.

The spatial configuration of the world automotive industry, and the role of particular emerging markets within it, has yet to be determined. Countries may well pursue strategies that are not entirely national, regional or global, and these strategies will interact with both the strategies of other countries and the strategies of the global auto manufacturers. It seems clear that the automotive industries of the emerging markets will be more integrated into the global automotive industry in the first decade of the 21st century than was the case of the 1980s. However, there will be considerable heterogeneity, and the balance of national regional and global tendencies will vary considerably.

THE EMERGING MARKETS AND THE TRIAD ECONOMIES

The discussion so far has concentrated mainly on the production, sales and trade of vehicles. However, the structuring of the emerging markets and the relationships between these markets and the Triad economies involve aspects such as design and sourcing. One most radical view of the advance of globalisation in the automotive industry would be to extrapolate tendencies seen within the EU to the global level. In the 1950s and 1960s, the European car industry consisted of a number of national industries, each producing cars to its own designs, using a national supply base and selling predominantly to the national market.[8] It is worth remembering that until the late 1960s, Ford and GM maintained largely independent operations in the UK and Germany. The two Ford subsidiaries did not produce a common model until the end of the 1960s. By the late 1990s, there had been a significant move towards a European motor industry. Ford, GM and Volkswagen had integrated design and sourcing across multi-country production systems. Markets, too, have steadily become more integrated. Of the European-owned mass producers of vehicles, only Fiat still concentrated more than half of its total European sales in its domestic base.[9]

The potential advantages of pursuing similar strategies at the global level are clear. Even if trade in vehicles and components remains limited, the use of standard designs and common suppliers across markets might provide significant cost reductions.

The question of design is discussed in Chapter 8 by Sugiyama and Fujimoto. This analyses the design of light vehicles by Japanese firms for the Indonesian market. The chapter examines how firms try to balance the often contradictory goals of adapting their products and activities to local requirements, and enjoying scale or scope economies through standardised global operations and resources. This analysis places product design in a dynamic framework of capability building, organisational learning and the external environment, which co-evolve over time. Chapter 8 shows how Japanese firms successfully adapted products to meet the evolving needs of consumers in Indonesia (which were themselves shaped by the products offered in the market), but then found after the East Asian crisis that an export-led strategy was rendered unfeasible by these same adaptations.

The discussion on the standardisation of design is also taken up in Chapter 9 by Guiheux and Lecler and Chapter 7 by Humphrey and Salerno. Guiheux and Lecler show how all of the Japanese assemblers in the ASEAN region have developed an 'Asian' car concept, designing vehicles more suitable for Asian markets, not only in terms of product (customer satisfaction) but also in terms of technological sophistication. These adaptations show just how difficult it is to produce vehicles suitable for markets with widely differing incomes and patterns of vehicle use. Similarly Humphrey and Salerno discuss the way vehicles are adapted to the needs of local markets in Brazil and India.

The issue of sourcing is also taken up by Humphrey and Salerno (Chapter 7) for the cases of Brazil and India. They show how assemblers show a strong preference for using follow sources (the same suppliers as used in the home country) in both markets. However, there are clear limits to the practicalities of follow sourcing. In some cases, it involves new, small-scale operations in unfamiliar environments, and assemblers are willing to shift to an alternative source, usually another transnational component supplier, when the follow source cannot supply at a competitive price.

Changes in design and sourcing strategy have a clear impact on the automotive industry in emerging markets. A strict application of follow design and follow sourcing reduces the possible input of locally owned firms into component design and production. Components are designed before production is planned in the host market, and transnational component manufacturers are in a strong position to obtain contracts from their transnational assembler customers. Even when there are design adaptations for the local market, these are usually carried out in the home country. Similarly, when follow sourcing is relaxed the assembler may choose another transnational supplier.

The consequence of these practices is that the boost to technological capability derived from the car industry in host countries is probably less at the end of the 1990s than 20–30 years earlier, when subsidiaries of transnational companies created local supplier networks and even developed models for the local market. While the process engineering skills required in the automotive industry have no doubt risen because of increasing quality requirements and product complexity, design and product engineering skills may be less in demand in emerging markets.

This is not to say that no innovation takes place within the emerging markets. In fact, some developments in these markets may have an important impact on the future shape of the global automotive industry. First, some emerging markets are privileged fields for organisational and social experiments. In some cases, they play the role of laboratories, where innovations can be tested out in favourable social conditions and away from the publicity and pressures of the core operations. Social security, trade-union rights and environmental rules are often some degrees below the ones one can find in central economies. Organisational innovations advanced in the emerging markets include changes in supplier–assembler responsibilities. In a few plants – like the VW Resende truck plant in Brazil, VW/Skoda's plant in the Czech Republic, GM's 'Blue Macaw' plant being built in Brazil, and others – the supplier is also responsible for the assembly of components and systems into the vehicle on the carmaker's final assembly line (Lung *et al.*, 1999). Social innovations include experiments in outsourcing, flexible allocation of labour, labour subcontracting and flexible working hours. These innovations can also be analysed by the companies in terms of their transfer back to advanced industrial countries or at least to put pressure on Governments and Trade Unions to cede more favourable conditions, as showed by the impact of Mexico and Central Europe on negotiating conditions in North America and Western Europe respectively.

The changes in assembler–supplier relationship appear to be more advanced in the new spaces than in Europe or in the USA. This raises the question of whether new spaces could be used for social and organisational experiments that could be further transferred to other plants around the world, mainly in the central economies. As far as social rights, trade-union organisation, labour legislation and welfare state systems used to be less developed in third world countries, it would be easy for the companies to experiment new social forms of production and work organisation in greenfield plants. Although the results of these experiments will not simply be transplanted back to operations in the central economies, it is clear that the experiments put pressure on the management, the staff and above all, the workers of traditional plants. The 1998 strike in GM components plants in the USA is related to this point. Some of the decision-makers for GM's North American operations had worked in GM's Brazilian operations, and they declared that they would like to introduce 'the Brazilian model' into the USA.

Secondly, automotive companies may be forced to innovate by the specific circumstances of emerging markets, but then apply this innovation more widely. An analysis of just such a change in the ASEAN region and its effects in Japan is provided by Guiheux and Lecler (Chapter 9). Low volumes of cars and pick-ups being assembled by Japanese producers meant that reproduction of the Japanese system – each assembler using its own, dedicated supplier – was uneconomic. Rather than replicate the structure of the components industry in Japan, where each major vehicle manufacturer maintained its own network of suppliers, companies such as Nissan and Toyota began to use common suppliers in the ASEAN region. Far from remaining as experiments dictated by local necessities, these new forms of supplier organisation have been transferred back to Japan, loosening keiretsu structures and changing relations between firms.

The optimistic view about the development of emerging markets is that enormous, untapped potential for vehicle production and sales exist. Huge populations are still relatively unmotorised by Triad patterns, and there is an insatiable appetite for car-based mobility and Western-style cars. Whatever the obstacles to the growth of the vehicle industry in emerging markets, and whatever the health and the environmental problems caused, they are unlikely to prevent the expansion of the vehicle industry, and they will not prevent some further globalisation of the industry. As the chapters in this book show, this process is already advancing extremely rapidly. However, the process will be unpredictable and unstable – subject to reverses and crises – and the outcomes will be more heterogeneous than a simple model of the inevitable advance of globalisation might suggest.

The industry is structured by three sets of factors. One set is largely the result of the policy choices made by the leading global automotive companies. These include investment and production strategies, follow design and follow sourcing, and assembler–supplier relationships. A second set of factors is largely outside of their control. These include the macroeconomic regional, sectoral and environmental policies adopted by governments. The third set of factors is the specific characteristics of production and demand in emerging markets. The future development of the automotive industry will be influenced by the ways in which the global strategies of the auto companies deal with these local realities.

Notes

1. The impact of the peso crisis on the Mexican auto industry and its position within NAFTA are discussed in Chapter 2 by Lung and Chapter 6 by Layan in this book.
2. In many cases, these restrictions are supported by established vehicle producers as a means of reducing competition from imports and completely knocked down (CKD) operations. See also the way in which NAFTA regulations disadvantage non-American producers in Mexico.
3. These tendencies are derived from the scenarios for the global industry put forward by Boyer and Freyssenet (1998).

4. International trade issues are discussed in Chapter 3 by Humphrey and Oeter in this book.
5. The category of IPMs is very similar to the category of PLEMAs (Periphery of Large Existing Market Areas) developed by Sturgeon (1997). The main difference lies in the word 'integration'. Some peripheral areas are integrated, but others are not. In the case of Eastern Europe, Poland has been integrated into the motor industry of the EU, but Romania has not.
6. Clearly, the EU and NAFTA are also quite different projects for regional integration, but the complexities of regional integration cannot be addressed here.
7. The main vehicle producers in the ASEAN region are, in order of production volumes in 1995, Thailand, Indonesia, Malaysia and the Philippines. In Mercosur, Brazil is by far the largest producer and consumer of vehicles, with Argentina a distant second. Vehicle production is negligible in Uruguay and Paraguay, the other two signatories of the Mercosur agreement.
8. Of course, this is an exaggeration, and the degree of fragmentation was always much lower for luxury cars.
9. Less than 40 per cent of total European sales of Renault and PSA were made in France in 1997. VW sales in Germany and Spain together accounted for less than half of total European sales (Fourin, 1998).

References

ADEFA (1999) Auto Industry Statistics, ADEFA – Asociación de Fábricas de Automotores de Argentina, Web Site – www.adefa.com.ar, accessed March 1999.
AMIA (1999) Auto Industry Statistics, AMIA – Asociación Mexicana de la Industria Automotriz (Mexico), Web Site – www.amia.com.mx, accessed September 1999.
ANFAVEA (1998) Anuário Estatístico 1998, ANFAVEA – Associação Nacional dos Fabricantes de Veículos Automotores (Brazil), Web Site – www.anfavea.com.br, accessed January 1999.
ANFAVEA (1999) Carta da ANFAVEA, January 1999, ANFAVEA – Associação Nacional dos Fabricantes de Veículos Automotores (Brazil), Web Site – www.anfavea.com.br, accessed February 1999.
BOYER, R. and FREYSSENET, M. (1998) *Le Monde qui a Changé la Machine.* Manuscript. Paris: Gerpisa.
EIU (1996a) *Motor Business Asia-Pacific.* London: Economist Intelligence Unit.
EIU (1996b) *Motor Business International: the Worldwide Motor Industry.* London: Economist Intelligence Unit.
FOURIN (1998) *Fourin's Automotive Forecast.* Nagoya: Fourin Inc.
LUNG, Y., SALERNO, M., DIAS, A. and ZILBOVICIUS, M. (1999) 'Flexibility through modularity: experimentations with fractal production in Brazil and in Europe'. In Lung, Y., Chanaron, J.-J., Fujimoto, T. and Raff,

D. (eds), *Coping with Variety: Flexible Production Systems for Product Variety in the Auto Industry*. Ashgate: Avebury.

STURGEON, T. (1997) *Globalization and the Threat of Overcapacity in the Automotive Industry*. Globalization and Jobs in the Automotive Industry, Research Note, 1. Cambridge, MA: MIT.

2 Is the Rise of Emerging Countries as Automobile Producers an Irreversible Phenomenon?

Yannick Lung*

INTRODUCTION

Trade magazines[1] have been rife with predictions that new countries are making a grand entrance onto the automotive industry's global stage, and this is also a recurring theme in the strategic plans made by automotive companies (car and component makers). Despite disappointment in the recent growth rates of the Central European, Latin American (Mexico, Brazil) and, lately, South East Asian markets, most observers today still appear to consider that the rise of the emerging countries is unstoppable. However, similar breakthroughs have already been widely announced on several different occasions, and even though they never really materialised, the top international experts (Altshuler *et al.*, 1984) have often been somewhat too quick to agree with these forecasts. It is, therefore, worthwhile asking whether or not the emergence of new automotive countries is an irreversible phenomenon. After having described the recent rise of the emerging countries, and after having analysed the factors involved, this chapter will explore the uncertainties associated with expectations for growth in these markets.

Announcing the rise of the emerging countries

First of all, it is important to determine whether there has really been an emergence of new countries in the global automotive industry. To do this, one must first study recent developments (since the early 1990s), and then take into account growth forecasts for the early 21st century. Above and beyond a general approach, analysis of a more disaggregated variety allows for some analytical fine-tuning by distinguishing between the different modes of international insertion applicable in each of these countries. Finally, the rush by car and component makers to these emerging countries must still be explained – everyone agrees that, despite the target markets' very real potential, this could soon result in the appearance of excess production capacities.

The rise of new automotive zones during the 1990s

In general, since the early 1990s, it has been possible to observe a stagnation of car production in the industrialised countries, and a concomitant increase in the emerging countries (Table 2.1). Globally, production in the traditional automotive countries (United States and Canada, European Union and Japan) has stagnated, although this statement should be relativised by the fact that none of these zones is at the same phase of the economic cycle: Japan has been in a recession since 1992 (production dropped by 2.5 million vehicles between 1990 and 1997); Europe has gone through a period of stagnation; and North America has been experiencing recovery (production having increased by 2.7 million vehicles over the same period). In any event, unlike predictions for the new players, the most optimistic forecasts for the traditional car making countries expect growth to reach only 1 or 2 per cent per annum in the next few years.

On the other hand, outside of these three zones, the 'Triad', there has been a remarkable increase: production in the rest of the world jumped by 58.7 per cent from 1990 to 1997, corresponding to the assembly of nearly 4.6 million extra vehicles. However, this significant increase was not across the board – for the most part, it has taken place in only a few countries: in particular, South Korea, Brazil, China, Mexico and India. In the oldest emerging countries, where there was already a car industry in the 1970s and 1980s, trends involved either continued growth (South Korea), or recovery (Brazil). During the period under study, these two nations doubled their production, assembling 2.7 million extra vehicles. If one also counts Mexico, where production doubled between 1988 and 1996, these three countries by themselves represented two-thirds of the growth achieved by emerging countries.

New and major players appeared in Asia (China, and to a lesser extent, India), and there were advances in certain countries in Central

Table 2.1 Motor vehicle production by continent

	1990 (000s)	1997 (000s)	Change 1997/90 (000s)	Index (1990 = 100)	1998 (000s)	Change 1998/97 (000s)	Rate of growth 1997–98 (%)
World	48 601	53 147	4546	109.4	51 932	−1215	−2.3
Triad	40 724	40 646	−78	99.8	40 790	144	0.4
European Union (EU)	15 597	15 294	−303	98.1	16 574	1280	8.4
USA & Canada	11 640	14 377	2737	123.5	14 166	−211	−1.5
Japan	13 487	10 975	−2512	81.4	10 050	−925	−8.4
Rest of the World	7 877	12 501	4624	158.7	11 142	−1359	−10.9
Latin America	1 835	3 166	1331	172.5	3 364	198	6.3
Mexico	*821*	*1 360*	*539*	*165.7*	*1 453*	*93*	*6.8*
Brazil	*914*	*2 070*	*1156*	*226.5*	*1 573*	*−497*	*−24.0*
East and Central Europe	2 788	2 024	−764	72.6	2 168	144	7.1
Russia & Ukraine	*1 917*	*1 164*	*−753*	*60.7*	*1 028*	*−136*	*−11.7*
Asia–Oceania[a]	3 036	6 077	3041	200.2	5 146	−931	−15.3
Korea	*1 322*	*2 818*	*1496*	*213.2*	*1 625*	*−1193*	*−42.3*
China	*536*	*1 578*	*1042*	*294.4*	*1 628*	*50*	*3.2*
India	*364*	*670*	*306*	*184.1*	*642*	*−28*	*−4.2*

Note: [a] Excludes Japan. Data for ASEAN region not tabled separately because of differences in data from different sources.
Source: Organisation Internationale des Constructeurs d'Automobiles (OICA).

Europe (Poland, Czech Republic), as older production units were replaced little by little by new models produced in factories which had been either totally retooled, or else created from scratch on green field sites. Finally, there was one situation of sudden transition, involving the collapse of state-owned industries in Russia and in Ukraine.

Optimistic forecasts predicted large increases in demand, especially for passenger cars. Sales in emerging markets were supposed to jump from 5.6 million in 1995 to 8 million in 2000, 10.6 million in 2005 and 13 million in 2010 – a level equivalent to European car sales in 1997.[2] Such forecasts need to be revised downwards substantially. Vehicle sales fell sharply in the emerging markets in 1998 (see Table 2.1) following successive financial and exchange rate crises: in Korea and the ASEAN countries in 1997, Russia in 1998 and Brazil in 1999. Such a huge reverse in the trend of demand growth in emerging markets requires a deeper analysis of the dynamics driving this growth.

Different modes of integration in the emerging countries

As a result of past events, and in light of what is being forecast for the future, the group of nations covered by the term 'emerging countries' seems to be a relatively heterogeneous category whose long-term outlook for growth largely depends on the modalities of their insertion into the international economy. Indeed, the strategy a company adopts depends on what it perceives to be the main issue regarding the national automobile policy of governments and their own vision of the future for these areas:

- integration of peripheral areas to one of the Triad poles (Eastern Europe, Mexico);
- participation in a process of regional integration (Mercosur, Asean); or
- building a national automotive industry which could, over the long run, compete with the traditional car-making countries (China).

Three different types of trajectory (see the introduction to this book: Chapter 1) can be differentiated by such an approach.

The emergence of new national vehicle industries

The first scenario – equivalent to a PAM – involves the creation of a national vehicle industry which benefits from the transfer of technology by multinational companies. Inspired by the Korean model, this perspective assumes the local market will become large enough to absorb production. Nevertheless:

- On the one hand, though it may be necessary to implement an export strategy to help support a nascent national vehicle industry, the national market itself remains the precondition for developing such a national vehicle industry (Table 2.2). Substitutions between domestic sales and exports (and vice versa) allow temporary adaptations to economic fluctuations and government policies, but in the long term the development of a national vehicle industry depends on the balanced growth of the two components of demand – see the examples of South Korea and, earlier on, Japan (Jenkins, 1995; Bélis-Bergouignan and Lung, 1994).
- On the other hand, foreign automotive companies (car and component makers) will not set up locally, or accept to transfer their technology, unless such a presence gives them privileged access to major markets. This can only be the case in countries featuring a large population and a small rate of car ownership, but which are committed to economic take-off. These have to be nations of continental size, such as China and India, or even Russia.

The Japanese, and, especially, the Korean experiences in creating a motor industry show how very important it is to stick conscientiously

Table 2.2   Export rate of motor vehicles production in emerging countries in 1997[a]

Countries	Production (000s)	Exports (000s)	Export/production (%)
Russia	1179.1	N/A.	–
China	1579.7	14.8	0.9
India	596.3	48.9	8.2
Brazil	2069.7	416.9	20.1
Argentina	446.3	210.4	47.1
South Korea	2818.3	1316.9	46.7
Poland	384.8	160.6	41.7
Czech Republic	368.4	241.5	65.5
Mexico	1359.5	988.1	72.7

Note: [a] Number of vehicles locally manufactured and assembled. Data not available for ASEAN region.
Source: OICA.

to an appropriate industrial policy, and especially to encourage the transfer and appropriation of the foreign technologies which will enable local companies to develop, little by little, their own competencies. In the motor industry, this orientation requires that particular attention be paid, once the [foreign] car makers have arrived, to the components industry, and that foreign investment be carefully controlled so as to ensure an effective transfer of technologies. This must be associated with a policy of training the local labour force, reinforcing the skills set available in all strata of local industry, and consolidating the state's means for intervention. Today, China is the country which best satisfies these criteria, but things are not as clear in Russia (owing to the country's social disintegration) or in India, which has seemingly committed itself to the path of liberalisation, but which has done so within its own particular context, keeping such a strict control over the process of deregulation that it is easy to imagine a reversal of this policy. On the other hand, in the aftermath of the Asian crisis, there has been a loss of credibility for the so-called 'national' policies of small countries like Indonesia. And even before this, Ukraine had been obliged to give up its wild dream of becoming a new player on the automotive industry's global stage, and has now had to satisfy itself with less ambitious projects.

Systems of pericentral regional integration

The situation in Brazil is like in other nations of continental size (China, and so on), but with the difference that Brazil is integrated into a specific regional organisation, Mercosur. This scenario can also be envisaged on a Commonwealth of Independent States (CIS)-wide scale for Russia and is developing in the ASEAN region (see Chapter 9 by Guiheux and Lecler). Regional integration of this type (ERM in the typology presented in the introduction to this book: Chapter 1), involving only emerging countries (Mercosur, ASEAN, CIS), allows for a division of labour to develop between the various members of the region. Companies integrate the management of their various entities throughout the area, and this generates a flow back and forth of goods and information. In the ASEAN zone, specific agreements on the car industry led to the building of such configurations (see Chapter 9). In Mercosur also, the trend has been towards a regional division of labour between Argentina and Brazil (Laplane and Sarti, 1999).

The tremendous growth of automotive trade between the two main members of Mercosur (Table 2.3) since the beginning of 1990s indicates clearly that this process leads to greater interdependence. Car makers have dedicated their assembly plants to specific models for the regional market: for example, small cars (Fiesta and Ka) are produced by Ford in Brazil (with the 1000c.c. engine adapted to the local 'popular car' market) while the medium-size Escort is produced in Argentina. The same kind of division of labour has been developed for mechanical components (transmission, engine) and other automotive parts by assemblers and suppliers.

These types of integration are the result of national commercial policies, and yet they have the particularity of being implemented by foreign multinational companies. In a liberalised context, this paradox makes it questionable whether such configurations are viable: will Mercosur be able to resist the attractiveness of the free trading North American pole, and will Asean be able to resist pressure from the International Monetary Fund (IMF) and the WTO? Moreover, above and beyond questions about the political willpower of a given government, there is the issue of its ability to play on rivalries between the companies trying to get established locally in order to increase their own autonomy. Back in the days when everyone was rushing to the emerging countries, the governments may well have been in a favourable situation – but if excess capacities do appear, it is very possible that the balance of power may in the future revert to the companies.

In this case, the relevance of strategies geared towards regional

Table 2.3   Automotive trade between Argentina and Brazil

Product	Year	From Brazil to Argentina		From Argentina to Brazil	
		Value[a]	*Share* (%)[b]	*Value*[a]	*Share* (%)[c]
Cars	1990	16.0	3.9	1.8	10.2
	1996	334.1	54.0	766.1	95.3
Parts	1990	43.9	8.2	51.1	40.1
	1996	534.8	41.0	273.5	77.2

Notes: [a] US$ million. [b] % of total Brazilian car exports. [c] % of total Argentinean car exports.
Source: Intal (in Laplane and Sarti, 1999).

leadership must be questioned. They were a success in Brazil, which, within the framework of Mercosur, had a conflicting relationship with Argentina – and they could be reproduced in other pericentral areas, such as in South Africa against the rest of the African continent, or in Turkey with respect to the Middle East. But the Triad's centripetal forces will probably not leave much room for configurations like these.

Peripheral integration

A third configuration corresponds to the integration of the new emerging countries into the centre, that is, into the Northern regions (IPMs). This is clearly shown by the example of Mexico's integration into NAFTA. The Mexican motor industry is nowadays totally oriented towards North America, which absorbs three-quarters of its production, whereas it had previously been oriented towards a protected domestic market (Carrillo, 1998). In certain respects, Mexico has reproduced the breakthrough achieved by the Spanish motor industry in Europe in the 1970s (see Chapter 6 by Layan). This is also the case for certain Central and Eastern European countries that have predicated the development of their automobile industry on their relations with the EU (Ruigrok and van Tulder, 1999). In Asia, although there are the two poles of Japan, and, more recently, of South Korea, the situation is less straightforward, despite the recent relocation of the components industry towards countries with low wage costs, whose competitiveness has recently been strengthened following the devaluation of their currencies.

Nonetheless, it is important to emphasise that this type of integration is not an example of a simplistic, centre-periphery type model, wherein low value-added activities are pushed out to the periphery. It is true that such tendencies do exist: thus 90 per cent of the wire harnesses which are fitted on North American vehicles are nowadays assembled in the *maquiladoras* along Mexico's Northern Border. However, the competencies of the local labour force are such that hi-tech activities can also be relocated in this area, so that the country is not reduced to screwdriver status. Again, the example of Mexico is instructive: Delphi built an engineering centre there, bringing together several hundred engineers and technicians with the goal of developing hi-tech components (Carrillo and Hualde, 1997). The IMVP survey comparing the productivity of assembly plants had focused on the remarkable performance of the Ford plant in Hermosillo (Womack *et al.*, 1990), and on the launch of the new Beetle 2 at the VW plant in Puebla, as indications of these countries' great ability to learn and to improve quality and productivity until international standards were reached.

Even if such changes remain limited to a spatial division of labour where peripheral countries are mainly specialised in the assembly of small cars and commercial vehicles, and in the export of components to the assembly lines for sophisticated models produced and sold in the industrialised countries, the long-term dynamic effects of the learning processes associated with the upgrading of peripheral plants to the highest standards of international competitiveness (productivity, cost, quality and flexibility) must not be underestimated.[3]

The oligopolistic game played by the companies

Given the prospects for growth, many companies have announced that they will be setting up in the emerging countries. In many cases, total investment in production capacities has at any one time exceeded the most optimistic forecasts for market growth. This mismatch was even more pronounced when growth did not actually materialise. Excess production capacities can suddenly appear, since, with their oligopolistic strategies, producers are quick to imitate their rivals, and they will announce that they are going to invest in production. One of many examples of this type of competition has been in Turkey, where in 1992–93, for a local market of some 300 000–500 000 vehicles, producers announced investments creating a yearly capacity of 1 million vehicles. The example of Vietnam is even more noteworthy: total yearly sales barely reach 2500 vehicles, yet producers are jostling one another in order to invest there. In Brazil, more than US$10 billion was invested in the vehicle industry between 1991 and 1997. The average annual investment was US$2 billion in 1995–97, compared to US$0.5 billion in 1985–87.[4] New assembly plants will increase capacity by up to 1.2 million vehicles per annum between 1997 and 2002 (see Chapter 7 by Humphrey and Salerno, Table 2.3), for a domestic market which peaked at 2 million units in 1997. Even the more optimistic forecasts anticipate that the 1997 sales peak will not be reached again before 2003. The new plants will create considerable overcapacity.

Thus, it seems unavoidable, and even rather predictable, that excess production capacities will appear in most emerging countries where car makers are rushing, dragging the component makers along with them. It is not that they are blind – this is simply the logical result of competitive processes in an oligopolistic industry (Galliègue, 1996).

The positions in the principal automobile markets (European Union, North America, and Japan) are nowadays relatively stabilised, even if certain reversals of fortune may occur over the medium term. There is so much competition, especially in the European and North American markets, that most car makers are forced to start price wars which devastate their commercial margins. In this environment, vehicle production makes little or no money – it can even make losses. The vehicle groups only make a profit thanks to their presence in segments where there are still some protected market niches (for example, light trucks for the 'Big Three' in the United States), or else because of their financial activities (Froud *et al.*, 1997). Manufacturing activities engender very low profits. Moreover, there is to be a thorough reorganisation of the sales networks – this has already been started in the United States, where new players have arrived on the scene, and it has been announced for Europe, where the privileged status of car distribution will soon come to an end (Jullien, 1998).

Given how saturated these markets have become, car makers can only survive if they drastically reduce their costs, and if they offer a wider and more diversified range of products. They have to aim for economies of scale and, at the same time, for economies of scope. The platform strategies announced by all the vehicle groups (see Chapter 4 by Freyssenet and Lung, Table 4.1) are an attempt to respond to these constraints through the production of global cars – these are products which share the same platform and the main mechanical components (commonalisation), but which can be adapted to the local market (Shimokawa, 1996). This trend also affects first tier suppliers, who try to spread out costs and benefit from economies of scale and scope both by using complex components (which necessitate major investments in R&D) in car models produced globally, and sometimes by using the same components on different models (made by the same or by other car makers). The search for modularisation is an attempt to respond to the new market environment.

Prospects for growth in the emerging countries offer car makers opportunities for profits which they cannot achieve in their domestic markets. By producing for these countries the same product, or a variation derived from the same model or from the same platform as in the industrialised countries, companies are hoping to take advantage of the commonalisation of components and platforms. By so doing, they hope to benefit from an increase in volume, from economies of scale and scope, and from a reduction of their costs in their domestic markets. It is truly a global industry, as defined by Porter (1986): the competitive position of a company in any one market depends on its position in the other markets. In this case, a company which is absent from the emerging countries, despite its vulnerability to their particular type of uncertainty, would be permanently penalised. It is very difficult to catch up with the first movers, and though the consequences of having decided not to set up in these countries might not be felt in the immediate future, they can be very costly over the long run. Moreover, staying away makes it easier for competitors to move into the new market and be in the privileged position of having an uncontested, dominant position: even if profits are not made in this new market, it may be possible to keep an already established competitor from improving profitability, and thus reinforcing its global position.

This is a result of the economic analysis of foreign direct investment in cases of imperfect competition (Aussilloux, 1998). In an oligopolistic industry, firms have a higher incentive to invest in foreign countries in a situation of demand uncertainty than in a stable environment, and they emphasisze the flexibility of their investment to reduce their sunk costs. They try to limit costs in view of the risk of overcapacity, or to export to other markets if domestic sales fall.

UNCERTAINTY IN EMERGING COUNTRIES

Car makers are rushing to get established and to acquire a solid position in the emerging countries. They are making major decisions – yet, they are totally uncertain as to how these markets are going to evolve. This is an uncertainty of the 'radical' kind, in Knight's (1921) sense of the word, for the car companies are operating in a decision-making environment in which it is not possible to calculate any probable outcomes whatsoever. This obviously detracts from the reliability of forecasts made by specialised institutions. It is very unlike the traditional Triad markets, where there is a smaller margin of error. In the Triad zones, there is relatively little strategic uncertainty, as most behaviour involves mimicry – this allows a company to anticipate its competitors' reactions. The three factors which are most difficult to anticipate in emerging countries are politics, changes in demand, and exchange rates. Therefore, these are the uncertainties which companies need to manage.

Political uncertainty: can the liberalisation of trade be reversed?

It is necessary to take historical precedents into account, especially between the First and the Second World Wars. The internationalisation of the automotive industry is nothing new, having been one of the industry's main characteristics since its inception – at several junctures in the past, international trade has accounted for an even higher proportion of sales than it does today (Bardou *et al.*, 1982). History thus reveals the ebb and flow of this kind of change, due in part to the economic, political and social tensions which it engenders (Hirst and Thompson, 1996). Since internationalisation in and of itself is incapable of creating the rules which might ensure its own growth and longevity, there were reactions against it – first the protectionist policies of the 1930s, and later (during the post-war boom), the national policies of 'autocentric' growth, carried out against the background of the *Pax Americana*. Globalisation has never been fully achieved – it is neither irreversible nor unavoidable.

Uncertainty of this type, essentially political in nature, is still prevalent today, both internally (relations with the local authorities) and externally (international exposure). With respect to internal uncertainty, one must take into account the socio-political context, as well as governmental instability. In addition, in numerous cases, corruption is a method of political regulation – and it can be difficult to deal with people who behave opportunistically. In small countries, the major multinational groups have some room for manoeuvre. For example, General Motors has been able to oppose the Philippine government's desire to create its own 'national' motor industry, and as an alternative solution, it has selected Thailand for a new assembly factory designed to service the South East Asian market. However, the balance of power is reversed in the larger countries, and this can sometimes force the major car manufacturers into costly agreements. The problem faced by Chrysler, which believed it had won a project to construct a minivan factory in China only to be pipped at the post by Mercedes in 1996, is only one of the many misadventures to which companies operating in certain emerging countries can fall victim.

With respect to external uncertainty, there is nothing irreversible about the latest wave of liberalisation, a trend which has dominated the final years of the 20th century, and which has brought about the negotiation of new rules governing international trade (WTO). These rules seek to eliminate tariff and non-tariff barriers to trade, either immediately, or else after a transition period of variable length. They have resulted in the abandonment of import substitution policies, and in the reduction of tariff barriers and quotas in countries like Mexico, Brazil and Australia, which have suddenly had to open their markets to international competition. The IMF has recently exerted pressure on the nations of South East Asia to force them to open their markets to foreign products, which implies the end of their national vehicle policies and could be a new step in the liberalisation of automotive trade.

The trend seems obvious, but it varies among different countries (see Chapter 3 by Humphrey and Oeter), and it can be stymied in situations of crisis. An example is the decision taken by the Brazilian government in 1995. When faced with an aggravation of its external deficit due to a sudden increase in imports, it decided unilaterally to increase tariffs on cars, first to 32 per cent, and then to 70 per cent, before adopting a system of quotas, applicable even to its partners in Mercosur. Even though these measures were later watered down following bilateral talks with Argentina, and multilateral negotiations with the WTO, the situation was unclear. The conflicts between the two countries over car-industry policies in the summer of 1999 indicate the vulnerability of South American regional integration. Other circumstances could easily lead to a reversal of the process of liberalisation, such as a nationalist reaction (for example, in Indonesia). The process of globalisation contains contradictions (see Chapter 4 by Freyssenet and Lung), that can generate the opposite tendency.

Market uncertainty

In addition to the political uncertainties that result from forces and processes that are greater than the motor industry alone, manufacturers have to face up to the uncertainty of demand. Several times over the recent period, car sales in the emerging markets have suddenly dropped. A more precise definition of the nature of these markets is thus required.

Is emerging market demand volatile or reversible?

The first question concerns the general trend in these markets: is demand for vehicles simply very volatile? In other words, is it likely over a short period of time to experience great annual variations, without there being any real reversal of the underlying trend? Nowadays, this is the hypothesis which is usually adopted for the Asian markets: despite the sudden drop in demand, investments are not being cancelled, they are simply being delayed. The influx of investments in Russia also attests to managers' expectations that, after the recent brutal drop in this country's income, lasting growth will return.

In this hypothesis, it is necessary to be present in these markets so as to take advantage of the expansion phase, when demand suddenly accelerates – but it then becomes indispensable to adopt methods for the organisation of production so that business can be cushioned against large fluctuations in activity. This flexible adaptation becomes possible when the labour force can be adjusted almost instantaneously. However, such an individual solution only makes the situation more difficult: if vehicle sales fall, excess labour in the motor industry would be laid off, reducing costs for the motor companies. However, such redundancies would reduce household incomes and aggregate demand, amplifying macro-economic fluctuations. This is a long way from the virtuous circle extolled in Fordism (Boyer and Freyssenet, 1999), where mass production and mass consumption are combined.[5]

Nevertheless, the volatility hypothesis seems over-optimistic if we consider the previous drop in emerging countries' demand. As indicated in Table 2.4, the reduction in vehicle sales is considerable (35 to 70 per cent, 50 per cent being the general case), and the time to recover the peak is long (6–10 years), or even indefinite (South Korea). None of these emerging countries that have faced such a fall has yet recovered its peak level, and the probability of a return to the previous trend in demand growth is low.

These findings provide support for a second hypothesis which argues that growth in the emerging countries can be reversed. Periods of overheating alternate with long periods of stagnation, or even of sharply lower demand. It would be mistaken blithely to reject such a scenario. The historical precedent provided by Brazil should not be forgotten: strong growth in the 1970s, followed by a period of stagnation (the 'lost decade'), before activity picked up again (see Figure 2.1). More recently, there is the Mexican example, where the level of sales reached in 1992 will not be seen again before 2003, at the very earliest. There could be a similar scenario in the countries of South East Asia, if the crisis there lasts. Thailand could be interpreted as a case of a trend of increasing vehicle production and sales being

Table 2.4 Falls in motor vehicle sales in emerging markets

	Motor vehicle new registrations		Change (reduction %)	Year[a]		Time to recovery[a]
	Peak (000s)	Minimum (000s)		Peak	Minimum	
Turkey	526	237	54.9	1993	1995	2000? (7 years)
Argentina	507	323	36.3	1994	1995	2003? (9 years)
Mexico	704	187	69.3	1992	1995	2003? (11 years)
Asean-4[b]	1448	654	54.9	1996	1998	2005? (9 years)
South Korea	1671	780	53.3	1996	1998	No forecasts
Brazil	1912	1528	20.1	1997	1998	2003? (6 years)

Notes: [a] Information and forecasts in July 1999. [b] Indonesia, Malaysia, Philippines and Thailand.
Source: OICA, Fourin.

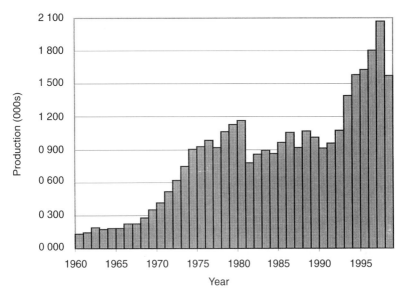

Figure 2.1   Production of motor vehicles in Brazil
Sources: ANFAVEA, OICA.

completely reversed. In 1996, local production peaked at 559 433 vehicles. It fell to 158 130 in 1998. The number of new motor vehicle registrations declined from 768 000 in 1995 to 201 055 in 1998.

The particularity of demand in the emerging countries

Extreme market segmentation explains in part why it is so difficult to
predict future demand for new vehicles in these countries. Historically,
in the industrialised nations, a steady and stable increase in demand
has been associated with the development of the middle classes –
because of their purchasing power, their need for mobility, and due to
the symbolic status of the car, households were led to spend a significant part of their extra income on the acquisition of motor cars
(Fordism).

These same conditions are not found in emerging countries. First of
all, households sometimes have access to a market for used cars, a
useful alternative to high priced new vehicles. The used car market,
which tends to be organised on a systematic, worldwide basis, is obviously crucial for the emerging countries. Secondly, it should be empha-

sised that the need for mobility can be satisfied otherwise than by privately owned cars. Transport can be collective – public transport and taxis – or individual – for example, two-wheeled vehicles (Godard, 1998). This is all the more true since the lack of a modern road infrastructure in the emerging countries hinders the diffusion of private cars – this is unlike the industrialised countries, where the rapid motorisation of households was enhanced by the road network built by the State.

Moreover, in nations of continental size, responsible for most of the growth in emerging country demand over the last few years (especially China and India), average income remains extremely low. The same models which are called entry-level in the European markets correspond to luxury vehicles in these markets – their quantity is limited, and their sales fluctuate. For example, in India, the so-called luxury models, equivalent to a Ford Escort, only represent 5 per cent of total car sales (Mukherjee, 1997). In Brazil, the growth in car demand during the 1990s was driven by the totally new segment of 'popular cars' (Norberto, 1999). These cars, with engines under 1000 c.c., represented 72.7 per cent of locally manufactured vehicle sales in 1998 – compared to 4.3 per cent in 1990. Finally, new car sales are sometimes mostly destined for taxi companies or for government employees – and not for private ownership: in China, less than 5 per cent of car sales are oriented towards households, compared to 55 per cent for taxis and commercial companies, 28 per cent for state-owned firms and government, and 12 for joint venture firms (Automotive Resources Asia).

In an environment like this, companies must put together adaptive strategies, but the presence of many manufacturers makes for more product variety, and consumers have become more demanding. The time when companies could simply sell obsolete products in protected markets has passed. A few years ago, obsolete models were being built and sold in the South (the Renault 12 and the Ford Taunus were still being assembled in Turkey in the mid-1990s), and they were being manufactured with worn-out equipment that had been shipped out from core country factories. Nowadays, the new products being built in the emerging countries are the latest versions of the same basic models as in the industrialised nations, and they may even be versions that were specifically adapted and developed for the Southern countries: the Fiat Palio, the Asian car and the three-box version of the Renault Clio 2 for example. Because of the low level of income in these countries (notwithstanding the recent rapid increase), and given the need to reach a significant sales volume in order to amortise investments, these models must be produced at a competitive cost (see above).

Global financial and exchange rate uncertainty

Growing international financial flows between countries, and in particular very short-term financial capital movements looking for high rates of return, is one of the main consequences of the globalisation process. Such short-term capital movements impose great pressures on currencies, especially in the more vulnerable emerging countries, and in recent years they have increased exchange rate volatility. In a matter of weeks, a national currency could lose 30 to 70 per cent of its value measured in US dollars. Most of the emerging markets have experienced this problem: Mexico in 1994 (50 per cent fall in a few days), the South East Asian countries and Russia in 1997–98 (30 to 70 per cent falls) and Brazil in January 1999 (40 per cent fall).

These fluctuations have pronounced short-term effects on domestic automobile demand:

- As the rate of interest generally rises to defend the national currency, this increases the cost of the credit that finances a large share of vehicle sales. Sales then fall.
- The general recession associated with financial crisis reduces economic activity, and pessimistic expectations arising from growing unemployment are followed by reductions in household consumption.

To evaluate the impact of interest rate changes – whose fluctuations are directly related to exchange rate policy – on vehicle sales, a simple theoretical model has been constructed using the least-square method. Considering the log–log adjustment of the direct relationship of vehicle sales (AUTOSALES, dependent variable) and the rate of interest (INTERESTRATE explanatory variable),[6] the following equation is constructed:

$$\text{Log (AUTOSALES)} = a \, \text{Log (INTERESTRATE)} + b$$

The parameter a can be interpreted as the elasticity of vehicle sales to the variation in the interest rate. The results are presented in Table 2.5. They show that interest rate fluctuations explain much of the fluctuations in vehicle sales in Brazil and in Mexico (elasticity equal to

Table 2.5   Regression of vehicle sales to interest rate

	a	b	r^2	Observation months
Brazil	−0.674	3.15	0.64	Jan.96–Jan.99
All vehicles	$(-7.96)^a$	$(25.05)^a$	63.41^b	$n = 37$
Mexico	−0.978	5.90	0.44	Jan.95–Dec.98
Cars and light trucks	$(-5.97)^a$	$(24.60)^a$	35.7^b	$n = 47$

Notes: [a] T value. [b] F value.

0.67 and 1 respectively). Uncertainty in exchange rates for emerging countries' currencies reinforce the uncertainty in demand.

Other medium- or long-term effects of exchange rates fluctuation must also be considered, as they have direct consequences on costs. Devaluation of the local currency has two well-known contradictory effects:

- rising prices for imported goods (components and vehicles);
- better price-competitiveness for exports.

As multinational investments in emerging countries are often – except in the case of the PAMs – oriented both towards the domestic market and towards exports, the effects of exchange rates fluctuations will depend upon the evolution of trade with the main foreign markets for local plants. Automobile firms could face many difficulties in cases of divergent tendencies in integrated regions: in NAFTA with the fall of the Mexican peso *vis-à-vis* the US dollar in December 1994; in the Mercosur with the downturn of the Brazilian real compared to the stability of the Argentinean currency, tied to the US dollar in the first half of 1999. To solve this kind of difficulties, interventionist policies are needed – US Treasury loans to Mexico in 1995, governmental negotiations between Argentinean and Brazilian Presidents in July 1999 – but these policies are not automatically engaged and their impact could be limited.

As it has a direct effect both on domestic demand and on costs and competitiveness, exchange rate uncertainty could discourage direct investment by multinational automobile companies in emerging countries. It reinforces their orientation towards strategies adapted to a world of high uncertainty.

Strategies for managing uncertainty in emerging markets

Vehicle makers are now in a difficult situation: despite all the uncertainty which can affect their expectations of how demand will grow in the emerging countries, it is imperative for them to be present in these countries if they want to capture market share for whatever turnover does actually materialise. In the current environment, where governments have kept certain forms of protectionism, it is necessary to build an assembly plant, or at least a CKD plant, in order to gain access to the local market. Companies which are not present can be severely punished. For this reason, car manufacturers can resort to different strategic options, depending both on the particular country under consideration, and on their own potential. Two main types of responses seem to predominate at the present time.

The decoupling of production and sales

The first orientation consists of decoupling production and sales through the creation of productive capacities which are designed to supply markets elsewhere than in the country where the vehicles are being assembled. The issue becomes one of exporting production, in variable proportions, towards other industrialised and/or emerging countries. This strategy is particularly adapted to areas on the periphery of the central, Triad zones. Mexico is the perfect illustration of this type of extroverted growth, and it is a perfect example of a textbook scissors effect: production and productivity grow at the same time as wages and local demand collapse (see Figure 2.2). Certain Central and Eastern European countries, like the Czech Republic, have not yet provided a clear illustration of this scenario, because local demand has continued to grow, but in the event of a downturn in domestic demand, a similar picture is likely to arise.

To a lesser degree, local production can accommodate great fluctuations (high volatility) of demand in the host country if market risks are spread among several emerging countries. This is the case in South East Asia and in South America, with their systems of regional integration, but such a strategy contains certain drawbacks because of the synchronicity with which regional crises tend to occur (the Tequila effect in 1995–96, the financial crisis in South East Asia in 1997–98). In addition to the issue of regional integration, companies can attempt to create links between entities located in the different emerging zones. By limiting the number of plants producing components which

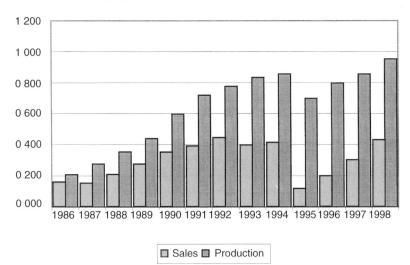

Figure 2.2   Sales and production of passenger cars in Mexico, 1986–98 (000s, units)
Sources: AMIA, OICA.

are sensitive to economies of scale, or by giving the responsibility for certain important tasks to particular poles of activity (for example, the development of specific models of vehicles adapted to the emerging countries), the issue becomes one of organising the flow of a number of products and services across a world-wide network (Humphrey, 1998). Given the many trade barriers which continue to exist between emerging countries, possibilities for creating organisations of this type at an international level are still limited. If the WTO continues to exert pressure in favour of even more deregulation by the year 2000, and given that this policy was strongly supported by the IMF when it was called in to help in South East Asia, it should in the near future be possible to develop a strategy emphasising the linkage of units in different emerging zones, especially since car makers have adopted strategies of global platforms and of commonalisation. This flexibility can also be attained by pushing variety management upstream, to the suppliers' doorstep.

The reduction of sunk costs

A second strategic orientation consists of limiting the sunk costs associated with investment, so that the company can withdraw without suffering any serious financial damage if expected sales do not materialise. This problem is akin to the financial constraint which affects car manufacturers who have been encouraged to set up in numerous emerging countries, yet who do not have sufficient funds to finance their multiple investments.[7] Several different solutions, which can work in combination, can satisfy this orientation.

The classical response to this type of situation consists of adopting a strategy of getting set up step by step, and of using different means to attain this end. A frequent method consists of first establishing a plant for CKD or Semi Knocked Down (SKD) vehicles, and of then transforming this into an assembly plant if sales attain the desired level. Moreover, with this strategy, it is possible to do a progressive learning, since assemblers can evaluate the local labour force's ability to adapt on the job (productivity, quality, involvement and so on), and they can assess the capabilities of the national components industry's local suppliers. This strategy may be useful if production volumes are low, but it is also risky if demand takes off – it may become impossible to catch up with competitors who were quicker to build production factories with sufficient capacity. This strategy is also vulnerable to the depreciation of the host country's currency. Import-dependent assemblers in ASEAN and Brazil were caught by devaluations in 1997 and 1999 respectively.

Another solution involves financing investment through an association with a local partner. This offers two advantages: on one hand, there is a lesser commitment of financial resources, and on the other hand, the indigenous partner, especially because of its familiarity with the local economy (socio-political networks, suppliers industry, distribution system, and so on), can offer competencies which supplement the technology transferred by the foreign manufacturer. Car makers are very reticent about this type of arrangement, as they cannot control the way in which decisions are made, and are thus forced to agree to compromises which they often consider to be suboptimal. Usually the manufacturers only resign themselves to solutions of this nature when they are forced to do so by rules governing foreign investment, and they try to get out of these restrictions as soon as possible (see the recent conflict over the control of the Indian company Maruti, or Peugeot's retreat from India and China). Nowadays car makers prefer another co-operative solution to reduce their own exposure to risk: one in which they associate with the components industry: the 'industrial condominium' (Salerno *et al.*, 1998).

Inasmuch as current forms of internationalisation are predicated on product convergence (global cars) and on the delegation of a growing part of activities to first-tier suppliers (who take on the role of system integrators), procurement management tends to take place on a world-wide scale – global sourcing (see Chapter 7 by Humphrey and Salerno). Suppliers who have won contracts to conceive, manufacture, and assemble a subsystem (suspension, seats, lighting and so on) in the car makers' country of origin are often asked to follow their clients when they set up in the emerging countries. Outsourcing activities allows the manufacturer to build a new assembly plant with a smaller investment: a growing percentage of total investment is allocated to suppliers who are asked to relocate near the new assembly plant in the emerging country (follow sourcing). More and more, car makers are forcing their partners to submit to this requirement if they want to win business in the core countries. Inversely, certain suppliers are trying to improve their relationships with the car makers by taking it upon themselves to relocate nearer to the manufacturers' factories in the emerging countries, hoping in the end to become a supplier in their country of origin.

To reduce their own financial investment, the suppliers themselves can associate with local partners, but they must then guarantee that they can reach international standards of competitiveness (productivity, quality, logistics and so on). As a result of this, there is a trend towards the distribution among a group of companies (the manufacturer and the main suppliers) of the risks of uncertainty which are specifically found in emerging markets. This system of mutuality is coupled with a process of socialization, since the car makers' investments often benefit from large sums of public money.[8] Together, these elements reduce the sunk costs which the manufacturer would have had to assume if expected sales had not materialised, an outcome which otherwise could have led to its departure. By making it easier for manufacturers to withdraw, entry barriers are greatly lowered, and this explains in part why companies are hurrying to get established in the emerging countries. It is not their short-sightedness which is at stake: they are often aware that the sum total of their accumulated investments will create overcapacity, but they hope that it is their competitors who will pay the price. When this is not the case, they make sure that they have a way out.

CONCLUSION

It would be exaggerated to talk about the 'mirage' of emerging countries, as their potential for growth is real, albeit not certain. However, it is important to relativise certain fabulous forecasts, and companies should be encouraged to define new methods for organising themselves internationally in ways which enhances their flexibility – this trait will be necessary if they are going to adapt, in these markets, to economic problems which might be foreseeable, but which are difficult to ascertain with precision. In turn, the companies' desire to cultivate an ability to adapt will certainly affect the way in which the motor industry is organised in the industrialised nations. The globalisation of the automotive industry is more than just the barely believable threat that operations will be relocated from the North to the South – it carries the seeds for a renewal of the whole sector's organisation, and the potential for transformations which will extend beyond the changes experienced in the 1980s, when Japanese methods of production were adopted. A new alchemy is being concocted for the organisation of production – and since this can be coupled with major technological changes (electric or hybrid vehicles), the landscape of the global automotive industry can be expected to experience a profound upheaval, even if this first occurs in the Triad nations, and not in the emerging zones.

Notes

* Translation by Alan Sitkin.
1. The monthly review *Automotive Emerging Markets*, first issued in 1997 by Financial Times Automotive, attests to this effervescence.
2. *Automotive Emerging Markets*, No. 2, 1997.
3. See Chapter 6 by Layan for a more extensive discussion of this point.
4. Information from ANFAVEA, the Brazilian Association of Vehicle Manufacturers.
5. In Fordism, demand grows in parallel with productivity growth through institutionalised procedures for increasing real wages (collective bargaining, social security and other indirect wages).
6. Monthly data. The proxy variable for interest rate is the interest rate on Treasury Bills for Mexico, and the inter-bank discount rate in Brazil.
7. The Korean car makers, especially Daewoo, had committed themselves to a strategy of all out investment throughout the emerging countries, but to do so, they had to take on a considerable amount of debt. The recent financial crisis revealed their vulnerability. They were forced to withdraw, and they even lost their autonomy.
8. The countries or regions which are likely to receive the new assembly plants are systematically placed in competition by the manufacturers. The national governments or local authorities are then forced to outbid each other in the provision of subsidies and tax exemptions. A consid-

erable proportion of the investment can be funded by the State (see the example of Ford 'Amazon' Project in Brazil), and the capital which the manufacturer must sink into the project is reduced by as much.

References

ALTSHULER, A., ANDERSON, M., JONES, D., ROOS, D. and WOMACK, J. (1984) *The Future of the Automobile: the Report of MIT's International Automobile Program.* Cambridge, MA: MIT Press.

AUSSILLOUX, V. (1998) *Investissement Direct à l'Etranger: Valeur d'Option et Valeur de Préemption.* Mimeo. Montpellier: LAMETA, Université de Montpellier.

BARDOU, J.P., CHANARON, J.J., FRIDENSON, P. and LAUX, J. (1982) *The Automobile Revolution: the Impact of an Industry.* Chapel Hill, NC.

BÉLIS-BERGOUIGNAN, M.C. and LUNG, Y. (1994) 'Le mythe de la variété originelle: L'internationalisation dans la trajectoire du modèle productif japonais'. *Annales (Histoire, Sciences Sociales),* No. 3, 541–67.

BOYER, R. and FREYSSENET, M. (1999) *The World that Changed the Machine.* Mimeo. Evry: GERPISA, Université d'Evry Val d'Essonne.

CARRILLO, J. (1998) 'The integration of the Mexican automobile industry to the USA: between policies and corporate strategies'. Paper presented at Sixth GERPISA International Auto Industry Colloquium, Paris, June.

CARRILLO, J. and HUALDE, A. (1997) 'Maquiladoras de tercera generacion. El caso de Delphi-General Motors', *Commercio Exterior,* Vol. 47, No. 9, 747–57.

FROUD, J., HASLAM, C., JOHAL, S. and WILLIAMS, K. (1997) 'Changing the area of the visible: a sector matrix for cars'. Paper presented to Fifth GERPISA International Auto Industry Colloquium, Paris, June.

GALLIÈGUE, X. (1996) 'Irréversibilités de l'investissement et valeurs d'option', *Revue d'économie Politique,* Vol. 106, 844–63.

GODARD, X. (1998) 'Eléments de débat sur l'extension de l'automobile dans les villes en développement', *Actes du GERPISA* (Université d'Evry-Val d'Essonne), No. 23, 35–44.

HIRST, P. and THOMPSON, G. (1996) *Globalization in Question.* Cambridge: Polity Press.

HUMPHREY, J. (1998) 'Assembler–Supplier relations in the auto industry: globalisation and national development'. Paper presented at the workshop Globalization of the Automobile Industry, Institute for Work and Technology, Gelsenkirchen, March.

JENKINS, R. (1995) 'The political economy of industrial policy: automobile manufacturers in the newly industrializing countries', *Cambridge Journal of Economics,* Vol. 19, 625–45.

JULLIEN, B. (1998) 'Les constructeurs américains face aux nécessaires mutations de la distribution. Quelles leçons tirer des rapides évolutions en cours aux Etats-Unis?', *Actes du GERPISA* (Université d'Evry-Val d'Essonne), No. 23, 77–91.

KNIGHT, F. (1921) *Risk, Uncertainty and Profit.* Houghton-Mifflin Company.

LAPLANE, M.F. and SARTI, F. (1999) 'Profit strategies in Mercosur: adaptability to changing conditions as a key factor for competition in unstable market'. Paper presented to the Seventh GERPISA International Auto Industry Colloquium, Paris, June.

MUKHERJEE, A. (1997) 'The Indian automobile industry: speeding in to the future'. Paper presented to the Fifth GERPISA International Auto Industry Colloquium, Paris, June.

NORBERTO, E. (1999) 'La révolution des petites cylindrées. Le marché nouveau des "voitures populaires" au Brésil'. Paper presented to the Seventh GERPISA International Auto Industry Colloquium, Paris June.

PORTER, M. (1986) 'Competition in global industries: a conceptual framework'. In Porter, M.E. (ed.), *Competition in Global Industries*. Boston, MA: Harvard Business School Press, pp. 15–60.

RUIGROK, W. and VAN TULDER, R. (1999) 'The integration of Central and Eastern Europe in car production networks', *Actes du GERPISA* (Université d'Evry-Val d'Essonne), No. 25, 119–54.

SALERNO, M., ZILBOVICIUS, M., ARBIX, G. and CARNERO, DIAS A.V. (1998) 'Changes and persistences on the relationship between assemblers and suppliers in Brazil'. *Actes du GERPISA* (Université d'Evry-Val d'Essonne), No. 24, 51–66.

SHIMOKAWA, K. (1996) 'Global sourcing, global product strategy in the world auto industry, and Japanese automakers' global strategy', *Keieishirim* (Hosei University), Vol. 32, No. 3, 1–16.

WOMACK, J.P., JONES, D.T. and ROOS, D. (1990) *The Machine that Changed the World*. New York: Rawson Associates.

3 Motor Industry Policies in Emerging Markets: Globalisation and the Promotion of Domestic Industry

John Humphrey and Antje Oeter*

INTRODUCTION

For much of the 1990s, vehicle production and sales grew rapidly in the emerging markets, while the vehicle markets of the Triad economies stagnated. From 1990 to 1997, vehicle sales in the major emerging markets grew by 92 per cent, and production by 99 per cent. Over the same period, sales and production in the Triad economies rose by 1 per cent and 4 per cent respectively (Fourin, 1998).[1] In this period, total vehicle sales in the Triad grew by 230 000, while sales in the major emerging markets grew by 3.9 million. Not surprisingly, production and sales in the emerging markets were expected to rise considerably in the early part of the 21st century.

The rapid growth of the vehicle industry in emerging markets took place in an overall context of increasing trade and economic liberalisation. Trade rose as a proportion of Gross Domestic Product (GDP) in these countries, and barriers to flows of goods and investment were generally lower at the end of the 1990s than they had been in the 1980s. Automotive industry trade regimes were significantly more open by the end of the 1990s. However, this in no way signified that governments in emerging markets had left the future of the motor industry in their countries to the play of market forces. This chapter will show that governments still actively sought to promote domestic vehicle production with a significant degree of local content.

It will be argued in this chapter that in the course of the 1990s governments in a number of emerging markets moved away from highly protective policies based on quantitative restrictions and prohibitively high tariffs. However, they continued to promote the motor industry through tariffs, licensing and TRIMs. The trade reforms agreed in the Uruguay Round not only reduced tariffs but also set a timetable for the phasing out of TRIMs. Local content and trade balancing requirements were deemed to be inconsistent with GATT provisions on national treatment, and trade and foreign exchange balancing requirements were held to constitute quantitative restrictions. WTO member countries were required to notify the WTO of GATT-inconsistent TRIMs, to phase them out within a set period (by 2000 for most emerging markets) and not to introduce new TRIMs in the interim (Low and Subramanian, 1998: 416).[2] However, as Sercovich (1997) has observed, the approach of deadlines for implementation of these agreements appears only to have intensified efforts to promote domestic motor industries in many countries. These efforts have been aimed at creating 'spaces' within which the domestic vehicle industry could not only flourish but also be prepared for a more liberalised trading environment.

A policy aimed at creating a domestic motor industry capable of competing in a future, more liberalised environment has three tasks:

- defining an 'automotive space' which is protected by policy measures acceptable to trading partners. This space might be national or regional;
- ensuring that the domestic motor industry is competitive within this space and able to attract FDI. The survival of the domestic motor industry depends upon its competitiveness within 'its' space and the attractiveness of this space for companies investing in the motor industry;
- preparing the domestic motor industry for a more liberalised trading environment. If tariffs are to fall and TRIMs to be phased out, then competition will increase and the motor industry should be helped to prepare for this.[3] This is important, not only because this liberalised environment will undermine inefficient local industries, but also because inefficient national motor industries impose a heavy burden on the rest of the economy.

In this chapter it will be argued that three distinct automotive spaces have been constituted in emerging markets: (i) highly-protected domestic markets; (ii) markets integrated into the production and sales systems of nearby Triad economies (the cases of Mexico and Central Europe); and (iii) regional markets, such as Mercosur.[4] Are these spaces viable, and will they create industries capable of competing in more open global automotive markets?

This chapter focuses on the passenger car and light commercial vehicle industry in six areas: ASEAN (Malaysia and Thailand only), Central Europe (Czech Republic, Hungary and Poland), China, India, Mercosur (Brazil only) and Mexico. It is divided into four sections. The next section discusses motor industry policies in the period up to the end of the 1980s. The third section examines policies in the 1990s, distinguishing between the automotive spaces outlined above. The final section considers the viability of the motor industries that have been created so far in emerging markets.

MOTOR-INDUSTRY POLICIES IN PRE-1990 PERIOD

In most emerging markets, motor industries were created in the context of broader import substitution industrialisation policies. The policies are summarised in Table 3.1. Brazil and Mexico moved rapidly to a high degree of local content in the late 1950s and early 1960s. India moved in the same direction at roughly the same time, although in a more autarchic fashion. In Thailand and Malaysia, the move to local production began later, in the 1970s, when local content regulations were imposed, and it was not until the 1980s that significant local content was achieved. In addition to the five countries listed in Table 3.1, the motor industries of China and Central Europe were developed behind protective barriers and in the context of State regulation of the economy.

In every case, quantitative restrictions, high tariffs and local content regulations were used to limit imports of built-up (BU) cars and oblige local assemblers to source at least some components domestically.[5]

Governments promoted local assembly and local production of components in order to generate employment, develop technological capabilities through spillovers into local industry and reduce the foreign exchange cost of imported vehicles and components. The shortcomings of such policies have been well documented.[6] The first stage, assembly of CKD kits, adds little to the local economy and is frequently characterised by model proliferation. However, in small markets, restricting the number of producers and increasing local content creates new inefficiencies through protection, monopoly and low volume production of components. Companies can still make a profit in the local market through charging high prices (see Chapter

Table 3.1 Motor industry policies in the import substitution period

Country	Start date	Policy
Brazil	1956	Ban on built-up cars (BUs) and move to 95% local content by weight for cars in five years. Quantitative restrictions on components available locally. No restrictions on ownership in vehicle or component sectors.
Mexico	1962	Ban on BUs. Local content fixed at 60%, increased to 65% for passenger cars in 1977. Quantitative restrictions on component imports. Initial proposals to limit number of firms and standardise parts between them not put into practice. Assemblers limited to final assembly and engines, and component companies had to be majority Mexican-owned.
India	1950s	Car industry subjected to controls applied more generally in manufacturing, including bans on BUs and completely knock down (CKD) kits, restrictions on foreign ownership, control of technology licensing agreements and a licensing regime which controlled the type and quantity of vehicles produced.
Thailand	1970s	Ban on BU imports after 1978. CKD tariff 112% in late 1980s. Local content requirement increased from 25% in 1977, to 35% in 1981, 50% in 1984 and 54% in 1987.
Malaysia	1970s and 1980s	Quotas and tariffs imposed on BU imports in 1966. Local content requirement increased from 10% by weight in 1972 to 35% in 1982. National car programme in 1983. Proton allowed to import CKD at reduced tariffs and pay reduced excise tax. Mandatory deletion list for components introduced in 1978 and quantitative restrictions introduced on a range of items. Restrictions on number of entrants to industry and models produced, and support for Malay ownership in the sector.

Sources: Brazil: Shapiro (1994); Mexico: Bennett and Sharpe (1984; 1985); India, Humphrey et al. (1998); Malaysia and Thailand: Abdulsomad (forthcoming) and information supplied by Kamaruding Abdulsomad.

9 by Guiheux and Lecler), but there is a cost for the economy as a whole.

One means of obtaining greater scale and also overcoming the problem of market size is to promote exports. Export promotion policies were developed with particular effect in Brazil and Mexico. In 1970, automotive exports from Brazil were less than US$10 million. By 1980, vehicle exports had risen to 13.5 per cent of domestic production, and exports of automotive products had reached US$1 billion. Similarly, the Mexican government began automotive export promotion in the 1970s. Further incentives were developed in the 1980s, and Mexico became a major export platform for US firms. In 1980, Mexico exported 18 245 vehicles, 3.7 per cent of total vehicle production. By 1990, vehicle exports had increased to 276 869 units, 33.7 per cent of total vehicle production.[7]

It is important to recognise, however, that these export promotion policies were pursued in the context of extensive protection of the domestic market. Although Brazil exported 187 000 vehicles in 1990, only 115 vehicles were imported. Similarly, Mexico imported 5376 vehicles in 1990 (less than 1 per cent of domestic vehicle sales), while exporting 276 869 units.

EMERGING MARKETS IN THE 1990s

Motor industry policies in the emerging markets changed drastically in the 1990s. Overall, policies continued to be driven by the same priorities – the motor industry should thrive in order to generate technological capability, foreign exchange and employment. The domestic industry should not be undermined by imports, and as far as possible it should not create a drain of foreign exchange. These gains were considered to outweigh the costs of protection.

These common policy aims have been pursued in quite distinct ways in different countries. In the introduction to this volume, three types of emerging markets were identified, PAMs, IPMs and ERMs. Each of these has a distinct approach to the creation of a viable auto industry.

Protected autonomous markets

The PAMs are those countries which continue to provide strong protection to the national market and the domestic industry. The clearest cases are China and India. Both countries have liberalised policy, particularly with regard to the participation of foreign companies in the motor industry, but protection remains strong. The policy regimes in force at the end of the 1990s were broadly similar to those adopted in countries such as Argentina and Brazil in the import substitution period. As can be seen in Table 3.2, both countries maintained high tariffs or quantitative restrictions on BUs, CKD and components. In India, imports of passenger cars remained almost entirely restricted: only 1681 new built-up cars were imported in 1997–98 (ACMA, 1999). In China, light vehicle imports were substantially reduced in the 1990s, falling from 31.2 per cent of sales in 1992 to 9.4 per cent in 1997 (Standard and Poor's DRI, 1999: 130). Automotive policies aimed to build up a domestic industry by attracting foreign capital to a protected domestic market, and the government closed off many of the channels that had been used to import passenger cars.

In both countries, the need for protection arose from the inefficiency of the domestic motor industry. The Chinese passenger car industry was both technologically backward and highly fragmented in the late 1980s. A large number of companies produced outdated models at low volumes, and the industry was completely incapable of meeting the burgeoning demand for cars. In India, the car industry was small and inefficient, and only one company, Maruti, produced passenger cars at a volume greater than 30000 units per annum.

Given the large potential size of both markets, both countries were able to maintain a high degree of protection for the national market while attracting considerable investment from transnational car companies. However, the degree of government intervention differed considerably in the two cases. In 1994 the China Automotive Industry Development Policies set out the objectives of creating a strong car industry with six or seven internationally competitive firms making passenger cars on a scale sufficient to supply 90 per cent of domestic demand. In order to achieve these goals, the government retained high tariffs on built-up vehicles and CKDs, and specified rapidly increasing local content. Further, the car industry was to contribute to industrialisation as a whole through technology transfer (Polly, 1998: 2), and to this end the government imposed controls on ownership and technology transfer for foreign companies in the sector. The number of new entrants into the assembly sector was restricted, and foreign companies were obliged to enter joint ventures as minority partners, with Chinese partners selected by the government.[8]

The highly interventionist nature of Chinese policies contrasts

Table 3.2   Motor industry policies in mid-1990s: protected autonomous markets

Policy	China	India	Malaysia
Imports of BUs	Licence and quota system abolished in 1994. BU tariff 80–100% in 1997 (less than half 1992 level). Tighter controls on special import channels	Almost complete ban; petrol-engined vehicles subject to tariff of 100%.	Quota on BU imports reduced from 10% to 5% of local production between 1989 and 1995. Imports subject to tariff between 40% and 200% according to engine size.
Imports of CKD and components	CKDs: 150% tariff (50% during first three years of operation). After third year of operation, tariffs on components dependent upon local content rate: 60–80% = 32% tariff 40–60% = 48% tariff under 40% = 80% tariff	CKD tariff, 48% in 1997. Components tariffs between 39% and 69% in 1997–98.	CKD tariff 42%, except for Proton and Perodua, 13%. Component tariff, 35%. Lower tariffs on imports from ASEAN region within BBC scheme. Proton and Perodua pay only half excise tax level of other firms.

	China	India	Malaysia
Local content requirement	Incentive to increase local content through tariff structure (see above). Local content guidelines indicate 40% in year 1, 60% in year 2 and 80% in year 3.	50% in first three years, 70% by end of fifth year.	Requirement increased between 1993 and 1996 from 40% to 60% for cars with engines under 1850cc and from 30% to 45% for larger cars. ASEAN components considered local.
Foreign exchange	Companies must generate foreign currency to cover import requirements.	Companies must generate foreign currency to cover import requirements.	None.
Number of companies	Entry strictly limited by Chinese government. Policy in 1998: target is 6–7 companies.	Unlimited as long as investment, local content and export commitments agreed.	Restricted entry of foreign assemblers
Ownership	Assemblers must be majority Chinese-owned. Component companies may have majority foreign ownership.	In effect, 100% foreign ownership allowed in assembly and component sectors.	Considerable privileges given to 'national' assemblers and support for Malay-owned companies.

Sources: China: Lee (1996), Ikeda (1998) and Polly (1998); India: Humphrey *et al.* (1998); Malaysia: Jayasankaran (1993), Rasiah (1998) and Abdulsomad (forthcoming).

markedly with those in India. While the domestic market was heavily protected, the Indian government made little attempt to influence the structure of the industry. Restrictions on foreign ownership were effectively scrapped, and wholly foreign-owned companies were permitted in both assembly and components. The government allowed any company meeting certain basic conditions about investment, foreign exchange, local content and exports to enter the market. This led to considerable fragmentation of production in an already small market. By mid-1999, nine new companies had joined the three existing assemblers to compete for a total market of under half a million cars per annum.[9]

The long-term prospects for the Indian and Chinese markets remain attractive. Their large populations and long-term potential for economic growth should eventually generate considerable demand for vehicles. However, car producers in both countries (with the exception of Maruti and VW-Shanghai) were still struggling to achieve sufficient scale to bring down the costs of local assembly and component manufacture. In China there is the political will to sustain the car industry, and even if China joins the WTO it is likely to continue promoting a local car industry. In India, already a WTO member, some conformance to Uruguay Round agreements is likely, and this may lead to a radical restructuring of the industry. This point will be discussed in the final section.

Malaysia provides a third case of a highly protectionist policy. From the mid-1980s, the government's strategy centered on the promotion of nationally owned assemblers. This strategy arose not only from the Malaysian government's support for Malay capital but also from its difficulties in persuading transnational car companies to increase local content. The government created Proton in 1983 through a tie-up with Mitsubishi and nurtured it through tariffs, quotas and preferential terms for CKD imports and domestic excise tax compared to other producers. Quotas on imports of components were also used to encourage domestic components production. The level of protection for the car industry rose in the 1990s, as can be seen in Table 3.2. The quota levels for CBU imports were reduced from 10 per cent to 5 per cent of local production, and the local content requirement for cars increased. These policies were taken further with the creation of a second 'national champion', Perodua, which produced its first car in 1994.

These policies clearly contravene WTO rules on quantitative restrictions and 'national treatment' (treating national and imported products equally within the domestic market), but the driving force for changes in automotive policies has been the East Asian crisis. In the context of the collapse of the domestic market, the continued inefficiency of the two national car companies and ASEAN free trade area (AFTA) integration plans, the government radically shifted its national car policy. Toyota took control of Perodua, and the government began seeking a minority partner for Proton. Greater integration with other ASEAN countries in the context of reduced overall protection for the region is now likely.[10] Malaysia is an example of how difficult it is to create an efficient car industry behind protective barriers.

Integrated peripheral markets

Mexico and Central Europe have taken a completely different route to developing the motor industry – integration with their Triad neighbours. In the case of Mexico, the NAFTA agreement has both recognised and reinforced the integration of the Mexican motor industry with the United States and Canada. In Central Europe (Poland, Hungary and the Czech Republic), the motor industry has been restructured and increasingly integrated with the European Union following the collapse of the Soviet bloc. In both cases, the late 1990s was a transition period towards complete integration into the production and sales spaces of the IPMs' Triad partners.

The integration of the Mexican motor industry with North America began in the 1980s, when export-oriented assembly and component plants were built in the north of Mexico. A combination of export promotion policies in Mexico and a search for cheap production sites by the Big Three US producers had turned Mexico into an important site for assembly of light vehicles for the North American market by the early 1990s.[11] However, the domestic market in Mexico remained protected by tariffs and local content requirements.

The NAFTA agreement will eventually abolish these restrictions, and light vehicles meeting the NAFTA local content requirement (which will increase to 62.5 per cent by 2002) will be traded freely within NAFTA. The NAFTA treaty provisions, summarised in Table 3.3, establish transitional arrangements. Up to 2004, only companies making light vehicles in Mexico can import vehicles into the domestic market, and these imports are subject to quotas and foreign currency balancing (Audet and VanGrasstek, 1997: 23).[12] Similarly, vehicles made in Mexico for the Mexican market must have at least

Table 3.3 Motor industry policies in mid-1990s: integrated peripheral markets

Policy	Mexico	Central Europe
Imports of BUs	Ban on BUs lifted in 1989; under NAFTA, tariffs on imports of BUs from Canada and the USA cut from 20% to 10%, and to be phased out by 2004 for cars, and by 1999 for light vehicles.	Import quotas in Poland and Hungary for new cars; ban for used cars over six years old in Hungary; tariffs on BUs gradually reducing from 11.4% in 1995 to zero in 2001 in Czech Republic and Hungary; reducing from 30% to zero in Poland by 2002.
Imports of CKD and components	No tariffs on 15% of components imported from the USA and Canada; increased to 54% of components within 5 years; no restrictions on intra-NAFTA trade after 2004; higher tariff rates for imports from other countries.	Tariffs for imports from the EU ranging from 0–7.3%, higher tariff rates for non-EU countries.
Local content requirement	Mexican value added to be reduced from 34% in 1995 to a 29% in 2003 and then completely abolished in 2004. However, the requirement for NAFTA value-added will rise from 50% to 62.5% by 2002.	60% of European manufactured content required to qualify for duty-free export to EU.
Foreign exchange	Assemblers must balance imports and exports until 2003.	Not applicable.
Number of companies	No restrictions	No restrictions.
Ownership	100% foreign ownership possible: ownership constraints being phased out.	100% foreign ownership now possible.

Sources: Central Europe: Sljivic (1995) and van Tulder (1998).
Mexico: Moreno Brid (1996) and Durán *et al.* (1997).

29 per cent local value added until 2003, and imported components for these vehicles must be balanced by exports of components or vehicles. Any surplus can be used to import cars, which are subject to a 10 per cent tariff until 2004. This policy allows an increasing division of labour between Mexico and North America (the USA and Canada) while both providing considerable support to the Mexican industry and benefiting companies with plants in both Mexico and North America. The Big Three US assemblers have been the main beneficiaries.

Mexico has proved an attractive location for vehicle assembly and labour-intensive components production. According to Lynch (1998: 21): 'Within North America, Mexico is at once an important site for low-skilled, labour-intensive production; has an export capacity in engines; and has emerged as an important source of assembled vehicles.' By the late 1980s, Mexico had a large trade surplus with the rest of North America in built-up vehicles, and a large deficit in automotive components and engines, and this pattern of trade has been strengthened by NAFTA.[13]

In some respects, Central Europe is moving towards a similar relationship with Western Europe, characterised by a high degree of regional integration and interdependence.[14] In the early 1990s, following the collapse of the Communist political and trading system, governments in central Europe looked to the EU for FDI and for their long-term political future. The new governments adopted 'hands off' industrial policies. No attempt was made to develop a common central European car policy, and in some respects it is easier for Central European countries to trade with the EU than with each other. Foreign investment was seen as the means to restructure ailing state-owned industries, and the three major passenger car producers in the region (Skoda in Czechoslovakia, and FSM and FSO in Poland) had been sold to foreign buyers by 1995.

As in the case of NAFTA, the integration process creates a regional market, with a European content requirement of 60 per cent for eligibility for duty-free export to Western Europe. Just as NAFTA favoured the US Big Three vehicle producers, so the European content requirement favoured the Western European car manufacturers against the Asian entrants, Daewoo in Poland and Suzuki in Hungary. Similarly, integration has been phased. Some quotas were placed on imports from Western Europe, particularly of second-hand cars, and phased reductions in tariffs up to 2001/2002 were agreed (see Table 3.3).

Table 3.4   Automotive trade between European Union (EU) and Central Europe,[a] 1996

Product	Exports to EU	Imports from EU
Passenger cars with engines <1500cc (units)	239300	146588
Passenger cars with engines >1500cc (units)	23914	150935
All vehicles (value, ECU million)	1202	2067
Parts and components (value, ECU million)[b]	601	936
Exports/production (%)	35.3	–
Imports/domestic sales (%)	–	49.0

Notes: [a] Trade between 12 EU members before enlargement in 1995 and the Czech Republic, Hungary and Poland. [b] Excludes engines, bodies and chassis with engines.
Sources: Imports and exports: Eurostat, EU trade statistics. Production and sales, EIU (1998).

Integration between the motor industries of Western and Central Europe has taken three forms. First, there has been increasing two-way trade in vehicles. Central Europe offers both growing domestic markets and low-cost production sites. Sales of passenger cars in the Visegrad countries (that is, Czech Republic, Hungary, Poland and Slovakia) increased by 12.5 per cent per annum between 1992 and 1997, reaching 730000 units in the latter year. A significant part of this market is being supplied by imports from Western Europe. Car imports from the European Union had been negligible in the 1980s, but they accounted for 49 per cent of sales in 1996 (Table 3.4). Central Europe is also exporting cars to the EU. Approximately one-third of all cars produced in 1996 were exported to the EU.

As can be seen in Table 3.4, Central Europe has specialised in small-car production. More than 90 per cent of car exports to the EU had an engine capacity below 1500c.c., and approximately 50 per cent were cars with an engine capacity under 1000c.c. exported from Poland.[15] Fiat Poland is fully incorporated in Fiat's European division of labour, concentrating on small-car production – primarily, the Fiat Cinquecento, but also the Palio (Fiat's car for emerging markets), for which Poland is Fiat's only European production site. Central Europe has begun to replace Spain as the Continent's preferred location for low-end car production.[16] Similarly, VW has positioned Skoda at the cheaper, more cost-conscious end of the VW range.

Secondly, a number of export-oriented engine and component plants have been built in Central Europe since 1990. The most notable examples are the Audi and Opel (GM) engine assembly plants in Hungary. These plants were constructed to assemble parts imported from plants in Germany for re-export back to assembly operations in Western Europe.[17] A further example is Ford's component plant in Hungary.

The development of a low-end car assembly plants and export-oriented component plants has certain similarities with the development of the Mexican vehicle industry in the 1990s. However, there are also clear signs of a new element in the regional division of labour – major investments in component manufacture for the domestic car industry in Central Europe. Both VW and Fiat have developed local supplier bases in Central Europe through a mixture of encouraging follow sourcing by major transnational component companies and the upgrading of existing local suppliers. According to Havas (1997: 217–18), 80 per cent of Skoda's bought-in components were sourced from within Czechoslovakia in the early 1990s, and an increasing proportion of these components were sourced from the wholly owned or joint venture companies set up by Western component manufacturers. Similarly, Fiat Auto Poland was increasing its sourcing from within Poland, but switching from locally owned suppliers to transnational companies (Havas, 1997: 218).[18]

In both Mexico and Central Europe, governments have looked to regional integration and FDI to provide scale and efficiency. This certainly helps to reduce inefficiencies in the motor industry. Governments expect to generate investment and employment in labour-intensive activities in the short term, and hope that eventually higher-skilled jobs will also be created.

Emerging regional markets

An alternative form of regional integration is the development of regions consisting solely of emerging markets. This section considers two countries, Brazil and Thailand, that have formed part of Mercosur and ASEAN respectively. Both countries have sought to increase the efficiency of their motor industries by reducing protection and increasing competitive pressures and by using access to the domestic market as a lever to promote investments by

Table 3.5   Brazilian automotive trade, 1989–97

		Exports		Imports	
Product	*Year*	*US$ million*	*% to Mercosur*	*US$ million*	*% from Mercosur*
Vehicles	1989	1506	5.2	4	1.0
	1991	871	26.1	196	18.4
	1993	1432	42.9	879	26.5
	1995	1075	40.4	3863	15.2
	1997	2494	50.2	3423	58.2
Components	1989	2270	4.4	920	9.7
	1991	2337	11.7	1095	12.1
	1993	3237	25.6	1767	22.9
	1995	3583	25.4	3309	22.3
	1997	4566	32.1	4791	17.3

Source: SECEX, calculated by the research programme, 'Globalização e Capacitação Tecnológica na Cadeia Produtiva do Mercosul', headed by Ruy Quadros and Sérgio Queiroz at the University of Campinas.

transnational companies. In both cases, regional integration schemes are designed to increase scale, but this has been much more effective in Mercosur than in the ASEAN region.

Brazil

Trade liberalisation and regional integration began to transform the Brazilian motor industry in the early 1990s. Quantitative restrictions were abolished, and by 1994 the tariff on BU passenger cars had fallen to 20 per cent. The Economic Complementation Agreement, signed in Buenos Aires in 1990, allowed for tariff-free trade in automotive products between Argentina and Brazil, subject to trade balancing and quotas (Roldán, 1997). The impact on trade of these measures is shown in Table 3.5. The reduction of the external tariff to 20 per cent and a resurgence of domestic demand led to a flood of imported vehicles. Imports of both vehicles and components grew substantially, and the trade deficit in vehicles reached US$2.8 billion in 1995. Although trade within Mercosur increased, most imports came from outside the region.

In response to the ballooning trade deficit, the Brazilian government introduced a new automotive policy, whose main elements are summarized in Table 3.6.[19] This policy protected the local assembly industry through greatly increased tariffs on cars from outside of Mercosur (quotas were also introduced, but later withdrawn in the face of WTO opposition), while reducing tariffs on components. It allowed assemblers with operations in Brazil to import capital goods, raw materials, components and built-up vehicles at reduced tariff rates, provided foreign exchange balancing requirements were met. This encouraged FDI in the assembly sector.

The new policy did not reduce trade in automotive products, but it brought the trade deficit under control and diverted trade in BU vehicles to Mercosur. By 1997, more than half of Brazil's vehicle imports and exports were traded with Mercosur.[20] Trade in components, however, remained predominantly with Europe and North America.

These policies, together with a buoyant internal market in Brazil, greatly increased the efficiency and scale of the industry. By 1995, small cars were being produced in large volumes. Fiat produced 233 000 units of the Uno Mille in 1995 and 267 000 units of the full Uno range. Similarly, VW produced 304 000 units of the Gol model (a Brazilian variant of the Polo), and GM 157 000 units of the Corsa (Carvalho *et al.*, 1997: 47 and 71).[21] At the same time, the low tariffs applied to components restructured the domestic components industry.

By the late 1990s, a genuine regional automotive production system was developing in Mercosur, based on a division of labour in vehicle and components production between Argentina and Brazil. The major assemblers, all of whom planned to have assembly plants in both countries by the year 2000, were beginning to produce different models and model variants in the two countries, and also to source major components from just one site in each country.[22] Nevertheless, intra-regional trade remained highly managed, and the motor industry was one of the main exemptions from harmonisation, reduction of external tariffs and free trade between Mercosur countries. The external tariff and effective rate of protection was much higher for vehicles than for any other product (Laird, 1997).

The success of this strategy is endangered by continuing uncertainty about policy. Motor industry policies have been the subject of repeated disagreements between Argentina and Brazil (Mortimore, 1998: 129–30), and tensions between the two countries increased

Table 3.6 Motor industry policies in mid-1990s: emerging regional markets

Policies	Brazil	Thailand
Imports of CBUs	Quantitative restrictions abolished in 1991. Tariff on BUs reduced from 85% in 1990 to 20% in 1994. Then raised to 70% in 1995. Will fall to the level of Mercosur common external tariff by 2000 (likely to be 35%); 50% reduction for companies assembling vehicles in Brazil up to 1999.	Quantitative restrictions abolished in 1991. Tariff for CBUs reduced from 100% in 1991 to 40–68% in 1997; temporary increase to 80% from October 1997 to 1999.
Imports of CKD and components	Tariff on components 16%, but reduced to 2.4% in 1996 for local assemblers, returning in stages to 16% by 2000. Tariff-free trade within Mercosur, but subject to import–export balancing requirements until 2000.	Tariff on CKD 20% (from formerly 112%); components tariff 42–60%. AICO scheme for ASEAN allows imports at 0–5% tariff, subject to certain conditions being fulfilled.
Local content requirement	60% calculated by value. Mercosur considered local content.	Local content 54%, and certain high-value items must be produced locally. To be abolished in 2000;[a] ASEAN considered local content.
Foreign exchange requirement	For each US$1 imported, $1 must be exported. For components imported at reduced tariffs, $1 in imports requires $1.50 in exports.	None.
Number of companies	No restrictions.	No restrictions. Ban on new plants lifted in 1993.
Ownership	No restrictions.	No restrictions on ownership. Companies participating in the AICO scheme must have 30% local ownership.
Incentives	Reduced taxes on small cars have led to a large expansion in this sector of the market.	No excise tax on pickups, compared to 35–40% tax on cars. Pickups a considerable part of local market.

Notes: [a] The phasing out of the local content requirement for cars was to be brought forward to 1998 as part of an agreement with GM. The postponement of this investment because of the East Asian crisis has meant that the government has returned to the original timetable.

Sources: Brazil: Bedê (1997) and Humphrey *et al.* (1998); Thailand: Rasiah (1998) and Abdulsomad (forthcoming).

considerably following the devaluation of the Brazilian Real in February 1999. This left the Argentine motor industry at a substantial competitive disadvantage, and further regulation of trade between the two countries seemed inevitable. A free market in automotive products within Mercosur is still some distance away.

Thailand

Thailand liberalised its automotive investment and trade regime in the 1990s (see Table 3.6), seeking to establish itself as the leading vehicle manufacturer in the ASEAN region. Quantitative Restrictions were abolished in 1991, tariffs on BUs, CKD and components were reduced, and a timetable for abolishing local content requirements was established. However, tariffs on passenger cars remained high, and local content requirements remained in force to promote the development of high value-added components industries.

The challenge facing Thailand, in common with other emerging markets, was to achieve scale. By the mid-1990s, both expertise and scale had been secured in the production of pickups, for which Thailand was the second largest global market in 1990. Isuzu, Mitsubishi, Nissan and Toyota all produced more than 50 000 units of their leading light (one-ton) pickup models (Automotive Industries, 1998) in 1995. These volumes, which are high for this type of vehicle, reflected both local vehicle use and local vehicle taxation, which exempted pickups from the 35–40 per cent sales tax levied on passenger cars. The situation for passenger car production was much less promising. It was fragmented across a large number of makers and models. The best-selling car, the Toyota Corolla, sold under 50 000 units in 1996, and 15 models competed in the subcompact, compact and midsize market segments (Siraprapapong, 1998: 40).

The search for scale was impeded by the isolation of the domestic market. Thailand did not become a major vehicle exporter (unlike Mexico and Brazil, see above). Vehicle exports from Thailand accounted for less than 5 per cent of total production in the early 1990s, and even just prior to the East Asian crisis less than 10 per cent of vehicle production was exported.[23] Similarly, exports of components were insignificant compared to imports. For every dollar of vehicles and components exported from Thailand in 1996, six dollars were imported (Bank of Thailand, 1998).

Regional integration in ASEAN did not increase scale, in large part because the various vehicle producers in the region continued to promote their own national industries. Trade in vehicles with the ASEAN region remained very limited, and the analysis by Guiheux and Lecler in Chapter 9 shows clearly that there was relatively little trade in components, in spite of the brand-to-brand complementation (BBC) scheme introduced in 1988. Guiheux and Lecler show that only 6 per cent of Thai automotive exports were directed to ASEAN countries in 1995. Similarly, in 1996, 85 per cent of vehicles and components imported into Thailand came from Japan and Germany (Bank of Thailand, 1998). Data at the firm level provided by Guiheux and Lecler support these findings. Japanese companies made little use of the BBC scheme, and Guiheux and Lecler do not expect the introduction of the AICO scheme to change this situation in the short term.

It remains to be seen whether the crisis that started in 1997 belatedly promotes regional integration or, in fact, encourages Thailand to seek a new role within a broader Asian division of labour. This point will be discussed in the next section.

HAVE MOTOR INDUSTRY POLICIES CREATED VIABLE EMERGING MARKETS?

In the introduction to this chapter, three aims for policy were defined: constituting 'spaces', ensuring the competitiveness of the domestic industry within them and preparing the industry for more liberal trading regimes. How far are the three different types of emerging markets along the road to achieving the third of these objectives?

The protected autonomous markets

The two large PAMs, China and India, were successfully constituted as national spaces. They have attracted foreign capital into the domestic motor industry, while isolating it from foreign competition. This policy could probably only be attempted now in large countries with low levels of motorisation. Their size is sufficient to make market access desirable to transnational vehicle producers, and their relatively low incomes mean that they are more likely to obtain exemptions and delays in the application of agreements on trade liberalisation.

However, most firms in the two countries produce vehicles in small, inefficient volumes, and any opening up of trade would certainly lead

Table 3.7   Production volumes for models at a single plant

| Country | Vehicle type | Production volumes (000s) | | | | |
		>100	50–100	20–50	<20[a]	Year
China	Cars	1	1	2	7	1995
China	Pickups, utility vehicles and vans	0	1	8	19	1995
India	Cars	1	1	1	9	1998
Malaysia	Cars	1	1	1	14	1995[b]
Malaysia	Vans	0	0	0	5	1995
Mexico	Cars	3	3	5	1	1997
Mexico	Pickups and utility vehicles	2	2	1	1	1997
Argentina	Cars	0	1	6	4	1997
Brazil	Cars	5	3	4	3	1997
Indonesia	Cars	0	0	1	13	1995
Indonesia	Vans and utility vehicles	0	1	2	10	1995
Thailand	Cars	0	1	3	7	1995
Thailand	Pickups	0	4	1	1	1995

Notes: [a] Excludes models with production of under 1000 units in the relevant year. [b] Data for Proton refers to 1997.
Sources: Automotive Industries (1998), except for India (ACMA, 1999) and Proton (Storey, 1998).

to a drastic restructuring of production. The extent of the problem is shown in Table 3.7, which calculates production volumes by model and plant. Table 3.7 shows that in India only one model of passenger car was produced in a volume greater than 100 000 units in 1997. This was the Maruti 800. The new entrants to the industry were all producing in very low volumes, and scales are likely to remain low while the domestic market is split between so many companies. A similar picture is shown for China. In 1995, 39 models of light vehicle were produced. Production of only one model exceeded 100 000 units in 1995 (the Shanghai-VW Santana), with two others exceeding 50 000 units. This is not a barrier to growth and profitability for car companies, as the market remains protected, but it demonstrates that without continued protection many assemblers and component manufacturers would not survive.

Such protection appears to be sustainable in China, in spite of increasing uncertainty about auto industry policies in 1999, but in

India it is probably not. The car industry was a key case for the liberalisation efforts in the 1990s and it is far from clear that the government will fight to keep high tariffs and foreign exchange balancing requirements. Some further integration of the Indian car industry into the global car industry seems likely. However, past protection of the industry may leave Indian firms unprepared for this.

Integrated peripheral markets

Mexico and Central Europe are being incorporated into the motor industries of North America and Western Europe. For these countries, the future of the motor industry depends upon providing competitive production locations for producers from the nearby Triad regions. Generally speaking, integration has solved the problem of scale in the IPMs. The data presented in Table 3.7 show that the majority of passenger car and light vehicle models assembled in Mexico attained volumes of 50 000 units or more in 1997. In spite of the decline in the domestic market resulting from the 1995 Mexican crisis, production increased in response to the dynamism of the North American market. While comparable data for Central Europe are not available, it is known that the leading Fiat and Skoda models are produced in volumes greater than 100 000 units, and Suzuki produces over 50 000 units per annum of its main model in Hungary. These findings on scale in the IPMs match those of Sturgeon and Florida (1999: 43), who show that average capacity of 60 assembly plants on the periphery of Western Europe and the USA was 155 000 units in 1996, considerably larger than in other emerging markets.[24]

The emerging regional markets

The ERMs face perhaps the most complex policy challenge, because they have to overcome national sensitivities to create a regional space while at the same time facing pressures to reduce regional protection. In the case of Mercosur, it has been shown above that considerable and effective integration of the auto industries of Argentina and Brazil was achieved by 1998. In the case of ASEAN, the regional space was not clearly constituted, and one of the reasons for this failure was the promotion of domestic motor industries by individual governments in the region.

How competitive are the two regions? It can be seen that Brazilian production has reached competitive scale. Table 3.7 shows that the Brazilian auto industry produced five models in volumes exceeding 100000 units in 1997. Production of these five models together exceeded a million units. While some models were produced in smaller volumes in 1997, the three models for which production was less than 20000 units had all been discontinued by the end of 1998. Volumes were lower in Argentina, in spite of increasing integration with Brazil, but should the Mercosur project develop further, one would expect Argentina to specialise in certain models, including light vehicles that can be produced profitably at volumes lower than those required for passenger cars.[25] Nevertheless, it is not clear that the car industry could continue to flourish without a tariff level of at least 35 per cent and continuing protection through TRIMs. While assemblers have been increasing local content above the levels required by government, abolition of the foreign exchange balancing requirement might lead to either large increases in component imports or reductions in exports.

In the case of ASEAN, scale continues to be a major problem. As can be seen in Table 3.7, most vehicles were produced in very low volumes in Indonesia, Malaysia and Thailand. Production of only one light vehicle exceeded 100000 units per year, while 50 vehicles did not reach a volume of 20000 units. One significant exception to the volume problem is in the assembly of pickups. Four models were assembled in volumes greater than 50000 units in 1995, which constitutes large-scale assembly for light vehicles in any part of the world other than North America.

Restructuring seems inevitable in the ASEAN region. On the one hand, governments in the region have made commitments to regional liberalisation by 2003 in the context of AFTA. The East Asian crisis has exposed the limits of the development of national auto industries, and policies are likely to be developed within the framework of AFTA, even in Malaysia and Indonesia, which promoted national auto producers.[26] However, two problems remain. First, the policy shift may not create efficient industries in the short period up to 2003. Secondly, even with regional integration, total vehicle sales in the region are unlikely to reach 2 million before 2005 (see Guiheux and Lecler, Table 9.6 in this volume). Regional integration will not be enough to secure sufficient scale. On the other hand, transnational companies are changing their strategies in ASEAN in response to the 1997 crisis. Dunne (1999) already sees signs of change. Following years of limited competition between Japanese producers enjoying the benefits of a fast-growing market, North American assemblers and component manufacturers are entering the region, and some of the smaller, locally owned manufacturers are leaving the industry. It seems likely that the global vehicle companies will look to regional integration as a means of making their investments more viable. There are clear signs of both a more strategic approach by companies to the regional division of labour (see Chapter 9 by Guiheux and Lecler, in this volume) and an increasing export role for some countries. This is particularly clear in the case of Thailand, where exports increased sharply to 66 788 units in 1998 (Fourin, 1999). Dunne (1999) predicts exports of 130 000 units in 1999, while other sources predicted that as many as 150 000 vehicles would be exported.

It remains to be seen whether the focus of the stronger countries and firms will be solely on the ASEAN market. As Guiheux and Lecler (Chapter 9) point out, the gains from regional integration within ASEAN are limited by the preferences for different vehicles within each market – cars in Malaysia, pickups in Thailand and vans in Indonesia. The route to increasing scale might be through a broader regional role within Asia, or even a trans-regional orientation.

Emerging regional markets or trans-regional markets?

The ERMs faced the biggest policy challenge at the end of the 1990s. The PAMs could expect some continuing protection, while the IPMs had committed themselves to integration with their Triad partners. The big question for the countries in Mercosur and ASEAN were, first, whether they could sustain regional spaces, and, secondly, whether such spaces would create industries efficient enough to provide low-cost locations in a more liberalised global automotive industry. In other words, could they find a broader, trans-regional role in the global automotive industry?

The case of Australia provides a clear example of how radical liberalisation of trade in automotive products might create an automotive industry with a broader trans-regional role, or might lead to decline and marginalisation. Until the late 1980s, Australia protected its car industry through tariffs on vehicle imports (set at 57.5 per cent in the mid-1980s), an import quota limiting vehicle imports to 20 per cent of domestic sales and a local content requirement of 85 per cent (with the remaining 15 per cent of content importable duty-free). The Australian value-added content of auto industry exports (vehicles, components, design, productive services, and so on) generated further rights to import equivalent values of automotive products duty-free.

At the end of the 1980s, the Australian Passenger Motor Vehicle Manufacturing Plan, also known as the Button Plan, drastically altered motor-industry policy.[27] It aimed to rationalise the industry and improve its efficiency through increasing international competitive pressures. Import quotas and local content requirements were abolished, and tariffs cut to 35 per cent by 1992, with a further reduction to 15 per cent by 2000.

The policy led to a rationalisation and increased import penetration. The number of car plants fell from eight to four, and a number of models produced in the country from 13 to five. Overall, auto production declined from 358000 passenger cars in 1987 to 274000 cars in 1992, recovering to 326000 units in 1997 (Fourin, 1998). In the early 1990s, import penetration in the passenger cars sector exceeded 40 per cent (Fujimoto, 1999: 39).

It seems clear that, given the small size of the market in Australia, the domestic industry could only survive without protection if local subsidiaries developed a role within the broader international division of labour of their parent companies. Therefore, the Australian strategy lets the future of the car industry be shaped largely by the production and sales strategies of transnational companies. Up to the mid-1990s, the results were mixed. Fujimoto shows that Nissan left the market, and Ford and GM adopted defensive strategies, merely rationalising production in order to survive. In contrast, Toyota began to develop a role for its Australian operations as 'one of the mid-sized hubs in Toyota's global manufacturing network' (Fujimoto, 1999: 47). Toyota imported vehicles and parts into Australia from Southeast Asia and the United States (as well as Japan) and exported parts to Turkey, South Africa and Southeast Asia.

This type of global network might develop much further in the context of greater trade liberalisation, transforming the role of ERMs. If investments in the car industry made initially to gain access to protected markets did, in fact, create efficient local subsidiaries in the ERMs, then transnational car companies might include them in enhanced inter-regional specialisation and divisions of labour. For example, Thailand might become a producer of light pickups for Asia, Europe and Oceania. Brazil might produce low-cost small cars not only for Latin America, but for Europe as well. The production of 'Third World' cars, such as the Fiat Palio and GM's Blue Macaw might be concentrated at just a few emerging market sites. In this case, the

ERMs would decline in importance as producers within them became more oriented to markets outside.

A second possibility is that the ERMs would become integrated into Triad-based regionalism. Mercosur opened negotiations with the EU in 1999 on the formation of a free trade area, while the USA would prefer to attract Mercosur into the sphere of NAFTA. Eventually, Japan may attempt to build a closer relationship with the AFTA countries.

A third possibility is that the ERMs will put a brake on regional and global integration in the face of the costs of restructuring. Continuing regional integration in ASEAN and Mercosur will involve major rationalisation and highly unequal losses between countries. National governments that have invested so much in the development of their motor industries will find such rationalisation uncomfortable. Managed trade within the region and protection for the regional motor industry as a whole may continue, particularly if developing countries are able to sustain their use of TRIMs at the WTO.

The restructuring of the automotive industry globally and in the emerging markets will continue to be strongly influenced by national and regional policies. Government intervention will continue to mould and direct the forces of global competition. However, the underlying problems of lack of scale and market volatility which have plagued emerging markets in recent years mean that the governments of these countries will have to balance their pursuit of national development strategies against the costs to the economy as a whole and the need to provide attractive markets and production sites for global vehicle companies.

Notes

*   The authors are particularly grateful to Kamaruding Abdulsomad of Lund University, Sweden and Peter Wad of the Copenhagen Business School for providing data on policy and sales in the SEAN region; to Brian McLaughlin of Rover, Denis Audet at the OECD and Chris Stevens at IDS for insights into trade regulations and policies; to Tim Sturgeon, director of the globalisation programme of the International Motor Vehicle Project; and to the Society of Motor Manufactures and Traders for providing access to car-industry statistics. The development of this chapter owes much to discussions with members of the GERPISA motor industry network. The production of this chapter would not have been possible without financial support from the Department for International Development of the UK government.

1. Triad economies: USA, Canada, Japan and Western Europe. Major emerging markets: ASEAN (Indonesia, Malaysia, Philippines and Thailand), China, India, Latin America (including Mexico) and Eastern Europe (excluding Russia). Further discussion of growth prospects in emerging markets can be found in Chapter 2 by Lung in this volume.

2. The GATT-inconsistent TRIMs already violated GATT agreements, but they could only be challenged through the disputes procedure. The Uruguay Round agreement on TRIMs allowed them to continue for a limited period, but set up a general mechanism for their elimination.

3. Just when and to what extent the WTO agreements will be enforced is hard to say. In the mid-1990s, some analysts predicted much more liberalised trading regimes by 2000/2002 (for example, Audet and VanGrasstek, 1997: 33). Other commentators and policy-makers believe that many TRIMs will survive well into the 21st century.

4. Mercosur is the regional trade grouping formed by Argentina, Brazil, Paraguay and Uruguay.

5. All references to trade in built-up cars refer to new cars. Trade in used cars is frequently subject to much greater restrictions (Audet and Van-Grasstek, 1997: 24–5).

6. For a strong critique of protectionist policies for the auto industry, see Wonnacott (1996).

7. Brazil data in this section taken from ANFAVEA (1998); Mexico data from Durán *et al.* (1997: 45). In the case of Mexico, increasing vehicle exports were accompanied by a radical shift in market orientation. In 1980, 98 per cent of vehicle exports were directed to Latin America and Europe. In 1990, 90 per cent of vehicle exports went to North America.

8. Car-assemblers also faced restrictions on the channels used for imports of vehicles and components, as well as controls on the distribution channels used for selling cars (Polly, 1998: 16).

9. See Chapter 2 by Lung, in this volume, for a discussion of why oligopolistic competition in the global automotive industry leads to excess capacity and the entry of many assemblers into markets of limited size.

10. See Chapter 9 by Guiheux and Lecler, in this volume, for an account of the impact of the East Asian crisis on the integration of motor industries in the ASEAN region.

11. See Carrillo and Lopez (1999: 95–7) for further discussion of the changing export profile of the Mexican auto industry.

12. One of the consequences of this policy is that companies such as BMW cannot export from their North American operations into the Mexican market because they do not export vehicles from Mexico. As a result, BMW has been forced to set up an inefficient local assembly plant which assembled only 2000 vehicles in 1998.

13. Mexico's experience in NAFTA shares some similarities with the integration Spain into the EU motor industry in the 1970s and 1980s. See the comparison between Spain and Mexico in Chapter 6 by Layan, in this volume.

14. This section focuses solely on the countries of Central Europe most integrated with the car industry of the European Union, the Czech Republic, Hungary and Poland. These countries are discussed in more

detail in Chapter 10 by Havas, in this volume. Quite different situations are found in the rest of Central and Eastern Europe. See for example the analysis in van Tulder (1998).

15.	While some investments have been made for the production of more sophisticated cars, such as the Audi TT sports car (see Chapter 10 by Havas, in this volume), these are only produced in small volumes.

16.	In the 1980s Spain was a major market for small cars and a major exporter of these cars to the rest of the European market. In the 1990s, Spanish car exports have shifted away from the smallest cars. Between 1988–90 and 1994–96, cars under 1 litre fell from 16.7 per cent to 5.5 per cent of Spanish car exports to the 10 non-Iberian members of the pre-enlargement EU.

17.	Opel's investment in an assembly plant for sports cars in Hungary shares the same characteristics.

18.	However, Balcet and Enrietti (1997: 28) show that Poland had a growing bilateral trade deficit in components with Italy in the period 1992–96.

19.	Details of this policy and the negotiations about the motor industry in the context of the Mercosur agreement can be found in Roldán (1997) and Vigevani and Veiga (1997).

20.	See Table 2.3 in Chapter 2 by Lung, in this volume, for data showing that the Argentine automotive exports were also mainly directed to the Brazilian market.

21.	See the next section for further discussion of this point.

22.	For a discussion of Fiat's division of labour between Argentina and Brazil, see Balcet and Enrietti (1999).

23.	In the first seven months of 1997, prior to the currency crisis, Thailand exported 19 017 vehicles – less than 7 per cent of total vehicle production (*Bangkok Post*, 28 August 1998).

24.	This figure is for the category of PLEMAs (Periphery of Large Existing Market Areas), developed by Sturgeon and Florida. This includes not only the IPMs, but also countries incorporated into the Triad in the 1960s and 1970s – Canada, Spain and Portugal. Average plant capacity in 212 plants in other emerging markets (including small markets such as Vietnam) was only 44 000 units.

25.	See also Chapter 7 by Humphrey and Salerno (in this volume) on modularisation as a strategy for producing vehicles efficiently at low volumes.

26.	The authors are indebted to Peter Wad of the Copenhagen Business School for these observations.

27.	This account is based on the description of the policy contained in the Industry Commission's 1996 draft report on how car-industry policy should be developed up to 2004 (Industry Commission, 1996).

Bibliography

ABDULSOMAD, K. (forthcoming) 'Promoting industrial and technological development under contrasting industrial policies: the automobile industries in Malaysia and Thailand'. In Jomo, K.S. and Rasiah, R. (eds), *Industrial and Technological Development in Malaysia*. London: Routledge, pp. 274–300.

ACMA (1999) *Automotive Industry of India: Facts and Figures, 1998–99*. New Delhi: Automotive Component Manufacturers Association of India.

ANFAVEA (1998) Anuário Estatístico 1998, ANFAVEA – Associação Nacional dos Fabricantes de Veículos Automotores (Brazil). Web Site – www.anfavea.com.br, accessed January 1999.

AUDET, D. and VANGRASSTEK, C. (1997) 'Market access issues in the automobile sector'. Paper presented to the conference on Market Access Issues in the Automobile Sector, Paris, OECD, July.

AUTOMOTIVE INDUSTRIES (1998) 1997 Worldwide Production Data, Automotive Industries (USA). Website – www.ai-online.com/stats/, accessed February 1999.

BALCET, G. and ENRIETTI, A. (1997) 'Regionalisation and globalisation in Europe: the case of Fiat Auto Poland and its suppliers', *Actes du GERISPA*, No. 20, 15–30.

BALCET, G. and ENRIETTI, A. (1999) 'La mondialisation ciblée de Fiat et la filière automobile Italienne: l'impact dans les pays de Mercosur', *Actes du GERISPA*, No. 25, 23–39.

BANK OF THAILAND (1998) *Bank of Thailand Quarterly Bulletin*, Vol. 38, No. 1.

BEDÊ, M. (1997) 'A política automotiva nos anos 90'. In Arbix, G. and Zilbovicius, M. (eds), *De JK a FHC: A Reinvenção dos Carros*. São Paulo: Scritta, pp. 357–87.

BENNETT, D. and SHARPE, K. (1984) 'Agenda setting and bargaining power: the Mexican state versus transnational automobile corporations'. In Kronish, R. and Mericle, K. (eds), *The Political Economy of the Latin American Motor Vehicle Industry*. Cambridge, MA: MIT Press, pp. 195–229.

BENNETT, D. and SHARPE, K. (1985) *Transnational Corporations versus the State: the Political Economy of the Mexican Auto Industry*. Princeton NJ: Princeton University Press.

CARRILLO, J. and LOPEZ, S. (1999) 'Relaciones cliente–proveedor de empresas automotrices alemanas en Mexico', *Actes du GERPISA*, No. 25, 93–104.

CARVALHO, R., QUEIROZ, S., CONSONI, F., COSTA, I. and DA COSTA, J. (1997) *Abertura Comercial e Mudança Estrutural na Indústria Automobilística Brasileira*. Report to IPEA. Campinas: Departamento de Política Científica e Tecnológica.

DUNNE, M. (1999) 'Asia After the Crash', Automotive Industries. Website – www.ai-online.com/, accessed March 1999.

DURÁN, C., PETERS, E. and TANIURA, T. (1997) *Changes in Industrial Organization of the Mexican Automobile Industry by Economic Liberalization*. Joint Research Program Series, 120. Tokyo: Institute of Developing Economies.

EIU (1998) *Motor Business International: the Worldwide Motor Industry*. London: Economist Intelligence Unit.

FOURIN (1998) *Fourin's Automotive Forecast*. Nagoya: Fourin Inc.

FOURIN (1999) 'Ajia jidosha sangyo' (The Asian Car Industry), *sekai jidosha sangyo*, Vol. 9, No. 1. Nagoya: Fourin Inc.

FUJIMOTO, T. (1999) 'Toyota Motor Manufacturing Australia in 1995: an Emerging Global Strategy', *Actes du GERPISA*, No. 26, 37–64.

HAVAS, A. (1997) 'Foreign direct investment and intra-industry trade: the case of the automotive industry in Central Europe'. In Dyker D. (ed.), *The Technology of Transition: Science and Technology Policies for Transition Countries*. Budapest: Central European University Press, pp. 211–40.

HUMPHREY, J., MUKHERJEE, A., ZILBOVICIUS, M. and ARBIX, G. (1998) 'Globalisation, foreign direct investment and the restructuring of supplier networks: the motor industry in Brazil and India'. In Kagami, M., Humphrey, J. and Piore, M. (eds), *Learning, Liberalization and Economic Adjustment*. Tokyo: Institute of Developing Economies, pp. 117–89.

IKEDA, M. (1998) 'Japanese, European and US auto manufacturers' strategy for Asia: with an emphasis on automobile production in China'. In Takahashi, Y., Murata, M. and Rahman, K. (eds), *Management Strategies of Multinational Corporations in Asian Markets*. Tokyo: Chuo University Press, pp. 161–74.

INDUSTRY COMMISSION (1996) *The Automotive Industry*. Draft Report. Canberra: Industry Commission.

JAYASANKARAN, S. (1993) 'Made-in-Malaysia: the Proton project'. In Jomo, K.S. (ed.), *Industrialising Malaysia: Policy, Performance, Prospects*. London: Routledge, pp. 272–85.

LAIRD, S. (1997) *Mercosur: objectives and achievements*. Mimeo. Geneva: World Trade Organisation.

LEE, C. (1996) 'Localisation strategy of a European firm in the Chinese market: the case of Shanghai Volkswagen from the Chinese perspective'. Paper presented to the 13th Annual Conference of Euro-Asia Management Studies Association, Tokyo, November.

LOW, P. and SUBRAMANIAN, A. (1998) 'TRIMs in the Uruguay Round: an unfinished business?'. In Martin, W. and Winters, L.A. (eds), *The Uruguay Round and the Developing Economies*. Washington, DC: The World Bank, pp. 413–34.

LYNCH, T. (1998) *Leaving Home: Three Decades of Internationalization by U.S. Automotive Firms*. IPC Working Paper, 98-007. Cambridge, MA: MIT Industrial Performance Center.

MORENO BRID, J. (1996) '*Mexico's Auto Industry after NAFTA: a Successful Experience in Restructuring?*'. Working Paper No. 232. South Bend: Kellogg Institute.

MORTIMORE, M. (1998) 'Getting a lift: modernizing industry by way of Latin American integration schemes: the example of automobiles', *Transnational Corporations*, Vol. 7, No. 2, 97–136.

POLLY, L. (1998) 'China's evolving automotive industry and market', *Industry Trade and Technology Review*.

RASIAH, R. (1998) 'Regulation and market structure of the car industry in Southeast Asia'. Mimeo. Kuala Lumpur: IKMAS.

ROLDÁN, M. (1997) 'Continuities and discontinuities in the regulation and hierarchisation of the world automotive industry: reflections on the Argentinian experience (1960s–1990s)', *Actes du GERISPA*, No. 20, 49–85.

SERCOVICH, F. (1997) '*Best practices, policy convergence and WTO 2000: race against time*'. Mimeo. Vienna: UNIDO.

SHAPIRO, H. (1994) *Engines of Growth*. Cambridge: Cambridge University Press.

SIRAPRAPAPONG, A. (1998) 'Automakers' production and marketing strategies in Thailand – impact of the financial crisis'. MSc Thesis. Bath: University of Bath, School of Management.

SLJIVIC, N. (1995) *Car Manufacturing in Central Europe*. FT Management Report. London: Financial Times.

STANDARD AND POOR'S DRI (1999) *Asian Automotive Industry Forecast Report*. New York: Standard and Poor's DRI.

STOREY, J. (1998) *The World's Car Manufacturers, Volume 1*. FT Management Report. London: Financial Times.

STURGEON, T. and FLORIDA, R. (1999) *The World that Changed the Machine: Globalization and Jobs in the Automotive Industry*. Final Report to the Alfred P. Sloan Foundation. Cambridge MA: MIT.

VAN TULDER, R. (1998) 'The integration of Central and Eastern Europe in car production networks'. Paper presented to the 6th Gerpisa International Auto Industry Colloquium, Paris, June.

VIGEVANI, T. and VEIGA, J. (1997) 'A integração regional no Mercosul'. In Arbix, G. and Zilbovicius, M. (eds), *De JK a FHC: A Reinvenção dos Carros*. São Paulo: Scritta, pp. 329–55.

WONNACOTT, P. (1996) 'The automotive industry in Southeast Asia: can protection be made less costly?'. *World Economy*, Vol. 19, No. 1, 89–112.

4 Between Globalisation and Regionalisation: What is the Future of the Motor Industry?

Michel Freyssenet and Yannick Lung*

INTERNATIONALISATION: THE 'FIN DE SIÈCLE' CHALLENGE FACING THE MOTOR INDUSTRY

If the challenge facing automobile producers in the 1980s was how to change their industrial model, that of the 1990s has been how to reorganise internationally. Of course, internationalisation has been one of the industry's characteristics since its inception, and international trade has accounted for a higher proportion of sales than it does today at several periods in the past (Bardou *et al.*, 1982). Globalisation has neither been achieved nor is it irreversible and unavoidable.

Yet the current tendency towards internationalisation differs from previous phases, and in particular, it differs from the situation in the 1970s and 1980s analysed by GERPISA in one of its initial research projects (Gerpisa, 1984). In part, this is due to the global context of deregulation and the emergence of new growth poles, but above all because of its origins. The clash between the industrial models used by companies and between national growth models seen over the last 20 years has destabilised the wage–labour nexus and, in turn, the markets of many mature countries, including countries that have benefited from this confrontation. Companies can no longer rely upon markets that are relatively predictable in terms of the level and type of demand.

Companies are therefore faced with the following choice: either to organise themselves in such a way that they can remain profitable in an unstable international economic environment while they await a possible homogenisation of competitive conditions in terms of products, capital and labour, or to seek out local and regional economic spaces in which they can recreate the conditions of regulated growth. Which process will win out? The analysis of international trade does not yet permit us to arrive at a clear conclusion. It is therefore necessary to undertake a detailed description of the internationalisation trajectories currently being followed by companies (producers, suppliers, distributors) in order to identify their strategic choices and to understand the outcomes.

This is an important question not only for automotive companies but also for our understanding of what is going to happen in the automotive industry. Either companies are going to adapt or transform their socioproductive model as a function of the new global context and the integrated regions that are being created, or they are going to focus on the areas that contain, or may in the medium term contain, the preconditions for the continued functioning of their existing model, or alternatively they will misunderstand or underestimate the choices before them, as a result of which their performance may well be seriously compromised. An understanding of the actions and outcomes of the actors who make up the automotive industry in all its aspects (productive organisation and employee relationships) therefore requires an understanding of the concepts and paths towards internationalisation being followed by each of them.

THE RECOMPOSITION OF GLOBAL ECONOMIC AND POLITICAL SPACE

The 1990s do not appear to be a mere continuation of the crisis that started in the early 1970s, but rather a new phase. It would appear that after having reduced the competitive gaps between them, vehicle producers and their suppliers are once more attempting to increase their production volumes and penetrate their competitors' markets. But this offensive is occurring in a global space which is undergoing a process of recomposition under the impact of four different, and sometimes contradictory, processes: financial globalisation, the liberalisation of world trade and deregulation, the constitution of regional entities around each pole of the Triad and finally the emergence of the newly industrialising countries, particularly in Asia. These are having a major effect on the automotive industry as they reinforce the global character of the competitive process.

Financial globalisation

While the internationalisation of the automotive industry remains undefined, particularly with regard to the form it takes (globalisation or regionalisation), financial globalisation has been largely completed, even if this process has not been accompanied by the development of a system of regulation appropriate to the new configuration. Even without evoking the systemic risks that make the whole world economy fragile (Aglietta *et al.*, 1990), companies are permanently subject to erratic fluctuations in exchange rates. These fluctuations have enormous impacts on company competitiveness and profitability, and can undermine the parameters of long-term industrial strategy, forcing changes in investment projects (Dohni, 1994). The three principal vehicle producing countries, the United States, Japan and Germany, have the three main currencies used in the international monetary system, the US dollar, the Yen and the Mark – now the Euro for the EU – which are immediately affected by the transactions of financial institutions and through which governments may try to create new competitive advantages.

Significant and sudden fluctuations in exchange rates affect not only the relationships between the three world regions but can also occur within regional spaces, such as the EU in the early 1990s. However, in the second half of the 1990s the most dramatic shifts in exchange rate parities have taken place in the emerging markets, with the collapse of the Mexican Peso late in 1994, then in South East Asia in 1997, Russia in 1998 and Brazil in 1999 (see Chapter 2 by Lung, in this volume).

Liberalisation of automotive trade

The wave of free trade which dominates the end of the 20th century has brought about the negotiated introduction of new rules to govern international trade. These rules seek to eliminate tariff and non-tariff barriers to trade, either immediately or after transition periods of varying length. The creation of a supranational regulatory body, the WTO, bears witness to the will to do this even if it is not yet powerful (especially given the prerogatives of the major economic powers, such as Act 301 in the United States). Both the major automobile powers and the smaller countries that have long been concerned to protect their national industry have been affected by the reduction, or indeed elimination, of barriers to trade in automotive products (vehicles and components) which has taken place in recent years.

As far as trade between the United States, Europe and Japan is concerned, tariff protection is almost non-existent and the other forms of protectionism, notably between Japan and its partners, will be phased out. The agreement reached between Japan and the EU to assure a voluntary restriction of exports by Japanese producers until the final opening of the European market on 1 January 2000 (Vigier, 1992) illustrates this trend. The abandonment of import substitution strategies has led to the reduction of tariff barriers and elimination of quotas in a range of countries (see Chapter 3 by Humphrey and Oeter, in this volume).

This tendency appears to be strong even if there have been some reversals in crisis situations. One example is the 1995 decision of the Brazilian government to increase tariffs on cars from 20 to 70 per cent and adopt a quota regime until this latter policy was ruled out by the WTO. A second example would be increased tariffs in Thailand following the 1997 crisis. The globalisation of competition is in practice leading to an erosion of the national bases of the automotive industry both in terms of final markets (increased imports and decline of national producers) and in terms of components (internationalisation of the components industry) which is making the situations of domestic companies and whole supply chains in every country more fragile.

Even so, the globalisation of competition does not imply the creation of a world automotive market. A world market presupposes that in various countries it is possible to find homogeneous products or product ranges and the same price for the final product (vehicle or model range) and for intermediate goods (production equipment and components), which would facilitate an international decomposition of the production process at the world scale. We are far from this situation, in part because the process of regional integration is continuing apace.

Regional integration

The internationalisation of economies is occurring largely within the framework of the construction of regional groupings. Integration in Europe is the most advanced case, with its economic and monetary union proceeding beyond the removal of barriers to trade to include the coordination of economic policies. The EU thus constitutes an integrated economic pole, particularly for the automotive industry, in which companies define their sales strategies and their production investments at the continental scale: Europeanisation (Hudson and Schamp, 1995; Bordenave and Lung, 1996). In North America, companies did not wait for the official creation of a free trade zone (NAFTA) in order to integrate their markets and production systems. Canada, which was always attractive for the US industry, benefited widely from the Auto Pact agreed with the United States as early as 1966, while North American investments designed to make the North of Mexico an export base began in the 1980s (Carrillo, 1990; Michelli, 1994; Chapter 6 by Layan, in this volume). The growth of regional integration in the Southern countries (Mercosur, ASEAN) is a more recent phenomenon and is of particular importance to/for the automotive industry, given the significance of economies of scale in the industry.

In a context of the globalisation of competition, companies are drawn to develop production activities in every region, including the Asia-Pacific zone, where the integration process is economically dominated by Japanese companies even if it can take institutional forms that do not recognise Japanese political leadership (for example ASEAN). At the scale of each of these regions, companies organise a division of labour that draws on the advantages inherent in each place with its specific competencies. This regional vertical division of labour is very clear at the European scale, in North America with the integration of Mexico and within the ASEAN countries (see Chapter 6 by Layan, and Chapter 9 by Guiheux and Lecler, in this volume).

The emergence of new car countries

The globalisation of competition is not limited to renewed direct competition among the main vehicle-producing countries (United States, Japan, Germany, Italy and France). It also includes the emergence of new spaces in the vehicle industry, both new markets given potential growth in demand and new production locations given advantages in terms of costs, particularly wage costs. These emerging regions and countries are the focus of the chapters in this book.

The car industry is thus greatly influenced by the recomposition of global economic and political space; the globalisation of competition is a powerful factor in determining the rhythms and forms of internationalisation by companies.

THE GLOBALISATION OF COMPETITION

Internationalisation in turn modifies the context of a competitive game which is dominated by three main characteristics. The first is the geographical redistribution of markets with the search for markets in industrialised and developing countries. The second is the reorganisation of production, which has transformed norms of production and trade. The third is the destabilisation and deregulation of the wage–labour nexus.

The search for markets

As far as demand for automobile products is concerned, the saturation of the mature markets in the industrialised countries stands in contrast to the recent dynamism of the newly emerging countries (see Chapter 2 by Lung, in this volume). The stagnation of the automobile market in the Triad countries is not simply a cyclical phenomenon (recession in Europe and Japan). It reflects a relative saturation of demand for cars with the rate of growth in these markets not exceeding 2–3 per cent per year over the long term. The utilisation of the car for personal journeys is made almost obligatory by the concentration of the population in urban agglomerations which are often poorly provided for in terms of public transport systems and where living spaces are predominantly dispersed (Orfeuil, 1994; Dupuy, 1995). Mobility can only be achieved through car use. The emergence of multiple car households raises the level of ownership and this leads to urban congestion and increased air pollution. The success of the car becomes a threat for its industry in the sense that the car is criticised as a cause of the ills of modern society.

With the threat of radical measures by the public authorities becoming increasingly credible, car producers are exploring new social uses of the car (such as car pooling) and boosting research into technical solutions through new functions or new products. If research into non-polluting vehicles (electric cars) does not come up with solutions soon, other ideas will be favoured, notably hybrid vehicles.

Hence new actors are emerging in the industry, such as electronics supplier companies. These actors may better be able to rethink, and thereby save, the principle of a self-propelled individualised vehicle that is diffused to the masses. In a deteriorating context, more radical innovations are likely to emerge outside the automobile industry from

actors less restricted than the vehicle producers by previous technological choices (see David, 1985, for a discussion of 'lock in'). In the
short term, intense competitive rivalries among car producers tend to
favour retention of their traditional paradigm. They are obliged to
respond to the saturation of demand with an increased segmentation
of markets, offering vehicles that are better adapted to new consumer
attitudes such as the combination of comfort and practicality of mini-
vans in Europe, light trucks (pick ups) in the United States and even
the urban minicar and its electric variants.

Given the saturation of such markets and the emergence of excess
production capacity (estimated to be more than 2 million units in
Europe) with the arrival of new producers, the manufacturers sought
out new markets in emerging countries. To be sure, markets in the
North continued to account for three-quarters of global automobile
sales in 1997, but the crisis of 1997 in East Asia and its consequences
for the emerging markets have intensified competitive pressures on
auto companies.

Industrial reorganisation

The car companies are confronted with this new competitive context,
and in recent years they have adopted new techniques to manage
production so as to permit quality, variety and productivity to
be increased simultaneously. Such structural changes arose out of differentiated trajectories (Freyssenet *et al.*, 1998) and as a function of
different time-scales in the creation of coherence within the new
'apparatuses' which link market relationships (productive organisation) and management of work (employee relationships).

This diversity of trajectories and the often underestimated plural-
ity of industrial models is a result of the different responses of producers to the new global norms of production and trade in the
automotive industry (Boyer and Freyssenet, 1999). Of particular note
is the relative levelling of quality gaps compared to the situation that
prevailed in the mid-1980s (MacDuffie and Pil, 1994), as well as the
relative homogenisation of model ranges once producers diversified
their models in order to be present in the same major market segments. At the same time, companies (both suppliers and producers)
have significantly increased factor productivity thanks to more efficient modes of organisation which have permitted the simultaneous
management of the main dimensions of production efficiency: quality,
variety and productivity. Significant increases in productivity have

been achieved recently, even if differences remain. Internationalisation therefore offers new opportunities to restore profit margins that have been reduced by price competition and to attempt to rediscover quasi-profitable situations.

There have been reconfigurations of industrial models (Boyer and Freyssenet, 1995), but only at the level of each company that has attempted a more or less complete process of creating internal coherence and external relevance from a variety of technical, organisational and managerial apparatuses and practices aimed at reducing the uncertainties of the market and the labour process. However, these local reconfigurations have not led to renewed macroeconomic coherence, and this has contributed to continuing uncertainties regarding the evolution of automobile markets.

The destabilisation of wage–labour nexus

The reorganisation of production has led to a contraction of employment in the car industry. This has been worsened by the draconian cost-reduction solutions adopted by both producers and suppliers in order to reinforce their price competitiveness. This process has been dramatic in countries where the sector plays a major role: in France for instance, over the past 15 years more than 100 000 jobs have been eliminated in the motor industry. The drop in employment has contributed to an accentuation of the social dichotomies resulting from the destabilisation and deregulation of the wage–labour nexus, notably through the crumbling of the systems for collective bargaining which had been created in the postwar period in different forms in different countries (Boyer, 1986). The reduction in employment in the motor industry has led to an increase in unemployment, both directly through redundancies and especially indirectly through cutbacks in the hiring of young people who have just finished their training. In single-industry regions centred on automotive production, the crisis has been particularly sharp, as for example in Detroit in the United States (Trachte and Ross, 1985), affecting the whole local economy and society. Certainly, the elimination of jobs in the assembly sector has sometimes been compensated by a rapid growth in the components sector and in the service sector. However, the precarious nature of the jobs created, the low levels of pay and the absence of collective bargaining may well lead to a decrease in workers' real wages (Sturgeon and Florida, 1999). In this context, the current questioning of the welfare state further accentuates social inequalities.

This situation tends to raise questions about dominant consumption behaviours and favours the development of new consumer attitudes, particularly new social uses for the car, and new expectations about products. Meanwhile, the diffusion of unemployment throughout Europe and the reduction of real wages in the United States are leading to the exclusion of part of the potential automobile market (Froud *et al.*, 1998). Social crisis reinforces the saturation of the car market and encourages producers to offer specific products to the low income clientele (Renault Twingo or Fiat Seicento). However, the shift in demand towards smaller cars jeopardises the profitability of producers because profit margins on these cars are lower than for luxury cars.

INTERNATIONALISATION TO REDUCE COSTS AND INCREASE VARIETY

Cost reduction and increased product variety remain two major objectives for vehicle companies wishing to strengthen their competitiveness – objectives that are, in fact, compatible in many circumstances (Jetin and Lung, 1996). Internationalisation lies at the heart of these challenges, as can be deduced from an analysis of the five main strategies producers are adopting to attain these objectives: the simplification of products (decontenting), the reorganisation of distribution, pressure on wages and flexibility of work, reducing the costs of components, and, naturally, the internationalisation of production.

The vogue for decontenting

Lately, the vogue within the automobile industry has been towards decontenting – the simplification of the product – by stripping the car of superfluous complexities. Such complexities directly increase costs through the cost of components manufacture or the 'complexification' of assembly; alternatively, indirect costs result from, for example, excessive weight or even the costs of managing an excessive variety of certain components. The necessary technical or managerial sophistication cannot always be justified, particularly when it remains invisible to the consumer and contributes no additional use value to the product. To a certain extent the vogue for decontenting is, in large part, a compensation for excesses on two levels: first, in terms of the introduction of new technologies aimed at improving comfort, quality or safety, which has led to a significant rise in the real price of cars recently (while real wages remained stagnant or even fell); secondly, through an excessive proliferation of model varieties and of variations for each model.

These excesses were particularly noticeable in Japan during the economic boom (bubble) of the latter half of the 1980s, so much so that the sudden change in the economic situation revealed an overengineering or fat design that has compelled producers to rationalise costs (Fujimoto, 1999).

Through a process of copycat competitive behaviour, the Americans followed suit, and then the Europeans imported this tendency, just as before with re-engineering or benchmarking. While decontenting is not a major factor in internationalisation, it may go some way towards facilitating it through a rationalisation of models and components from a global perspective (parts sharing, fewer platforms).

The reorganisation of distribution

Prior to the vogue for decontenting, another strategy adopted by producers to curb costs was the reorganisation of distribution systems. There is much room for manoeuvre in this domain, given that marketing and distribution costs account for close to a quarter of the selling price (excluding taxes) of a vehicle. The concern to curb distribution costs is not only an outcome of competition among producers but also a reaction to the appearance of potential new competitors in the car distribution sector. Producers are having to take account of the shift towards the sale of new vehicles by new large independent distribution groups such as AutoNation in the United States, the effects of competition on services linked to distribution from specialised automobile repair groups (such as Kwik-Fit and Midas) and the effects of deregulation of distribution in Europe (Chanaron and Jullien, 1999).

Car producers have, therefore, been forced to rethink their distribution systems by testing new forms of distribution, notably at the launch of innovative products (for example, with the marketing of the Daimler–Mercedes Smart urban minicar). Nevertheless, experimentation has been limited, and restructuring largely confined within particular countries, even in Europe. Distribution practices are rooted in a strong institutional inertia, reflecting not only the impact of national regulations but also the cultural practices of consumers, as illustrated by the traditional distribution system in Japan. In this context, one might speculate on the possible emergence of large international distribution companies that might become a threat to the automobile producers (Jullien, 1999).

Pressure on wage costs

The third avenue for producers to curb their costs is well known: containing or reducing wage costs. While these costs represent only a small part of the value of the automobile (7–10 per cent), companies are permanently concerned to limit the growth of direct and indirect wages paid to car workers (or to social welfare institutions) so as to avoid cost inflation. While the indexing of wages to prices – whether tacit or recognised in collective agreements – characterised the golden age of Fordism, de-indexation is now the norm, and the tendency is to vary wages as a function of the company's economic results as a form of profit sharing. Producers are also attempting to obtain a fresh start from their employees and unions with regard to modes of organising work, reconfiguring the employee relationship in order to obtain greater internal and external work flexibility. External flexibility involves the various means of facilitating the quantitative adjustment of employment levels as a function of the short-term economic situation: hiring and laying off, seasonal adjustments to weekly working hours over the course of a year, and so on. This concern may be compatible with claims made by unions for shorter working hours, and hence negotiations between union and management may permit progress in this area. Volkswagen has, therefore, at least temporarily, conceded a 28.5 hour week to its German workers, which has allowed the company to deal with a surplus labour force. However, what is also at stake in such negotiations is often the internal flexibility of labour through the redefinition of modes of involving workers, notably within a teamwork framework (Durand *et al.*, 1999), the intensification of work, and schedules that allow the longer use of equipment (for example night and week-end shifts) so as to accelerate the rate at which it is amortised.

In order to reinforce their positions during these negotiations (whether explicit or implicit) and obtain concessions from their employees, most companies make use of a double threat:

- The first is relocation of production operations abroad. Widely used throughout the 1970s against workers in the car industry in the United States (towards Canada and then Mexico) and Great Britain (relocation to Spain), this strategy paid off. The same tendency is currently operating in Germany. While the traditional advantage of German industry (its non-price competitiveness) is crumbling under the impact of growing foreign competition, particularly from Japan, its high salary costs make the idea of relocation abroad increasingly credible. Most of the car producers operating in Germany have obtained significant concessions from the unions (VW, Mercedes, Opel, Ford). In a reversal familiar to history, after having been associated with threats to British workers (Bordenave and Lung, 1988), Spain has now itself become threatened by the prospects of relocation from Southern to Eastern Europe.

- The second threat is the externalisation of production of components previously undertaken internally, when suppliers are able to offer the same products at lower costs and with a wide adaptive flexibility (volume, quality, just-in-time, technical competencies, and so on).

Pressure on the supplier industry

Pressure on suppliers is another basic strategy in the car industry aimed at reducing costs, given that almost 70 per cent of the value of a car is produced by the components industry and subcontractors. With the reinforcement of price competition, producers have, therefore, turned to their suppliers in the search for significant price reductions.

The rationalisation of the supplier industry should accelerate therefore, particularly under the impact of the globalisation of this sector which constitutes one response to the various pressures placed upon it. Companies have to reinforce their technological competencies if they are to design components with a high technology content (electronics, composite materials, and so on); use high technology processes, and supply products to the highest quality standards, not only in terms of absence of defects but also in terms of product integrity (characteristics in use). Hence, there are strong pressures to innovate. These competencies have to be consolidated when producers delegate a growing proportion of the design, production and assembly of components, and even whole functions and subsystems of vehicles, to their suppliers. Suppliers, therefore, need both improved competencies and lower costs, which constitutes a force for relocation of labour intensive activities to countries and regions with low wage costs, such as the peripheries of the Triad.

Global sourcing is becoming a leitmotiv; this involves a special supply relationship between the producer and the supplier (often the sole supplier of the component in question) which supplies all of its client's factories, wherever they are located worldwide (see Chapter 7 by Humphrey and Salerno, in this volume). The assembly lines may be supplied by components imported from a global factory or by products manufactured at a supplier factory located in the same country or region as the assembly plant. Global sourcing permits both:

- reliance on a supplier of international scale, which has the requisite capabilities (Chandler, 1992) since it has developed basic competencies and possesses adequate financial resources to invest in research and development and to innovate by offering new components;
- costs-cutting thanks to economies of scale permitted by increased production volumes.

Hence the concentration of the supplier industry (Chanaron, 1999) appears to be accelerating through merger and acquisition tendencies operating at the global scale. The criss-cross flows of investment across the Atlantic are reinforcing the presence of American suppliers in Europe, and the European industry has tried to respond by investing in the United States and around assembly factories being built in emerging countries. Internationalisation continues the industrial concentration already taking place under the impact of the restructuring of supplier relationships through the adoption of hierarchical patterns (Chanaron, 1995; Helper and Sako, 1999). This is not to be interpreted as an alignment with some Japanese model of supplier relations; Japan itself is being affected by a questioning of traditional supplier relationships (Guiheux and Lecler, Chapter 9, in this volume; Lecler, 1998).

At any rate, globalisation has become the key word for a car-supplier industry, which is now being thoroughly restructured by this race to global scale. The outsourcing of a significant proportion of production and the growing diffusion of modular assembly (Lung *et al.*, 1999b) reinforce the role of the major multinational supplier companies. With their specific technological competencies and extensive financial resources, they can negotiate on an equal footing with the car producers. This will stimulate changes in power relationships between the participants in the car system and lead to a reconfiguration of relationships between producers and suppliers.

The internationalisation of production

Finally, and more directly, cost reductions may be based on the internationalisation of production. Internationalisation permits companies to benefit from economies of scale, as firms relocate to emerging countries and simultaneously maintain a presence in the markets of the industrialised countries. In practice, at constant volumes, the production and sale of the same products across different markets, rather than the sale of country- or region-specific products, leads to economies of scale. The global car strategy takes up the attempts to create a world car by the Americans in the 1970s as a response to successful Japanese incursions into various markets (Maxcy, 1981). The aim is to produce and market a vehicle in the major markets (particularly those of the Triad) which responds to the expectations (sometimes diverse) of consumers in these markets, sharing a number of components while accepting local adaptations. This strategy, which was initiated by Ford (Bordenave, 1998), is now being taken up by General Motors. To a certain extent, Japanese companies are involved in an inverse tendency with their strategy of local adaptation of models while they had previously marketed an homogeneous product throughout all their markets (on global localisation for Honda, see Mair, 1994).

If we accept that there is a relative convergence of car markets, 'commonalisation' and the sharing of principal components fit in with the automobile producers' strategy to reduce the number of platforms used at the global scale (Table 4.1). The idea is to distribute, over a greater volume, the growing costs of designing an ever increasing number of models the life cycles of which are reduced due to the accelerated pace of product replacement. The platform strategy permits cost reduction to be reconciled with the greater variety that results from the competitive battle: the new products in the industrialised country markets (minivan, urban minicar) and the special vehicles that some producers offer in the emerging markets can be developed on the same platform, which reduces design costs and the lead time (time to market), and increases economies of scale for shared components.

Hence the Palio, developed on the platform of the Fiat Uno model, may be produced in volumes up to 1 million in the new car emerging

Table 4.1   Platform strategies

Car group	Brands	Number of world-wide platforms (passenger cars only)	
		mid-1990s	*planned*
Volkswagen[a]	VW, Audi, Seat, Skoda	16	4
Fiat	Fiat, Lancia, Alfa-Romeo	7	3
PSA	Citroën, Peugeot	6	3
Renault[b]	Renault	5	3
Nissan	Nissan, Infiniti	24	5
Toyota	Toyota, Lexus	20	7
Ford[c]	Ford, Lincoln, Mercury, Jaguar	24	16
General Motors	Chevrolet, Buick, Oldsmobile, Pontiac, Cadillac, Saturn, Opel, Vauxhall, Saab	14	7

Notes: [a] Except luxury brands (Bentley, Bugatti, Lamborghini).
[b] Excluding the Dacia subsidiary in Rumania. [c] Number of platforms for passenger cars and light trucks – before the take-over of Volvo.
Sources: Automotive trade press and company reports.

countries of the South and in Eastern Europe (Balcet and Enrietti, 1997, 1999; Camuffo and Volpato, 1999). Similarly, Chapter 9 by Guiheux and Lecler and Chapter 8 by Sugiyama and Fujimoto, in this volume discuss the development of Asian cars for South East Asian markets by Japanese producers. Increased variety involves a broadening of the product range through an increased number of models and variants and accelerated product replacements. This increased variety cannot, however, be permitted to generate excess costs, and this leads the producers:

- to utilise components and platforms to the maximum (commonalisation, platform strategy);
- to conclude alliances with competitors for low volume vehicles and components (de Banville and Chanaron, 1999);
- to delegate a significant proportion of development, production and even assembly to suppliers. This externalisation reduces financial commitments and therefore the risks run by the producer.

The evolution of the car product

These developments assume both a certain convergence among the principal markets so that platforms can be shared among models which respond to the different expectations of consumers, and a technical development of the product towards a modular vehicle concept. Here, there are two contrasting conceptions of the automobile product. From one perspective, the car is a product-system. Several examples illustrate this proposition: the way the vehicle holds the road does not depend only on the steering but also on a chain of reactions within the whole vehicle; vibration and acoustic characteristics are determined by numerous components and the way they are arranged. The car is a product system in the strong sense of the word system: the characteristics of the vehicle are more than the sum of the characteristics of the parts. The increasing demands of consumers for quality (product integrity) should lead producers to design low volume yet better adapted products.

From a contrasting perspective, the car product is considered to be modular; it can be reconfigured, at least partially, by modifying the various subassemblies. This is the conception of the car which prevailed at the inception of the industry with a separation between the design and production of the chassis on the one hand, and that of the body and the fitting of the interior on the other, or again that of the engine and the mechanical components. This conception has been maintained in the truck industry and perfectly corresponds to the demands of commonalisation and the delegation of design, production and the assembly of subsystems to suppliers. Given the specificities of the truck industry, the first experiments took place in an assembly factory for Volkswagen trucks in Brazil (Marx *et al.*, 1996). Modular assembly is now diffusing, especially in greenfield sites in emerging countries (see Chapter 7 by Humphrey and Salerno, in this volume).

These developments position product design and the organisation of design at the heart of current restructuring processes. Product development at the global scale implies new methods in relation to different markets and in the management of relationships between the different services and departments involved in the design of a world car. The aim is to have all employees belonging to different services (for example marketing and design) and who are located in different world regions (for example marketing employees in Europe and the United States) working together. The platform-based strategy, and more broadly the modular vehicle, also entail the redefinition of organisational and design methods, to the extent that the early involvement of suppliers in the development of new products becomes the norm (Laigle, 1995; Lecler *et al.*, 1999). Following the restructuring due to the introduction of simultaneous and concurrent engineering techniques (Clark and Fujimoto, 1991; Midler, 1993; Jürgens, 1999), globalisation may bring about new changes to the organisation of product development by car producers.

WHICH STRATEGIES OF INTERNATIONALISATION?

The success of the internationalisation of car companies and their suppliers will depend upon their aptitude for facing the multiplicity of uncertainties about markets and employee relations. Moreover, the survival and position of companies will depend on the success or failure of this internationalisation. Hence the working out of internationalisation strategies will largely determine company futures. These strategies can initially, at least, be grouped into three major scenarios: (1) global homogenisation at one extreme, (2) regional heterogenisation at the other extreme, and (3) regional diversification/global commonalisation as an intermediate outcome.

The global homogenisation scenario would correspond to the case in which the liberalisation of global trade prevailed over the processes of creating more restricted economic spaces, with all car markets or at least the most important among them tending to homogenise, with employment conditions converging under the impact of constraints that were common to all. At this point, the decision to create a global model range would be relevant, whether a full range or a niche range. This scenario assumes that the reduction or elimination of customs duties is not substituted by other restrictions on trade, notably local content requirements. In the medium term at least, companies should invest where they want to sell, though even in this case the creation of a world model range is by no means impossible.

In this context, a strategy of internationalisation might consist of specialising production operations and regions in one segment of the model range, either for components or for finished vehicles, in order to benefit from maximum economies of scale. Given that each region is specialised in one segment, one can imagine that each local subsidiary might have its own particular socioproductive system without this affecting the coherence of the whole, unless the differences were profound that they produced significantly different income distributions and therefore different car markets. This would undermine the hypothesis of an homogenisation of global demand.

The intermediate scenario, regional diversification/global commonalisation, presupposes that without attaining complete homogenisation both product markets and work share certain fundamental traits across the different world regions, only being differentiated by secondary factors. In this framework a strategy of sharing principal components (global commonalisation) and platforms and a relatively similar policy regarding the basic elements of workplace relationships would enable companies to offer both differentiated regional product ranges and workplace relationships with regional specificities which would still be targeted at the same ends, for example, flexibility and polyvalence.

This scenario would lead to a centralisation of platform design and the creation of an overall employment policy and would lead to a globalisation of components production and, consequently, of the supplier industry. At the same time, it would be accompanied by a regionalisation of model design, locally derived from global platforms, and of course of their production. Autonomy would remain in the determination of concrete modalities for workplace relationships as a function of the local context (with respect to rules regarding wage determination, for instance). One might imagine that production could be transferred between regions if necessary, since each factory would assemble different models on shared platforms. Global planning of production programmes might therefore be envisaged. Ford and Honda display some of these characteristics.

Finally, in the regional heterogeneity scenario, homogenisation clashes more directly with the creation of differentiated regional complexes. In this hypothesis, it is the dynamic of regional integration that prevails, including the integration of countries at different levels of development and with somewhat different competencies. Within each region this dynamic produces a specialisation and concentration which relaunches growth. However, regional integration may assume different forms. These include simple free trade zones (in which economic and social power relationships are permitted to work themselves out) or true economic, political and social integration (in particular, involving a controlled policy to increase the purchasing power of the population).

Markets and work would be so different, and permanently so, between world regions that product ranges and employment policies would be specific to each region, except for interregional trade in some niche markets. This scenario could tolerate the persistence of less internationalised companies, which would remain local players with an intricate knowledge of the regional market and great agility. However, given the handicaps which this type of company would experience (see above), this scenario seems to support a multiregional configuration: regional subsidiaries would have great autonomy in terms of their product strategies, but the group would exercise financial control and probably distribute knowledge and experience between the different regions. Here we recognise 'Multi Regional Motors', described as the optimal form of international organisation in Chapter 8 of *The Machine that Changed the World* (Womack *et al.*, 1990) in contrast to the 'global company'. Our intention, therefore, is to question the idea of the globalisation of the car industry (Solvel, 1988; Chanaron and Lung, 1995) and to explore the hypothesis that the creation of new economic regions and their coexistence will produce new heterogeneities that go beyond short-run or apparent convergences. This viewpoint is justified because they are constituted by different economic, political and social processes. Consequently such processes can be contradictory and lead to social and political tensions with uncertain outcomes. They will therefore enter competition maintaining or endowing themselves with particular advantages. Car companies therefore coordinate their activities across the different regions of the world according to approaches which fit their internationalisation strategy. The variety of configurations is greater when the scopes of activity of different companies have different contours and are heterogeneous. Even when faced with the same environment, companies organise themselves in different ways depending upon their own history, their previous learning and their strategic horizon.

Hence, while the two principal American producers, Ford and General Motors, have had parallel internationalisation trajectories for more than 70 years, operating in the same regions according to very similar chronologies, there have been significant differences throughout this history (Dassbach, 1989), as there are today (Bélis-Bergouignan *et al.*, 1996). With its Ford 2000 plan, Ford has launched the global integration of its activities with a transregional configuration based on local competencies (United States, Europe, Japan). GM is following its rival, but it remains within a bi-regional structure with GM North America on the one hand and Opel, in charge of the rest of the world, on the other. A similar variety of structures can be seen among Japanese firms (Boyer and Freyssenet, 1999); the idea that they are converging towards a single model of globalisation may be disputed.

Following this, it is necessary to examine the development of the new regions involved in the internationalisation of companies – in other words, the emerging countries or regions which are being created – if we are to understand the likelihood of success of the various internationalisation strategies. For each type of region we need to know how markets work and what institutional frameworks (in particular state intervention) are evolving. Beyond this overall framework, we need to identify the problems being encountered by companies, given their international structures and industrial models, the solutions they have discovered and their performance in each location. It would appear essential to analyse the impacts of investments on host regions as functions of the modalities of local penetration (relationship with the local industrial fabric or position in the international division of labour organised by a multinational company, for instance), particularly with regard to the development of the technological potential of these emerging countries.

Note

* Translation by Sybil H. Mair.

References

AGLIETTA, M., BRENDER, A. and COUDERT, V. (1990) *Globalisation Financière: L'aventure Obligée*. Paris: Economica.
BALCET, G. and ENRIETTI, A. (1997) 'Regionalisation and globalisation in Europe: the case of Fiat Auto Poland and its suppliers', *Actes du GERPISA*, No. 20, 15–30.
BALCET, G. and ENRIETTI, A. (1999) 'La mondialisation ciblée de Fiat et la filière automobile italienne: l'impact dans les pays du Mercosur', *Actes du GERPISA*, No. 25, 23–40.
DE BANVILLE, E. and CHANARON, J.J. (1999) 'Inter-firm relations in alternative industrial models'. In Lung *et al.* (1999a), pp. 364–90.
BARDOU, J.P., CHANARON, J.J., FRIDENSON, P. and LAUX, J. (1982) *The Automobile Revolution: the Impact of an Industry*. Chapel Hill, N.C.
BÉLIS-BERGOUIGNAN, M.C., BORDENAVE, G. and LUNG, Y. (1996) 'Global strategies in the automobile industry', *Actes du GERPISA*, No. 18, 99–115.
BORDENAVE, G. (1998) 'Globalization at the heart of organizational

change: crisis and recovery at the Ford Motor Company'. In Freyssenet *et al.* (1998), pp. 211–41.

BORDENAVE, G. and LUNG, Y. (1988) 'Ford en Europe: crises locales, crise globale du fordisme'. *Cahiers de recherche du G.I.P. Mutations industrielles*, No. 17, Paris.

BORDENAVE, G. and LUNG, Y. (1996) 'New spatial configuration in the European automobile industry'. *European Urban and Regional Studies*, No. 4, 305–21.

BOYER, R. (ed.) (1986) *La Flexibilité du Travail en Europe. Une Etude Comparative des Transformations du Rapport Salarial dans Sept Pays de 1973 à 1985*. Paris: Editions La Découverte.

BOYER, R. and FREYSSENET, M. (1995) 'L'émergence de nouveaux modèles industriels'. *Actes du GERPISA*, No. 15, 75–142.

BOYER, R. and FREYSSENET, M. (1999) 'The World that Changed the Machine.' Mimeo. Evry: Université d'Evry Val d'Essonne, GERPISA.

BOYER, R., CHARRON, E., JURGENS, U. and TOLLIDAY, S. (eds) (1998) *Between Imitation and Innovation: the Transfer and Hybridization of Productive Models in the International Automobile Industry*. Oxford: Oxford University Press.

CAMUFFO, A. and VOLPATO, G. (1999) 'From lean to modular manufacturing: the case of the Fiat '178' world car'. *IMVP Globalization Research Report*. Cambridge, MA: MIT.

CARRILLO, J.V. (1990) 'The restructuring of the car industry in Mexico: adjustment policies and labor implications'. *Texas Papers on Mexico*, No. 90-05.

CHANARON, J.J. (1995) 'Constructeurs/Fournisseurs: spécificités et dynamique d'évolution des modes relationnels'. *Actes du GERPISA*, No. 14, 9–22.

CHANARON, J.J. (1999) 'Globalisation, division internationale du travail et relation constructeurs-fournisseurs'. *Actes du GERPISA*, No. 25, 5–21.

CHANARON, J.J. and JULLIEN, B. (1999) 'The production, distribution, and repair of automobiles: new relationships and new competencies'. In Lung *et al.* (1999a), pp. 335–63.

CHANARON, J.J. and LUNG, Y. (1995) *L'Economie de L'Automobile*. Paris: La Découverte.

CHANDLER, A.D., Jr. (1992) 'Organizational capabilities and the economic history of the industrial enterprise'. *Journal of Economic Perspectives*, Vol. 6, No. 3, 79–100.

CLARK, K.B. and FUJIMOTO, T. (1991) *Product Development Performance: Strategy, Organization, and Management in the World Auto Industry*. Boston, MA: Harvard Business School.

DASSBACH, C.H.A. (1989) *Global Enterprises and the World Economy: Ford, General Motors and IBM: the Emergence of the Transnational Enterprise*. New York: Garland Publishing.

DAVID, P.A. (1985) 'Clio and the economics of QWERTY'. *American Economic Review*, Vol. 75, No. 2, 332–7.

DIRKS, D., HUCHET, J.F. and RIBAULT, T. (eds) (1998) *Between External Shocks and Internal Evolution: Towards New Phase in Japanese Management Practices*. Berlin: Springer-Verlag.

DOHNI, L. (1994) 'Investissements Directs Extérieurs et Mouvements des Cours de Change'. Doctoral thesis. Pessac: Université Bordeaux I.

DUPUY, G. (1995) *Les Territoires de L'Automobile*. Paris: Anthropos.

DURAND, J.P., STEWART, P. and CASTILLO, J.J. (eds) (1999) *Teamwork in the Automobile Industry: Radical Change or Passing Fashion?* Basingstoke: Macmillan.

FREYSSENET, M., MAIR, A., SHIMIZU, K. and VOLPATO, G. (eds) (1998) *One Best Way? Trajectories and Industrial Models of the World's Automobile Producers*. Oxford: Oxford University Press.

FROUD, J., HASLAM, C., JOHAL, S., JULLIEN, B. and WILLIAMS, K. (1998) 'Accelerating household inequality and braking business opportunity: a comparison of motoring demand in the UK and France'. Paper presented at Sixth GERPISA International Auto Industry Colloquium, Paris, June.

FUJIMOTO, T. (1999) 'Capacity building and over-adaptation: a case of fat design in the Japanese auto industry'. In Lung *et al.* (1999a), pp. 261–85.

GERPISA (1984) 'L'internationalisation de l'industrie automobile'. *Actes du GERPISA*, No. 1. Published in *Cahiers de l'IREP-D*, No. 6, Grenoble.

HELPER, S. and SAKO, M. (1999) 'Supplier relations and performance in Europe, Japan and the US: the effect of the voice/exit choice'. In Lung *et al.* (1999a), pp. 286–313.

HOOD, N. and VAHLNE, J.E. (eds) (1988) *Strategies in Global Competition*. Stockholm: Selected papers from the Prince Bertil Symposilim at the Institute of International Business.

HUDSON, R. and SCHAMP, E. (eds) (1995) *Towards a New Map of Automobile Manufacturing in Europe? New Production Concepts and Spatial Restructuring*. Berlin: Springer-Verlag.

JETIN, B. and LUNG, Y. (1996) 'Un ré-examen critique de la relation entre variété et modèles industriels à partir de l'industrie automobile'. Paper presented to Journées de l'AFSE 1996 L'empirique en économie industrielle, Caen, April.

JULLIEN, B. (1999) 'Does the fundamental restructuring of car retailing imply internationalization of industry players?' Paper presented to the Seventh GERPISA International Auto Industry Colloquium, Paris, June.

JÜRGENS, U. (ed.) (1999) *New Product Development and Production Networks: Global Industrial Experience*. Berlin: Springer-Verlag.

LAIGLE, L. (1995) 'De la sous-traitance classique au co-développement'. *Actes du GERPISA*, No. 14, 9–22.

LECLER, Y. (1998) 'Recession and globalisation: what future for Japanese industrial Keiretsu?' In Dirks *et al.* (1998), pp. 183–285.

LECLER, Y., PERRIN, J. and VILLEVAL, M.C. (1999) 'Concurrent engineering and institutional learning: a comparison between French and Japanese auto part makers'. In Lung *et al.* (1999a), pp. 314–34.

LUNG, Y., CHANARON, J.J., FUJIMOTO, T. and RAFF, D. (eds) (1999a) *Coping with Variety. Flexible Productive System for Product Variety in the Auto Industry*. Aldershot: Ashgate.

LUNG, Y., SALERNO, M., ZILBOVICIUS and CARNEIRO DIAS, A.V. (1999b) 'Flexibility through modularity: experimentations with fractal production in Brazil and in Europe'. In Lung *et al.* (1999a), pp. 224–58.

MACDUFFIE, J.P. and PIL, F. (1994) 'The international assembly plant study: round two preliminary findings'. Paper presented to the IMVP Research Briefing Meeting, Berlin, June.

MAIR, A. (1994) *Honda's Global Local Corporation.* Basingstoke: Macmillan.

MARX, R., SALERNO, M. and ZILBOVICIUS, M. (1996) 'The modular consortium in a new VW truck plant in Brazil: new forms of assembler and suppliers relationship'. Paper presented to the Fourth GERPISA International Auto Industry Colloquium, Paris, June.

MAXCY, G. (1981) *The Multinational Motor Industry.* London: Croom Helm.

MICHELLI, J. (1994) *Nueva Manufactura, Globalización y Producción de Automoviles en Mexico.* Mexico City: Faculdad de Economia, Universidad Autonoma Metropolitana.

MIDLER, C. (1993) *L'Auto Qui N'Existait Pas. Management des Projets et Transformation de L'Entreprise.* Paris: InterEditions.

ORFEUIL, J.P. (1994) *Je Suis L'Automobile.* Montpellier: Editions de l'Aube.

RUIGROK, W. and VAN TULDER, R. (1995) *The Logic of International Restructuring.* London: Routledge.

SOLVEL, O. (1988) 'Is the global automobile industry really global?' In Hood and Vahlne (1998).

STURGEON, T. and Florida, R. (1999) *The World that Changed the Machine: Globalization and Jobs in the Automotive Industry.* Final Report to the Alfred P. Sloan Foundation. Cambridge MA: MIT.

TRACHTE, K. and ROSS, R. (1985) 'The crisis of Detroit and the emergence of global capitalism'. *International Journal of Urban and Regional Research*, Vol. 9, No. 2, 186–217.

VIGIER, P. (1992) 'La politique communautaire de l'automobile'. *Revue du Marché Unique Européenne*, No. 3, 73–111 & No. 4, 73–126.

WOMACK, J.P., JONES, D.T. and ROOS, D. (1990) *The Machine that Changed the World.* New York: Rawson Associates.

5 Mobility at a Price: Motor Vehicles and the Environment in South and South East Asia

Shobhana Madhavan

This chapter analyses the environmental impact of vehicle use in South and South East Asia and the range of policy responses available to reduce this impact. The countries of South and South East Asia are very disparate in terms of economic development. Over the last three decades these countries have experienced growing urbanisation and affluence, although this growth has been unevenly distributed, both spatially and over time. While levels of car ownership remain generally low compared to Western Europe or North America, high rates of growth of traffic in cities have led to congestion on roads and environmental damage from atmospheric pollution, noise and land use impacts.

Transport sources, especially road transport vehicles (private and public, formal and informal) are a dominant source of air pollution, responsible for various types of impacts – localised and global, short and long term. Although the share of private motor transport in environmental damage in developing countries is less than that of developed countries it is by no means negligible. While technological advances – stimulated by regulatory requirements – have improved the environmental performance and energy efficiency of motor vehicles, in developing countries vehicles still tend to be more polluting and less energy efficient than in more developed countries, due to a combination of factors: obsolete technology, vehicle longevity, poor maintenance and poor road surfaces. Congestion also adds to the quantity of emissions and hence to pollution levels.

Major cities in developing countries are experiencing serious environmental pollution as a result of emissions from motor vehicles, which account for around 90 per cent of carbon monoxide emissions

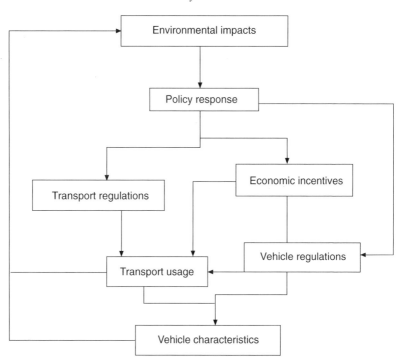

Figure 5.1   Environmental impacts of motor industry policies

in urban areas – and the overall environmental impact of pollutants is complicated by synergistic effects, such as the formation of ground level ozone from nitrogen oxides and volatile organic compounds (VOCs). Proportions of pollutants emitted depend upon the flow, speed and composition of traffic.

This chapter examines the role, and the environmental impacts, of motor vehicles, with reference to the analytical framework set out in Figure 5.1. It covers a range of countries in South and Southeast Asia with varying levels of economic development.[1] The study covers the period from the late 1980s to around 1997; it does not include the effects of the financial crisis in South East Asia on motor vehicle sales, and so on, as it is far too early to detect any effects that this crisis may have had on long-term trends. The chapter focuses on the analysis of the key indicators, and consequences, of growth in demand for motor vehicles. This is viewed in the broad context of the transport system and the interface between transport and environment policies. The chapter concludes with a case study on India, which brings together the main issues and the strands in policies which seek to mitigate the environmental consequences of rapid growth in motor vehicle traffic.

THE ANALYTICAL FRAMEWORK

Transport is both a major area of economic activity and a key sector in terms of its effects on the quality of the environment. Road transport is a major employer and a principal source of environmental problems. The environmental impact of motor traffic depends on the stock and usage of motor vehicles, and on environmental damage per vehicle; the latter may be reduced by improved vehicle technology, but growth in traffic will tend to increase environmental damage. With traffic increasing in most Asian countries, environmental and transport policy measures are needed to reduce or contain the adverse effects of traffic growth.

Figure 5.1 illustrates schematically the process whereby perceived environmental impacts of transport prompt a policy response. This involves measures to influence transport usage, including changes in regulations affecting provision and use of infrastructure, and the deployment of economic incentive measures, such as fuel taxes. These measures, together with regulations governing vehicle construction and use, affect the design and specification of vehicles; and the environmental impacts of transport depend in turn upon the characteristics and usage of vehicles.

CHARACTERISTICS OF THE TRANSPORT SYSTEM

While there is considerable diversity, in general, Asian countries have levels of income and vehicle ownership which are lower than in Western Europe. Consequently, there is more reliance on non-motorised transport and on public transport, although rising incomes tend to increase ownership and use of motor vehicles, particularly of two wheelers. Due to infrastructural deficiencies and, in some instances, high levels of polluting emissions from two wheelers and from ageing vehicles, the environmental impact of traffic is proportionately greater than in Europe.

Most of the countries covered by this chapter have substantial

Table 5.1   Projected urban population and urbanisation in Asian countries

	Urban population (000s)			% Urban	
	2000	*2020*	*% Increase*	*2000*	*2020*
Bangladesh	27172	58317	115	21	34
China	438236	711698	62	34	49
India	286323	498777	74	28	39
Indonesia	85458	146176	71	40	55
Malaysia	12767	20395	60	57	68
Pakistan	57792	123489	114	37	50
Philippines	43985	69862	59	59	70
Sri Lanka	4434	8148	84	24	35
Thailand	13057	22049	69	22	33

Source: GNP: Asian Development Bank, 1999; remaining figures derived from World Resources Institute, 1998: 274–5.

urban populations; and urbanisation is projected to increase in the first 20 years of the next century (see Table 5.1). This has important implications, both for the development of transport systems and the environmental impacts of transport, with reference to atmospheric pollution and pressures on land use.

The evolution of transport systems in cities in developing countries can be traced to historical patterns of land use, location of economic activity, city structures and inward migration from rural areas. Usage of different modes of transport is a function of socio-economic characteristics of households, cost and also availability of different modes. Compared with urban centres in developed countries, the main cities of Asia tend to have high population density, and low car ownership and road network density. A recent study of 35 cities worldwide included seven Asian cities (Bandung, Bangkok, Guangzhou, Jakarta, Manila, Singapore and Surabaya) with average population density of 11.3 persons per sq. km (compared with a 35 city average of 6.9), car ownership of 52 per 1000 population and road network density of 4.7 km of road per sq. km (the 35 city averages were 309 and 9.6 respectively) (derived from Ingram and Liu, 1997: Appendix Table 5.3).

The comparatively low vehicle and road network densities of Asian cities might suggest that the negative impacts of motor vehicles are lower than in Europe. However, high population densities, and

growing demand for travel, generate pressures in cities which generally have limited scope for absorbing growth in vehicle traffic, and
consequently are prone to traffic congestion. Many Asian cities are
approaching, and in some case may have reached, a crisis point where
transport is both highly inefficient and environmentally damaging.
There are essentially two lines of response to these developments: new
road construction, which is liable to generate further traffic growth,
and traffic restraint. Both of these are politically challenging, particularly if measures are needed to avoid, rather than respond to, a crisis.

South and South East Asia is a heterogeneous region, and the countries covered by this chapter vary considerably in their levels of prosperity and their vehicle ownership and use. A broad distinction can
be made between the more populous, and less prosperous, countries
(Bangladesh, China India and Indonesia) and those (including
Thailand, Malaysia and Taiwan) which have – until recently – enjoyed
the rapid economic growth characteristic of the so-called 'tiger'
economies. GDP per capita in 1998 ranged from $261 (Bangladesh)
to $15 082 (Taiwan). There is also great variation in the development
of, and pressures upon, infrastructure. In the larger and less prosperous countries, the populations are predominantly rural, notwithstanding the large cities in those countries; vehicle densities (measured by
vehicles per road km) are also low compared to Thailand, Malaysia
and Taiwan. A further indicator of transport infrastructure development is the proportion of road length which is paved – ranging from
just over 7 per cent in Bangladesh to 97.5 per cent in Thailand (which
also has a high vehicle density). Taiwan stands out from the rest in
terms of population density for both cars and people. These indicators are summarised in Table 5.2.

The proportionate size of the vehicle population, and its composition also vary, as is shown by Table 5.3: while Bangladesh had less than
one vehicle per thousand people in 1997, Taiwan had almost one
vehicle for every four people.

The modes of transport in the region differ in certain important
respects from those in developed countries. Firstly, non-motorised
transport (NMT) modes (also referred to as para transit and intermediate transport) such as bicycles, rickshaws and cycle rickshaws
constitute the predominant mode in almost all developing countries
accounting from 25 to 80 per cent of trips (Replogle, 1992: 1–3). While
NMTs offer benefits (a personalised form of transport, low cost, use
renewable energy) and are well suited for short trips, and cause no
atmospheric pollution, they belong to the economist's category of

Mobility at a Price

Table 5.2   Key motoring indicators, 1997

	GNP per capita	Population/ km²	Urban population as % of total	Cars/km²	Paved road as % of total	Vehicles/ km of road
Bangladesh	270	938.2	15.7	1.0	7.2	1.0
China	860	131	26.2	0.2	–	7.8
India	390	325.3	25.5	1.4	50.2	3.7
Indonesia	1110	108.4	30.6	0.5	–	11.8
Malaysia	4680	62.9	49.8	9.8	75	43.3
Pakistan	490	176	32	1.4	57	6.2
Sri Lanka	800	242	48.8	2.6	18	11.6
Taiwan	n/a	665.4	n/a	127.3	85.5	261
Thailand	2800	121.3	18.2	2.9	97.5	70.1
Developing country average	n/a	50.4	42.3	1.3	37.2	13.6

Source: Pemberton and Puckering (1998: 31–3, 56–7, 96–7, 102–3, 118–19, 144–5, 186–7, 190–1).

Table 5.3   Total motor vehicle population, 1997

	Motor vehicle population	% of Asia total	Vehicles per 000 population	Vehicles per person (index Asia total = 100)
Bangladesh	107 500	0.08	0.9	2
China	7 320 000	5.31	6.1	14
India	7 267 000	5.27	7.9	19
Indonesia	4 128 000	3.00	21.5	50
Malaysia	4 221 472	3.06	208.3	490
Pakistan	1 324 000	0.96	10.5	25
Sri Lanka	459 528	0.33	25.7	60
Taiwan	5 237 511	3.80	243.9	573
Thailand	5 730 646	4.16	94.3	222
Total	35 795 657	25.98	13.3	31
Total Asia	137 800 770	100	42.6	100

Source: SMMT (1998: 135).

inferior goods in so far as the demand for them is inversely related to income growth: access to personal transport, frequency of trips and modal choice are determined by income levels.

Patterns of income inequality in developing countries, especially in urban areas, account for the continuing presence of such modes in

Table 5.4   Vehicles per thousand population, 1994

	Asia[a]	Africa	Western Europe	World
Private cars	14	22	359	137
Commercial vehicles	12	11	59	42
Motorised two wheelers	24	2	44	23
All vehicles	51	35	462	202

Note: [a] Excluding China, Japan and Russia.
Source: Schwela and Zali (1999: 4).

cities despite attempts by transport and urban planners to eliminate them from the transport system. Rising incomes have led to growth in demand for NMTs. Bicycle ownership in China (where about half the total bicycle stock is in cities) increased 50 fold between 1952 and 1985 to 170 million, and is projected to rise to 500 million by 2000. In urban areas of Bangladesh cycle rickshaws account for some 30 000 passenger miles and about 100 ton miles of freight movement in 1992; and the cycle rickshaw fleet in Bangladesh is expected to reach 1 million by 2000. For the lowest income group in Delhi, 40 per cent of work related journeys in the 2–8 km range were made by bicycles. In Indonesian cities *becaks* (pedicabs) account for a major share in urban mobility despite attempts to ban them (Replogle, 1992: 1–2).

Secondly, in many cities in developing countries public transport buses (run by state undertakings or large private corporations), with technical capacities between 70–100 passengers, account for the major proportion of total journeys. We can infer from studies undertaken in the 1980s that in major cities public transport accounted for 35–50 per cent of total journeys (Hilling, 1996: 206–8). The contribution of public transport to total travel demand in most developing country cities is inadequate and the continuing presence of NMTs is witness to the lack of adequate provision by public transport.

Thirdly, in most of Asia the rates of motor vehicle ownership in proportion to population are well below the world average. Even Africa has a substantially higher rate for cars, although not for commercial vehicles. In contrast, Asia has a fairly high rate of ownership of two wheel vehicles (see Table 5.4).

Fourthly, the age of vehicles is an important indicator of vehicle

Table 5.5   Age distribution of the car parc, 1997

	<7 years	7–12 years	>12 years	Average age
Bangladesh			70	15+
China	64.7	23.7	11.6	4.2
India	42.6	23.7	33.7[a]	7.6
Indonesia	38.8	23.6	37.6	8.1
Malaysia	37.5	14.6	47.9	10.3
Pakistan	32.7	24.6	42.7	
Philippines	36.9	24.4	38.7	15+
Taiwan	62	37.4	0.6	4.8
Thailand	61.1	20.9	18	4.6

Note: [a] 25-year-old cars are not uncommon.
Source: Pemberton and Puckering (1998: 37, 57, 97, 103, 119, 145, 148, 187, 191).

technology, energy efficiency and environmental performance. The age profile of the vehicle population varies considerably between countries: in Bangladesh, 70 per cent of the cars are over 12 years old, while the figure for Taiwan is less than 1 per cent – see Table 5.5. However, this is not necessarily related to economic development as measured by GDP, since rapid growth in the vehicle population from a very low base (as for example in China) will result in a relatively new vehicle stock.

CAR OWNERSHIP: THE INFLUENCE OF GOVERNMENT POLICIES

Governments have often been ambivalent towards the motor vehicle, and particularly the car, industry. On the one hand cars have been regarded as import-intensive luxuries which a developing country can ill afford; on the other hand the vehicle industry is a key sector in a modern industrial economy, and often an important export sector. The latter view has long been prevalent in the so-called 'tiger economies', and has now gained more general acceptance. Nevertheless, there remains a tendency towards protectionism, emphasising import substitution rather than global competitiveness; this is manifested for example in customs duties, even in countries like Bangladesh where

Table 5.6   Import duties and other taxes: Asian countries, 1998 (%)

Country	Engine capacity (c.c.)	Cars: built-up	Cars: knocked-down
Bangladesh	0–850	45	45
	850–1000	45	45
	1001–1300	60	60 (Other tax 15)
	over 3000	60	60 (Other tax 150)
Pakistan	up to 1000	110	40
	1000–1300	130	40
	1300–1800	160	40
	over 1800	275	40
Malaysia	all sizes	140–300	up to 80[a]
Taiwan	all sizes	25[b]	25
Philippines	all sizes	30[c]	3
Thailand	up to 3 litres	42	
	over 3 litres	68.5	
China	under 1500	100	
	over 1500	120	
India	all sizes	40	(+40 additional duty)

Notes: [a] Imports subject to 10% sales tax. [b] Plus 25% commodity tax.
[c] Includes semi knocked-down.
Source: Pemberton and Puckering (1998: 38, 58, 99, 146, 150, 188, 192).

there is no indigenous industry and all passenger cars are imported. Customs duties are also an adjunct to local content policies which again is part of indigenisation programmes in most developing countries. In most countries a distinction is made between imports of 'built-up' and 'knocked-down' cars, and duties often vary with engine capacity; in Indonesia duty on 'knocked-down' cars varies with local content of the final output. Rates of import duty for cars are shown in Table 5.6 and (for Indonesia) Table 5.7.

In addition to import duties countries levy additional taxes both at the national and local levels. Consequently, car prices are still relatively high in Asia (see Chapter 9 by Guiheux and Lecler, in this volume, which shows that vehicle prices in the ASEAN region were 50–100% more expensive than in Japan).

Historically, policy-makers have shown little interest in the use of fiscal measures to restrain traffic growth. While there is the potential to do so, the levying of duties and taxes has more to do with raising

Mobility at a Price

Table 5.7   Import duties and other taxes: Indonesia, 1998

	Local content (%)	*Rate of duty (%)*
Cars: knocked-down,	<20	65
depending on local	20–30	50
content	30–40	35
	40–50	20
	50–60	10
	>60	0
Cars: built-up		200 (Additional luxury tax depending on category)

Source: Pemberton and Puckering (1998: 104).

revenue, protecting local industry and monopoly profit than with giving a disincentive for vehicle ownership.

The incidence of duties and other taxes, together with the degree of liberalisation, also has an impact on the nature of vehicles sold and produced in South East Asia. In some countries, demand for vehicles is heavily skewed towards pickups and vans. In Thailand and Indonesia, passenger cars accounted for only 28.6 per cent and 10 per cent of total light vehicles sales in 1995 (see Chapter 8 by Sugiyama and Fujimoto, in this volume). In the case of Thailand, there is no excise duty on pickups, compared to the rate of 30–40 per cent on passenger cars.

GROWTH IN VEHICLE NUMBERS AND TRAFFIC

Notwithstanding continuing import restrictions, some – but not all – Asian countries have recently experienced very rapid growth in the car market – see Table 5.8. In India, Indonesia and Malaysia the increase in new car registrations was in the region of 20 per cent per year between 1992 and 1997, while Sri Lanka suffered a severe decline. Taiwan and Thailand showed little change in registrations of passenger cars between 1992 and 1997. In the case of Thailand, this was due, in part to the fact that the East Asian crisis had a more immediate impact on car registrations, as can be seen in Table 5.8. In Indonesia and Malaysia, the impact of the crisis only became evident in the 1998 registration figures.

Table 5.8   New passenger car registrations[a] in Asian countries, 1992–97

	1992	1993	1994	1995	1996	1997	% Change, 1992–97	Annual change %
India	203881	244628	281577	394178	479760	474387	132.7	18.4
Indonesia	30341	32684	401412	37921	43914	73215	141.3	19.3
Malaysia	110289	120735	151063	224991	275693	307907	179.2	22.8
Sri Lanka	9355	7829	7745	6206	4742	4643	–50.4	–13.1
Taiwan	282992	268317	283222	282232	263960	268060	–5.3	–1.1
Thailand	121488	174169	155670	163371	172730	132060	8.7	1.7

Note: [a] New registration refers to vehicles brought on the road for the first time and also used vehicles.
Source: 1994–97: SMMT (1998: 112–13); 1992–93: SMMT (1998: 116–17, Table 40).

Car use has also increased substantially. In China, total passenger kilometres driven grew on an average of over 10 per cent per annum between 1979 and 1993. Total passenger km in 1993 were 785 billion amounting to 700 km per person per year (compared with the US figure of 13000 km), a 40 per cent increase over the 1990 figure. Passenger kilometres are projected to quadruple between 1991 and 2010 (OECD, 1996: 109–10). There has been a corresponding increase in the number of vehicles. The number of small cars grew from less than 250000 in 1980 to almost 1.3 million in 1990. Over the same period the number of buses tripled, and the number of motorcycles increased 17 times. By the year 2000 the number of small cars is expected to reach 4 million but this would still leave China with a low ownership rate, at 250 people per car (OECD, 1997: 10, 110).

ENVIRONMENTAL IMPACTS OF MOTOR VEHICLES

Local atmospheric pollution – much of it from transport sources – is a serious concern in cities in developing countries, where children may have exposure equivalent to smoking two packets of cigarettes a day. Air pollution has various components, and the relative contributions of different types of motor vehicles also vary depending on the composition of the vehicle stock and traffic conditions. Examples are given in Table 5.9, which shows motorcycles and trucks as the major emission sources in Surabaya, Indonesia; they were also significant sources in Bangkok, although emissions of carbon monoxide and lead were mainly from cars.

In China, emissions from road traffic have risen rapidly in the main

Table 5.9   Main sources of motor vehicle emissions, by pollutant: Surabaya and Bangkok

	Surabaya		Bangkok	
	Main source	*% of motor vehicle emissions, 1991*	*Main source*	*% of motor vehicle emissions, 1989*
Nitrogen oxides	Diesel trucks	56	Diesel trucks	48
Hydrocarbons	Motor cycles	78	Motor cycles	54
Carbon monoxide	Motor cycles	52	Cars	72
Organic particulates	Diesel trucks	92	Diesel trucks	88
Lead	Diesel trucks	51	Cars	77
Sulphur	Diesel trucks	75	Diesel trucks	77

Source: Schwela and Zali (1999: 149, 178).

cities, and control of these emissions in the future is a major challenge for policy-makers (OECD, 1996: 125). Road traffic passenger km increased by over 13 per cent per year, and road freight tonne km by almost 15 per cent, between 1981 and 1993. Projected annual increases between 1993 and 2010 are over 8 per cent (passenger) and 11 per cent (freight). The annual rate of growth in energy consumption is projected at approximately $6\frac{2}{3}$ per cent (OECD, 1996: 111), this would imply that approximately half the growth in road traffic will be offset by increased energy efficiency.

Motor vehicles in China are among the most polluting in the world, with low emission standards (approximating to 1970 US standards) and outdated technology combining with deficiencies in the road infrastructure. Vehicles in Beijing generate as much pollution as those in Los Angeles and Tokyo, which are 10 times more numerous. In the main cities of China, cars are largely responsible for high atmospheric concentrations of carbon monoxide, nitrogen oxides, ozone and lead (leaded gasoline is still in use, but is being phased out) (World Resources Institute, 1998: 118).

In Taipei (Taiwan), motorcycles account for more than half of the motor vehicle population, and offer a convenient form of transport in a densely populated and congested city. Emissions per km from a four stroke 50 c.c. motorcycle engine are higher than for a 2 litre car engine – typically 2.7 times higher for carbon monoxide and 6.7 times higher for hydrocarbon and nitrogen oxides (Chiu and Tzeng, 1999: 128). One possible development, examined by Chiu and Tzeng (1999), is the introduction of electrically powered motorcycles. Transport sources – and motor vehicles in particular – do not only contribute to localised environmental damage. They are major contributors to greenhouse gas emissions. Although climate change is a global phenomenon, the contributions vary considerably between countries. Per capita energy consumption is well below the levels of developed countries; China and India together use little over half the energy consumed in the United States. China would have per capita carbon dioxide emissions some $7\frac{1}{2}$ times higher than at present if its emissions were at the current US level (calculated from World Resources Institute, 1998: 344–5). An important reason for lower energy consumption and greenhouse gas emissions in developing countries is their lower ownership of motor vehicles. For instance, the US figure for vehicles per capita exceeds those of Malaysia (by a factor of three), of Indonesia (by a factor of 58) and China (by a factor of 127); for Bangladesh the factor is a staggering 843.

According to climate change analysts, developed countries account for two-thirds of total greenhouse gas emissions. However, within two or three decades developing country emissions will surpass those from developed countries. Much of this will come from transport sources: there is considerable scope for growth in the number of motor vehicles, especially in populous countries, such as China and India, which now have low rates of vehicle ownership. A UNEP study found high energy/GDP elasticities, and an elasticity for CO_2 emissions with respect to GDP close to unity, for a group of developing countries (including India, China, Thailand, Indonesia) (Bruce *et al.*, 1995).

Whatever the problems of scientific uncertainty and problems of measurement and evaluation it is important to note some of the likely consequences of climate change for developing countries. Based on a number of country studies, the Working Group on Climate Change (Bruce *et al.*, 1995: 218) noted the estimate of 'damage' for a doubling of CO_2. Subject to a number of simplifying and controversial assumption these are:

World impact: 1–2 per cent of world GDP
Developed countries: 1–1.5 per cent of GDP
Developing countries: 2–9 per cent of GDP

These relate to land loss leading to displacement of people, loss of coastal ecosystems, and generally losses in industrial and agricultural production. In the case of Bangladesh the road and rail link between Dhaka and Chittagong/Khulna would be disrupted by a rise in sea level: a 100 cm rise would affect 1460 km of roads. For a 1 m rise in sea level in India about 5763 sq. kms of land and 4200 km of road would be lost. The annualised cost (including loss of land) of this event is estimated to be 1 per cent of GNP.

THE POLICY RESPONSE

The policy response to environmental impacts has essentially two elements. Transport policy measures seek to relieve congestion through road improvements, to encourage switching to less polluting modes, and to restrain car use through traffic management measures. A further distinction can be made between restraint on vehicle ownership and vehicle use: there may be more scope for the latter (especially in congested urban areas) than for the former.

Environmental policy measures aim to counteract the consequences of the use of motor vehicles – examples of such measures include incentives for use of unleaded petrol and installation of catalytic convertors.

The formulation and implementation of these two types of policies usually rest with different government departments and with different tiers of government in developing countries (as in developed countries) leading to great complexity in administration. The implementation of policies in these two areas may in turn be constrained by other policies, such as urban development, and or land use policies. For instance, possibilities for road construction and upgrading in cities and metropolitan areas are clearly limited because of pressures on land use.

Transport policy

Transport policy in developing countries is geared to the perceived requirements of economic and social development, with elements of transport planning, land use planning, and urban development. The main aims of transport policies are concerned with the provision of road and rail services for the bulk of the population, the emphasis being on accessibility rather than mobility. Rapid rates of growth in population impose additional pressures. Transport policy measures to support road and rail networks are given priority over other demands in most of the countries under study. The dichotomy between urban and rural areas gives rise to different forms of transport provision to meet the needs for access and mobility.

Specific measures to control the use (and ownership) of cars occupy a relatively small role in transport planning and development, given that with low rates of car ownership (see Tables 5.2, 5.3 and 5.4) car travel provides mobility only for a minority. Again, policies to control the use of cars are applied to urban areas in so far as the problems of car use are manifest mainly in the major cities.

Import duties, registration fees and car taxation generally have as their primary objective the raising of revenues rather than restricting ownership and use. While the above measures lie mainly under the jurisdiction of central governments, others are administered by state or local governments, including police departments. These include traffic management systems (area traffic controls, priority bus lanes) and measures to restrain the use of cars such as road pricing. There is considerable variety of measures and much complexity in administrative procedures.

In Western Europe measures are advocated to change the modal split, switching journeys from cars to buses and trains. Atmospheric pollution can be reduced by a transfer of traffic to bus and rail. This can have a direct benefit (reduced energy consumption and hence reduced carbon dioxide emissions) related to higher energy efficiency of these modes, and an indirect effect on polluting emissions through relief of traffic congestion (which increases the efficiency of vehicle use). On average, pollutant emissions per passenger km are lower for bus and rail than for cars, and a transfer from cars to public transport would – other things being equal – tend to reduce emissions, provided that vehicle occupancy is sufficient to outweigh higher levels of emissions per vehicle in public transport modes. In developing countries, the proportion of journeys by car is relatively very low: the problem facing policy makers is to respond to a growing demand for car travel and ownership which will come with increasing prosperity. The potential savings from modal switch must not be exaggerated given that car travel accounts for a small proportion of passenger miles and for the vast majority of the population there is no choice but to use public transport.

With present levels of vehicle usage, measures to facilitate traffic flow – by changing road layout and traffic management – have some scope for improvement in urban environmental quality. However, growing traffic volumes will tend to counteract any gains: average vehicle speeds in central Bangkok are between 6–10 km/hour, and at the busiest intersection traffic can sometimes move at only 0.8 km/hour (du Pont and Egan, 1997: 27). One policy approach, which so far has been applied vigorously only in Singapore, is to deter car usage by stringent charges and taxes. In Singapore import duties and taxes account for 70–80 per cent of the cost of buying a new car, and (with petrol costing around $3 per gallon) the monthly cost of operating a car is in the region of $400. Restrictions on car use are effected by means of area licensing to prevent congestion (Singapore has had such a system since 1975), parking charges and restrictions, and electronic road pricing (a pilot scheme has been tried in Singapore) (du Pont and Egan, 1997: 28). Singapore is exceptional in its successful implementation of this approach; there must be doubts as to the feasibility of instituting similar measures in other Asian cities.

Environmental policy

The magnitude and costs of the environmental problems caused by motor transport have been the subject of many studies: so have the possible solutions to the problem (for examples, see Schwela and Zali, 1999). Recent environmental protection requirements are beginning to address the problem of pollution. Governments (and in some instances the car industry) in developing countries have adopted measures to reduce emissions.

These include the purely technical (improved vehicle technology, choice of fuel, inspection and maintenance, emissions testing, the installation of catalytic convertors) and non-technical (traffic management, measures to encourage the use of public transport). Other measures such as scrappage schemes, and (except in Singapore) road pricing have yet to assume a significant role in managing pollution caused by automotives.

Policy measures serve a variety of objectives, in addition to environmental protection, relating – *inter alia* – to fiscal policy, economic development and safety. There are also trade offs between environmental objectives: for example the use of catalytic convertors to reduce local atmospheric pollution leads to an increase in fuel consumption and hence in greenhouse gas emissions.

There is evidence of concern in Asia. Vehicle emission standards have been considerably tightened in India (see below), and tougher emission rules in Chinese cities are leading to investments by foreign firms in the production of catalytic converters for passenger cars (AutoAsia, 1999). Countries in South East Asia have instituted legislation to limit environmental impacts of vehicle use: examples include Malaysia's 1974 Environmental Quality Act (amended 1985 and 1996), and regulations on Clean Air (1978), Control of Lead Concentrations in Motor Gasoline (1985) and Motor Vehicle Noise (1987) (Tan, 1998a), and Indonesia's 1992 Act on Road Traffic and Transportation and 1993 Decree on Emission Standards for Vehicle Exhaust Gas (Tan, 1998b).

ENVIRONMENTAL PRESSURES AND MOTOR VEHICLES: INDIAN EXPERIENCE

The motor vehicle industry in India is an interesting case study particularly so because it shares a number of characteristics with the industry in developing countries in South East Asia. Building on the momentum for development established since the advent of the Maruti in the 1980s, the period from the early to the mid-1990s saw rapid growth (see chapter by Humphrey and Salerno, in this volume). All sectors of the industry recorded around 30 per cent growth in sales during this period. The sectoral composition includes cars, commercial vehicles, utility vehicles, two wheelers and three wheelers. While cars account for approximately 10 per cent of total vehicles, two wheelers consisting of scooters, motorcycles and mopeds are by far the predominant forms of personal transport.

Most travel in cities is by public transport – which is a reflection of economic circumstances, rather than the quality of the service provided. The bus is the dominant urban transport mode, especially outside the four largest cities which have substantial suburban rail networks. In the past decade the number of motorised two wheel vehicles has grown very rapidly in Indian cities, at annual rates ranging from 10 to 15 per cent (Dalvi, 1997: 172–3).

Indian industry has been subject to political controls and planning mechanisms, either directly through government ownership, or through licensing measures which directed investment and placed limits on capacity. Within this framework, passenger transport has been dominated by public sector undertakings, which include the railways, the main airlines and many bus operators. Many bus services are operated by State Transport Undertakings, which have often been given political directions by state governments to accord priority to uneconomic rural routes rather than to urban services; private operators have been insufficiently regulated, and the overall result is inadequate and uncoordinated services. Road freight, although not nationalised, has been subject to heavy taxation and regulation, particularly affecting interstate traffic (Padam, 1998: 2–3).

This historical inheritance is now subject to fundamental change, with moves towards economic liberalisation. There are far reaching implications for road transport: privatisation lessens the constraints on bus operations, deregulation increases the scope for road haulage, while the relaxation of industrial licensing has led to expansion of motor vehicle production.

In general, liberalisation can be expected to increase road traffic. Economic growth, and restructuring, will stimulate transport intensive forms of consumption, while markets for vehicles and transport services become increasingly contestable. Considerable growth has already been observed in the number of private motor vehicles. Barriers to entry in road haulage are reduced, stimulating competition and efficiency; a similar effect can be anticipated in passenger transport, although operators may no longer be obliged to provide uneconomic services.

Growth in traffic is of course constrained by the extent of infrastructure provision: if road capacity is under continuous and sustained pressure, the traffic using the roads will be subject to severe congestion, discouraging further growth. However, there are also problems in providing additional capacity: experience in Europe suggests that highway construction tends to generate traffic, particularly in urban areas, intensifying pressures on land use and the environment.

There are various demand projections for motor vehicles (including two wheelers) in India by the year 2000: the high ends of the forecasts range from 4.7 million units (McKinsey/EIU) through 5 million (DRI) up to 5.5 million (Morgan Stanley). These imply market growth of the order of 10–20 per cent between 1995 and 2000; and the projected growth rates are generally higher for cars than for other vehicles. Meanwhile, planned growth in production capacity is so massive (up to 5–8 million units by 2000) that there are doubts as to whether demand (even at the high forecast levels) will be sufficient to avoid excess capacity (Shah, 1996: 4.01–5.13).

Nevertheless it is anticipated that the demand for personal and freight transport will grow with increasing economic prosperity (the growth rate is predicted to be around 5 per cent) and a sizeable market of the affluent middle classes. Other forces leading to increasing demand for personal transport are inadequate provision of public transport facilities and the relatively low share of railways in passenger movement in most cities.

The increase in personal transport use is not only an issue for cities. According to the National Council of Applied Economic Research, demand for motor vehicles in rural areas must not be underestimated (NCAER, 1996). Rural demand for motor vehicles is at present concentrated in the utility vehicle segment. Analysis of the economic situation in rural India reveals a number of factors which might lead to convergence between urban and rural areas in terms of demand for motor cars amongst the more affluent segments of the population.

Rural areas in India contain about 600 000 villages spread across 3.29 million sq. km. Rural economic activity and social organisation give rise to distinctive travel patterns and travel needs. Trip patterns differ in rural areas: while walking is the principal mode motorised vehicles are largely used to travel long distances and for social purposes. Households of higher social and economic standing travel more frequently and over longer distances. The proximity of rural areas to cities and the availability of public transport are important factors determining the number of trips undertaken (Madhavan, 1983).

Private motor transport is used predominantly by large farm households, which constitute only a very small per centage of total farm households. But these households (the number of middle and high income households more than doubled between 1987/88 and 1993/94) have a high proportion of local spending power, due to their ownership of land, the use of technology in farming and their social and political status. These are multiple vehicle households (cars are a status symbol) whose influence and resources require, and enable, them to maintain their links with towns and cities – and hence their need for personal motor transport. The poor quality of motorable roads has not altogether deterred the use of motor cars in rural areas.

Marketing strategists have begun to recognise the importance of rural markets for consumer goods, including consumer durables. Systematic surveys in the 1980s and mid-1990s have shown that rural markets account for a significant part of the sales of bicycles, radios, table fans, motorcycles, TVs, radios and so on. The penetration of the media, and the availability of a wide range of manufactured goods are beginning to change lifestyles and influence tastes. The big attraction of the rural market is its sheer size: and this is now combined with improving economic prospects. The ultimate basis for optimism over rural demand for private cars lies in the dreams and aspirations fanned by the media and the film industry.

In urban areas environmental concerns are increasingly acute. Pollution from suspended particulates is a particularly severe problem in major cities, while WHO guidelines are exceeded for other pollutants such as sulphur dioxide, lead, carbon monoxide and nitrogen dioxide (Schwela and Zali, 1999: 23–7). Controlling emissions from automobile engines has become mandatory under the Indian Motor Vehicles Act 1988 (Amendment) which came into effect in July 1989. The government now requires the industry to adopt fuel efficiency norms set for different types of vehicles. For passenger cars below 1000 c.c. under test conditions vehicles should achieve 22 km per litre at 25 km per hour. Although there are fiscal incentives available to manufacturers to achieve fuel efficiency these are in the form of concessions on import duty and will cease to be available once products and processes are fully indigenised.

Other regulations introduced by the 1988 Motor Vehicles Act include the fixing of age limits for scrapping of vehicles and measures to raise standards of driving. Seat belts are to be made compulsory on front seats in all new cars. Fines for all vehicles which do not meet emission standards have been raised from Rs50 to Rs1000. Some 22 new Safety Standards have been formulated under the Central Motor Vehicles Rules (Rule 124). There is a wide gap between the existence of laws in the Statute book and their actual implementation: some states and some transport departments are more vigorous in enforcing the laws. But there has recently been a noticeable change in public attitudes towards traffic infringements, especially in the light of the intervention by the Supreme Court in matters relating to air pollution from motor vehicles.

Vehicle emission standards in India now follow those set in Europe. The specification presently being adopted is known as the 'Euro I' standard, which limits carbon monoxide emissions to 2.72 g/km. Although it is envisaged that the standard will eventually prevail nation wide, in the first instance cars sold in Delhi were required to meet the Euro I standard from 1 June 1999. Vehicles which do not meet this standard can still, for the time being, be sold elsewhere in the country, but in practice manufacturers are likely to design all their new models to conform with the standard.

Environmental protection has become an area of judicial activism, as the courts have sought to ensure that legislation is actually enforced (see for example Desai, 1998). In a recent judgement, the Supreme Court brought forward from 2005 to 2000 the date for implementation of Euro II standards (with a carbon monoxide emission limit of 2.2 g/km) for cars sold in Delhi, and set quotas for sales of vehicles meeting the Euro I standards in the interim period. These developments tend to favour new multinational entrants such as Hyundai, Daewoo, Mercedes and Toyota, which have the technological capability to meet the stricter norms. The dominant manufacturer, Maruti had no models which meet the Euro I standard in 1999 (Environmental Concerns, 1999: 46). To remedy this shortcoming, Maruti signed a Memorandum of Understanding with Suzuki to introduce three new models (the 1600 c.c. Baleno, a new 800–1000 c.c. Alto, and a 1000 c.c. 'Wagon-R' model) by May 2000, with a total investment of Rs12 billion (approximately $300 million); furthermore the Gypsy model was to be upgraded to Euro II standards by May 2000 (*The Hindu*, 10 August 1999). Another indigenous manufacturer, Mahindra & Mahindra, produces vehicles which do not meet the Euro II standard, and one of its best selling models, the Commander, does not even comply with Euro I; however, the Commander is being modified to Euro I level (at an estimated cost of Rs4000 – approximately $100 – per vehicle), and there are now plans to upgrade all models to the Euro II standards by April 2000 (*Times of India*, 26 August 1999). By 2000 a new vehicle should have emission levels 96 per cent below the level for an equivalent pre-1989 vehicle (see Table 5.10).

Table 5.10 Emissions of pollutants from new and existing vehicles in India, tons per day, 1989, 1996, 2000

	New vehicles	Emissions/thousand vehicles (tons per day)	
		Existing vehicles	% reduction
1989	200	1444	86
1996	63	1344	95
2000	13	969	99

Source: Derived from Shah (1996).

Table 5.11   Sales and stock of vehicles,[a] India, 1989, 1996, 1997, 2000

	New vehicle sales (000s)	Vehicle stock (000s)	Sales as % of vehicle stock
1989	337	3888	8.7
1996	738	6905	10.7
1997	749	7550	9.9
2000 (projection)	950	9200	10.3

Note: [a] Excludes two- and three-wheeled vehicles.
Source: 1989, 1996, 1997 Pemberton and Puckering (1998: 97); 2000 derived from Shah (1996).

The overall effect of new vehicle standards depends – *inter alia* – on the turnover of the vehicle stock, and the rate at which existing vehicles are replaced. The number of new vehicles relative to the existing vehicle stock is now comparable with Europe – in 1997 vehicle sales were 9.9 per cent of the total *parc* (see Table 5.11), above the UK figure of 8.3 per cent (calculated from Pemberton and Puckering, 1998: 97, 199). However, there is a large number of older vehicles, such that the average age of vehicles is $7\frac{1}{2}$ years (see Table 5.5 above) with one-third more than 12 years old.

The car industry is on course to achieve low emission levels by the development and use of new engines, modern fuel systems and modern engineering systems. Although the future scenarios include the development and use of electric cars, in the immediate future efforts will be concentrated on achieving the norms set for achieving a reduction of emissions by 1996 (transitional norms) and achieving the goals set for 2001 by the Ministry for Environment.

To meet the new emission standards, vehicles must incorporate technologies such as fuel injection, oxygen sensors, and electronic engine management. Most new vehicles are based on models developed by multinational manufacturers, and already incorporate technology for use of lead free petrol. Since 1995, catalytic converters have been fitted in new vehicles sold in the four main cities (Delhi, Calcutta, Chennai and Mumbai); and the convertors (and supplies of unleaded petrol) are becoming increasingly common throughout the country. However, the increased availability of low lead fuel is not an unmixed blessing, since its use in a vehicle designed for leaded fuel can accelerate the wear on valves, tending to reduce engine efficiency and increased polluting emissions (Reddy, 1999: 165).

The resulting environmental improvement will of course be much less dramatic: new vehicles are only a small proportion – well under 10 per cent – of the vehicle stock. Given the longevity of the vehicle stock, there will be a large number of vehicles on the roads designed for low (or non existent) emission standards for many years to come. Much also depends on proper maintenance of vehicles, particularly engine tuning and cleaning, and also of the catalytic convertors; this in turn requires development of an infrastructure with technicians who have equipment and skills suited to the increasingly complex technology of modern vehicles. Furthermore, the use of fuel adulterated with kerosene or hexane, which is not uncommon in India, can drastically affect a vehicle's performance: in a recent instance it was found that 80 per cent of diesel vehicles had failed emission tests solely due to adulterated fuel and badly clogged filters (Reddy, 1999: 165–6).

In meeting environmental objectives, the Indian motor industry will have to overcome a very large number of obstacles not to mention the considerable resource costs entailed in the quality of fuel production and setting up adequate distribution networks for improved fuels. Supplies of unleaded petrol are limited and engines for passenger cars are being produced primarily for petrol. All this calls for massive investment in petroleum production and infrastructure for its distribution.

However, the constraints do not end here. A large number of changes will have to be made to achieve efficient traffic management both through traffic engineering and modifying driver behaviour. These will include effective levels of traffic management in the major cities of India to keep vehicles moving. There is an urgent need for statutory provisions for fitness certification and maintenance of vehicles. Testing systems will also have to be in place to reflect and to register compliance with requirements. Finally, improvements in road engineering and regular maintenance of roads are essential if reduction in pollution levels are to be achieved. Physical infrastructure, and its operation, also affect vehicle performance. With a given traffic volume, environmental performance is positively related to the quality of road surfaces and layout, traffic management and road user discipline.

The intensity of usage of inter-urban roads has been increasing. The length of India's road network increased fivefold between 1951 and

1991, while the vehicle population grew by a factor of seventy (Parikh, 1997: 223). Over the same period, the split between road and rail changed dramatically: road freight increased from 21.5 per cent to 70.1 per cent of the road plus rail total; for passenger transport the respective percentages are 37.8 and 84.5 (Padam, 1998: 16). The central government has devised a plan for a Rs1300 billion, 13000 km, 'National Super Highway' network, to be developed by the private sector on a 'Build, Operate and Transfer' basis. State governments are also planning similar schemes for inter-urban highways.

The future of urban traffic is more problematic; experience has shown that improvements to facilitate traffic movement can lead to generation of additional traffic, which tends to negate environmental improvements. So although environmental standards for motor vehicles will greatly reduce polluting emissions per vehicle, this improvement will, on present trends, be offset by rapid growth in the vehicle population. Given the need for communication and mobility in a modern economy, the key issue is how to accommodate this requirement in a manner which does not have unacceptable effects on the environment and the quality of life. A transport policy response to this issue would focus on the efficiency of transport modes in terms of the benefits of mobility in relation to the social (rather than solely the private) costs. Efficiency in this sense is encouraged if user costs for specific modes were to reflect more closely and precisely the pressures arising from their use of scarce environmental capacity. The process of cost internalisation can be promoted through mechanisms such as emission related vehicle taxes, congestion charges, and parking controls and charges. At the same time, land use and infrastructure planning can seek to reduce the need for travel (this approach has been pursued by the UK government – see DoE, 1994).

So, while economic liberalisation removes direct government controls, transport operators and users should assume increased responsibility for the wider consequences of their activities. There would still be an important role for motor vehicles, but they would not dominate the urban environment, and there would be a complementary relationship with alternative modes. There is as yet little evidence that transport policies have taken account of these broader issues; the concern has been mainly with liberalisation and deregulation and the relief of infrastructural deficiencies in order to accommodate increased traffic: while these are important, they can ultimately be self-defeating (see Dalvi, 1997: 308–9).

The fundamental question is whether governments (at national and state levels) have the political will to set policies on a course which could be seen to confound popular aspirations. Globalisation may be perceived – crudely – as bringing the benefits of technologies and lifestyles currently enjoyed in America. The multinational motor vehicle producers have been attracted by the prospect of a large, hitherto underdeveloped, market – to the extent that India has more major manufacturers than the United States! Clearly there is a general expectation that rising living standards will increase personal mobility and the quantity and variety of products and services consumed. The rational long-term policy response must be to channel these aspirations to ensure that they are not ultimately self-defeating; but, as the experience of western Europe suggests, this is a major challenge. Indian policy-makers at least have the advantage that the 'car culture' is less entrenched, and land use is much less car oriented, than in Europe or America.

CONCLUSION

South and South East Asia contain markets with established records of growth and huge future potential. In some parts of the region (notably Taiwan) motor vehicle ownership rates are broadly comparable with Europe, while other markets – particularly in the more populous countries – are much less developed. Nevertheless, this growth potential is constrained by the effects on the quality of life: already, even where vehicle ownership rates are low, urban areas suffer from the environmental impacts of vehicle use. Countries in the region have responded by raising vehicle emission standards; but it is doubtful whether this response will be sufficient in the longer term. Therefore, the major policy challenge is to find other means of curbing the impact of the car.

The case study of India highlights the issue of how to reconcile, on the one hand, the role of the motor vehicle industry as a major sector of the economy, and road transport as a key factor in economic development, and on the other hand, environmental concerns which will inevitably intensify unless appropriate measures are taken to restrain vehicle usage. To prevent an eventual crisis, transport, land use and environmental policies have to ensure that mobility requirements are met without unacceptable environmental damage. However, this anticipatory approach is politically difficult because it will be perceived as confounding aspirations associated with the spread of vehicle ownership which have indeed been encouraged by the government's new industrial policies.

Note

1. This chapter focuses mainly on the following countries: Bangladesh, China, India, Indonesia, Malaysia, Taiwan and Thailand.

Bibliography

ASIAN DEVELOPMENT BANK (1999) *Asian Development Outlook 1999.* Oxford: Oxford University Press.

AUTOASIA (1999) 'Cleaning up in China'. *AutoAsia*, January/February 1999, 26.

BRUCE, J.P., LEE, H. and HAITES, E.F. (eds) (1995) *Climate Change 1995: Economic and Social Dimensions of Climate Change.* Cambridge: Cambridge University Press.

CHIU, Y.-C. and TZENG, G.-H. (1999) 'The market acceptance of electric motorcycles in Taiwan: experience through a stated preference analysis'. *Transportation Research*, Part D 4, 127–46.

DALVI, M.Q. (1997) *Transport Planning and Policy in India.* Mumbai: Himalaya Publishing.

DESAI, A. (1998) *Environmental Jurisprudence.* New Delhi: Vikas Publishing House Pvt. Ltd.

DoE (1994) *Planning Policy Guidance Note 13.* London: Department of the Environment.

DU PONT, P. and EGAN, K. (1997) 'Solving Bangkok's transport woes: the need to ask the right questions'. *World Transport Policy & Practice*, Vol. 3, No. 1: 25–37.

ENVIRONMENTAL CONCERNS (1999) 'Indian cars must meet Euro emission norms, orders apex court'. *Environmental Concerns of India*, May: 6.

HILLING, D. (1996) *Transport and Developing Countries.* London: Routledge.

INGRAM, G.K. and LIU, Z. (1997) 'Motorisation and Road Provision in Countries and Cities'. Paper presented at Harvard University, Cambridge, Mass.

MADHAVAN, S. (1983) 'What kind of transport for the informal sector in developing countries? Some questions for transport planners'. *Manchester Papers on Development*, No.7, 53–92.

NCAER (1996) *Indian Marketing Demographics: the Consumer Class.* New Delhi: National Council of Applied Economic Research.

OECD (1996) *China in the 21st Century: Long-term Global Implications.* Paris: OECD.

OECD (1997) *Climate Change: Mobilising Global Effort.* Paris: OECD.

PADAM, S. (1998) *Transport Sector in India: a Status Paper.* Pune: Central Institute of Road Research.

PARIKH, K.S. (1997) *India Development Report, 1997*. Delhi: Oxford University Press.

PEMBERTON, M. and PUCKERING, D. (1998) *World Auto Atlas and Directory*. Banbury: Pemberton Associates.

REDDY, C.M. (1999) 'Diesel vs. petrol: a question of quality'. *The Hindu Survey of the Environment '99:* 161–6.

REPLOGLE, M. (1992) 'Bicycles and cycle rickshaws in Asian cities: issues and strategies'. Paper presented to the Sixth World Conference on Transport Research, Lyon, July.

SCHWELA, D. and ZALI, O. (eds) (1999) *Urban Traffic Pollution*. London and New York: E & FN Spon.

SHAH, S.G. (1996) *Shaping the Indian Automobile Industry*. Mumbai: Association of Indian Automobile Manufacturers.

SMMT (1998) *Motor Industry of Great Britain 1998 World Automotive Statistics*. London: Society of Motor Manufacturers and Traders.

TAN, A.J. (1998a) *Preliminary Assessment of Malaysia's Environmental Law*. Singapore: APCEL.

TAN, A.J. (1998b) *Preliminary Assessment of Indonesia's Environmental Law*. Singapore: APCEL.

WORLD RESOURCES INSTITUTE (1998) *World Resources 1998–99*. New York: Oxford University Press.

6 The Integration of Peripheral Markets: a Comparison of Spain and Mexico

Jean-Bernard Layan*

Since the mid-1980s, the Mexican motor industry has experienced exceptional growth, with annual vehicle output having exceeded the one million mark since 1996 (Table 6.1). This period of expansion, which was sparked off when the big North American companies decided to build a series of assembly facilities in the country, has been sustained by an export boom towards the United States. From an analytical point of view, these events have become a classic example of the Triad having integrated its periphery into its core, and they have come to symbolise a type of industrial development which the present article will from now on refer to as 'Integrated Peripheral Markets'.[1] Mexico is not the only country to have lived through this kind of experience. During the 1970s, the Spanish motor industry also followed a similar trajectory. At the beginning of that decade, Spain had been producing 500 000 vehicles annually – but by 1997, this number had soared to 2.5 million (Table 6.2), and the country had caught up with France as Europe's second largest vehicle producer, far ahead of Italy and the UK. More than 80 per cent of the production of foreign companies in Spain has been exported to the countries in the European heartland.

As the 20th century draws to a close, the global economy has entered a phase of regionalisation, and this has changed the nature of the relationships which govern international trade. Mexico's and Spain's successes are a prime example of this phenomenon, even if they preceded the two countries' entry into their respective regional blocks, and are therefore neither the automatic consequence of Spain's having joined the European Community, nor of Mexico's membership in the newly founded NAFTA. In both instances, industrial integration preceded the official opening up of a core commer-

Table 6.1   Motor vehicle production and exports by type: Mexico, 1980–98 (units)

	Production			Exports			
	Cars	Commercial vehicles	Total	Cars	Commercial vehicles	Total	Export as % of production
1980	303056	186950	490006	13633	4612	18245	4
1985	267358	191322	458680	20398	39198	59596	13
1990	598093	222464	820557	249921	26016	275937	34
1995	699312	237888	937200	598803	183873	782676	84
1996	799557	426808	1226365	635906	342239	978145	80
1997	853197	508833	1362030	591485	396707	988192	73
1998	952909	499938	1452847	590648	386325	976973	67

Sources: GNFAC and OICA.

Table 6.2   Motor vehicle production and exports by type: Spain, 1970–98 (units)

	Production			Exports			
	Cars	Commercial vehicles	Total	Cars	Commercial vehicles	Total	Export as % of production
1970	450426	88706	539132	–	–	–	–
1975	696124	118040	814164	154072	17095	171167	21
1980	1028813	152846	1181659	470248	36593	506841	43
1985	1230071	187533	1417604	761887	68798	830685	59
1990	1679301	374049	2053350	1066009	183550	1249559	61
1995	1958789	374998	2333787	1537182	275105	1812287	78
1996	1941716	470593	2412309	1537023	389983	1927006	80
1997	2010266	551213	2561479	1640397	451138	2091535	82
1998	2216571	609492	2826063	1742234	494270	2236504	79

Sources: GNFAC and OICA.

cial zone to its less developed periphery. There are further parallels, as well. The present study will carry out a comparison which will demonstrate how Spain and Mexico both 'emerged' in a similar manner, and how this process led to their following two closely related modes of insertion into the international system.

In both Spain and Mexico, economic integration was only feasible because of a planned reorientation of industrial policy, and because of a conscious decision to open up the countries' trade networks. Yet, the real motor behind the expansion of Spain and Mexico's motor industries lay in the convergence of the spatial strategies which the sector's top companies, led by the 'Big Three' American companies, began to follow. Ford and General Motors, as well as the European and Japanese firms which were to follow in their footsteps, needed to offset increased competition in their core markets. This led them to attempt to reduce their labour costs and increase the flexibility of their workforce. Their priority became the relocation of their activities, with the periphery becoming responsible for manufacturing relatively standardised components, and for assembling bottom-of-the-range products. However, this hierarchical specialisation, in which the Spanish and the Mexican motor industries took on a subaltern role, was no industrialisation of obsolete or 'secondhand' production. Nor did it involve a relocation of products which had entered the last phase of their product cycle, as was thought by Vernon (1966): the techniques and modes of organisation which were developed in these new industrial plants were usually at the forefront of modernity. In fact, some of these new facilities even pioneered the organisational innovations which often occur when a new product is manufactured. Indeed, firms often saw their new peripheral transplants as an opportunity for the territorial management of various types of industrial risk, including those which stemmed from chaotic trends in demand, or from employee resistance to changes in the organisation of work.

Nevertheless, the growth of the automotive sector of these two major Hispanic nations has profoundly modified the very economic and social environments in which their industries were born. This transformation has caused a certain amount of ambivalence, but nevertheless, companies have had to take note of it. On one hand, the differences between the core spaces and their immediate periphery are no longer very pronounced, and this has led some firms to lose a part of their initial interest in the periphery: delocalised units of production have pressured core installations into accepting flexible wage schemes, and into adopting more reactive principles of organisation. On the other hand, the periphery's accumulation of competencies has created new perspectives for the future, and these have already caused a marked change in Spain and Mexico's mode of insertion into the global economy.

THE COMMON ORIGINS OF INTEGRATED PERIPHERAL MARKET TRAJECTORIES

The motor industries in Spain and in Mexico seem to have gone through a veritable renaissance. For once, the strategic development of firms has been in tune with those political changes which radically modified the regulatory framework framing a nation's productive activities.

Changes in the model of industrialisation

The two industrial transformations in question were not only sparked off by economic factors – political and institutional issues also had a bearing on events. Both Mexico and Spain shifted from a policy where the shelter of protectionism was used in order to achieve industrialisation via import substitution, to a different strategy, based on the promotion of exports and on free trade. However, we should not forget that earlier economic policies in Mexico and Spain did have a positive effect on the way in which the two countries' industrial infrastructure would develop.

The shared dream of a national motor industry

For almost 20 years, these two major Hispanic nations experienced a modest but tangible industrial expansion, safe behind the solid barriers of a protectionist system. The regime of General Franco, nationalist and authoritarian as it was, considered autonomous industrial development as a means for restoring a small part of the Kingdom of Spain's past glory. To succeed in this endeavour, the regime opted for an isolationist policy which associated a strict quota on imports with the requirement that the majority stake (a massive 90 per cent) in domestic companies be kept in Spanish hands. From the late 1940s onwards, a policy of limiting the imports of finished vehicles served as a launching pad for a truly national type of automobile production. Two local companies, SEAT in Barcelona and FASA in Valladolid, operated under manufacturing licences, on behalf of Fiat and Renault respectively. They shared the Spanish market, which at that time was comprised of just a few tens of thousands of new vehicles each year. Then, in the 1960s, Citroën set up in Vigo, Chrysler in Madrid, and British Leyland near Pamplona. Production started to grow at a high rate (more than 25 per cent annually), and reached more than 300 000 units per year in the early 1970s.

In Mexico too, an inwardly focused strategy of industrialisation was at work from the early 1960s onwards. This was an expression of a tradition of economic and political independence which had been given a new impetus by the writings of analysts such as Raúl Prebisch and other United Nations Economic Commission for Latin America (UNECLA) economists.[2]

The Mexican government helped its national motor production along by prohibiting the importation of finished vehicles, by setting minimum percentages of local content, and by requiring that Mexicans hold a majority stake in the capital of supplier firms. Vehicle production itself was assumed by five subsidiaries of foreign companies (Ford, GM, Chrysler–Automex, Volkswagen–Promexa, and Nissan), and by two joint ventures in which the Mexican state held a majority stake (Willy–VAM, together with AMC, and DINA, which operated under a licence from Renault and Fiat). All of these production plants were run within the confines of a few extremely integrated industrial complexes that were located in the middle of the country, in a 100 km radius around the capital, Mexico City. This system attained a modicum of success: production increased sevenfold in 15 years, jobs in the sector rose by a factor of six, and 80 per cent of all materials used in automobile assembly were domestic in origin (Carrillo, 1993). In 1980, the automotive sector accounted for more than 6 per cent of all manufacturing in Mexico, against only 2 per cent in 1960 (Micheli, 1994).

All in all, these two regimes of inwardly-focused growth may have had their limitations – but they undeniably served as a springboard for the subsequent period, with its emphasis on exports. Moreover, this type of industrialisation introduced modernity into countries whose earlier traditions had been agricultural; and it served to educate generations of technicians, qualified workers, and even the entrepreneurs who were to become necessary if industrial expansion was to take place at a later date.

The multinationals exerted considerable pressure for a change of policy

Policies reflecting the wishes of entrepreneurs and networks of influence that represented the interests and ambitions of the new ruling classes led to a complete remodelling of the institutional framework which encompassed the productive sectors in these two major Hispanic nations. Despite a facade of allegiance to earlier principles, there had been radical changes in the countries' social, political, and ideological orientations, and these were reflected in the new environment. In the late 1960s, a new generation of technocrats, educated in major universities abroad (for the most part, in the United States), arrived at the head of the economic ministries in Madrid. This group was responsible for the reorientation of Spain's economic and industrial policies, a trend which would be continued, and even amplified, by the democratic governments which came after Franco. However, the main reason behind the substantive changes to the regulations which controlled the vehicle sector was that the multinationals, and Ford in particular, exerted continuous pressure on the Spanish state. In the early 1970s, after years of effort and in exchange for the construction of a large assembly plant near Valencia, Henry Ford II was able to secure that three decrees, called the 'Ford laws', be adopted in response to his group's demands: direct control over the venture's capital; a significant reduction in local content levels; and lower customs duties on parts. Later, when GM–Opel built a plant near Zaragoza towards the end of the decade, there was yet another reduction in the percentage of local content, another drop in customs tariffs, and a cancellation of vehicle import quotas.

Technocrats educated in major American universities also invaded the upper echelons of the Mexican administration, and took over some key posts in the PRI, the country's (quasi-) single party. Mexico's presidents during the 1980s, de la Madrid and Salinas de Gortari, were no longer party chieftains, as had been their predecessors; rather, they were Harvard-educated economists who wanted to change their country's industrial policies. Here again, reforms were considered to be indispensable: not only did the market's small size and excessive variety make it impossible to amortise an inexorable growth in physical assets, but the requirement that tools and hi-tech components be imported worsened the trade gap each and every time that vehicle demand accelerated. The automotive sector represented in and of itself one half of Mexico's trade deficit in the early 1980s, at the same time that the country was sinking ever deeper into a full scale financial crisis (Micheli, 1994).

A need for foreign currency was already behind the creation in 1965 of the *maquiladora* sector, which benefited both in Mexico and in the United States from a status akin to that of an enterprise zone. Restricted at first to the Northern border areas, this status was extended in 1972 across all of Mexico. The success of the maquiladora sector influenced many of the reforms which occurred in the late 1970s and early 1980s. At first sight, the series of laws which regulated this sector seemed to have preserved the main principles of the earlier strategy of import substitution; yet, they all received the go-ahead from the major American companies – and for good reason. These texts may have perpetuated that part of the previous system which held that imports to Mexico had to be offset by a provision of foreign currency – but they also progressively lowered the rates of local content, thus transforming what had been a cumbersome constraint on production into a simple financial compensation, a foreign transaction which was much easier to manage. This change would serve as the basis for the major automotive groups' first large scale investments in export-oriented plants, and especially in facilities where motors were to be produced (Carrillo, 1993). After Mexico joined the GATT in 1986, deregulation became systematic: most restrictions on production and trade were cancelled and customs duties were greatly decreased. Open borders and liberalisation became the country's new policy, culminating in the signature of the NAFTA between the United States, Canada, and Mexico, in 1986. NAFTA would 'little by little' get rid of most of the remaining regulations, and as part of this new framework, the United States would demand a reduction of the percentages of local content (24 per cent), while paradoxically setting a 62.5 per cent rate of preference for North American products: a protectionist measure which, at least for Mexico, was a step backwards on its road to free trade.

The new regional associations only exerted a limited influence

The 1980s were marked by the creation of new regional trading blocks (NAFTA, Mercosur, AFTA), and by the widening and deepening of what has today become the EU. Even though Mexico and Spain each occupied the same southerly position within their respective regional constellations, in neither of the two countries was membership in these continental common markets the principal cause of the rise in automobile output. In fact, the investment decisions which sustained the rapid growth of the automotive sectors in Mexico and Spain preceded by more than a decade the countries' membership in their respective continental institutions. However, from very early on, the actors (the governments and large companies) incorporated the possibility of membership into their analyses and medium-term decisions – as much a rational expectation as a self-fulfilling prophecy. For example, at the same time that Spain was organising its entry into the EEC, its government was carrying on negotiations with Ford (Seidler, 1976). Later on, the major firms' relocation strategies were able to gather strength from Mexico and Spain having integrated the trading networks in their respective regions – and this enhanced the industrial integration of the firms productive networks across Europe and North America.

Note that the industrial expansion of the world's two largest Spanish-speaking countries was not necessarily caused by their having opted for a system based on free trade. In order to be successful, this desire to find a way into the international division of labour needed to converge with the strategies of localisation which a number of firms were following.

The strategic plans followed by the firms

In both Spain and Mexico, industrial development was essentially the consequence of a strategic reorientation which had been undertaken by the major North American groups. These firms were able to use the variable of space in order to solve their commercial or productive problems. Of course, other firms from Europe and Japan also came to play an important part in the industrial expansion of the Triad's periphery – but these were competitors who were already present in these protected markets, and who would later be forced to adapt to the new intrusion. The three large US vehicle makers continued to play a leading role in the definition of new spatial strategies.

The leading role played by the 'Big Three'

The renewed interest by the three major North American vehicle groups in Spain and in Mexico was directly linked to the recurrence of internal crises which were caused by a worsening of their market positions, especially in the American market. These crises were engendered by the competitive tensions which crop up when a macroeconomic environment has been massively disrupted.

The market became considerably more competitive after the first oil shock: shrinking demand stimulated competition at the same time as the energy crisis increased the general public's interest in small, economy vehicles, a Japanese and European speciality. Ford was badly hurt by this situation. From 1973 to 1975, the number of vehicles it produced dropped by 22 per cent, sales by 12 per cent, profits by half, and over a period of just a few months, 12 per cent of its workforce was laid off. In this context, it was to Ford's advantage to set up in Spain – it hoped to gain access to a market which was rapidly growing, and which was also relatively protected, at least for the foreseeable future. Together with the decision to manufacture the Fiesta in Valencia, this implantation symbolised the company's diversification towards small cars, a product which was greatly in demand because of the energy crisis, and which constituted the dominant segment in the Southern European markets. Above all, setting up in Spain allowed Ford to overcome the problems it was having with the workforce at its plants in Britain, which had become a constant battlefield for the company (Bordenave and Lung, 1988). The same logic would also lead GM to the same conclusions, in essence, following Ford's lead. As a first step, GM's component-making subsidiaries established plants at Cadiz and at Logroño – then, after a long hesitation over the relative merits of taking over an existing facility versus building a new one, GM would 'in 1982' finally decide to open up a small vehicle plant near Zaragoza (for the Opel Corsa).

A parallel chain of events was taking place in the North American market, where the local firms' positions continued to worsen, and where the Japanese had captured more than 20 per cent of the annual market in new vehicles. The second oil shock, and the advent of monetarism which followed it, made the situation even worse: Chrysler almost went bankrupt, AMC was purchased by Renault, and Ford went through the longest and most serious crisis it had ever known (Bordenave, 1995). At first, the Mexican solution was a logical response on the part of corporate leaders whose distorted view of the Japanese success story had lead them to believe that all they had to do was control their labour costs (Womack, 1990). From the mid-1970s onwards, GM, Ford, and Chrysler, via their component-making subsidiaries, were already benefiting from the lower salaries being paid to workers in the maquiladoras.[3] Far from feeling that the system of monetary compensation which was in effect during the late 1970s was a constraint on them, the Big Three saw it as an opportunity, for it coincided with the opening of the Mexican market to those companies who were ready to build export-oriented plants. By deciding to build motor assembly facilities, the companies were able to reap a triple benefit: they were running a labour-intensive activity requiring a less qualified workforce; they could organise a system of subcontracting which would be easy to relocate; and they were producing high value-added products. This latter aspect was particularly attractive in light of the fact that they were required to provide a financial compensation for imports. In 1982 and 1983, Chrysler and GM set up shop in Ramos Arizpe, whilst Ford chose Chihuahua (plants with an annual capacity ranging from 400 000 to 450 000 units). GM's decision to also build vehicle assembly plants should be seen as a continuation of the Southern Strategy which it had followed during the 1960s, when it had already sought to obtain the cost advantages which are inherent to an implantation in virgin territory for industrialisation (Rubenstein, 1992).

The construction of greenfield plants in the North of Mexico offered the added advantage of allowing the companies to experiment with 'Japanese techniques', while limiting social risks through the phenomenon of extraterritoriality. In the early 1980s, many people back at the Detroit headquarters started to believe that Japan's competitive advantage had been based on the superiority of Japanese productive organisation. Indeed, Ford made overtures to Mazda. This industrial collaboration would lead to the joint construction of a plant at Hermosillo, capital of the state of Sonora, on the US border. In 1986, with materials which had been sent over from Japan, hundreds of Japanese engineers started up the production of the Mercury Tracer, a clone of the mini-compact Mazda 323 (Shaiken, 1990). As in Spain, this was a case of Ford trying to find a solution to the fundamental crisis of its labour relations – and like in Europe, the strategy would be crowned with success. The performances of the Mexican plants, and of the Hermosillo facility in particular, would play a decisive role in changing the attitudes of the UAW union leaders – people who, because of their sense of patriotism, and despite the absence of any institutional support, would later come out in favour of mobilising workers against these technological and organisational mutations (Babson, 1998).

The Big Three fulfilled the role of a 'first mover'. This was because American firms had long been involved in the process of internationalisation, and were therefore quicker to spot both changes and new opportunities. Moreover, because of their greater size, and their longer track record, their ambitions were more global – and this enabled them to modify, by their very presence, the industrial structure, and the nature of competition in the countries where they became established.

The competitors adapt in response

The three American companies' investments in Spain and in Mexico caused the competitive conditions in these emerging vehicle markets to change radically. The sudden arrival of Ford, and then of GM, precipitated a retreat from Spain by Chrysler, British Leyland, and Rover, who either sold their plants, or simply abandoned their stakes. Even more symbolic was Fiat's disengagement from its stake in SEAT at a time when this company was in deep trouble. Inversely, another pioneer, Renault, adapted to the new situation, and even worked to reinforce the sector's trend towards external growth through a massive investment programme. In fact, Renault would use the modernisation of its Spanish plants as a springboard for renovating the rest of the group; the company overtly used the competition between its Spanish and French plants as a weapon in its battle to obtain a loosening of the 'social rigidities' back in France (Layan, 1997). Even so, FASA's integration into the rest of the group did not harm its penetration of the local market, and Renault soon became the leading brand in Spain.

Similar events were taking place in Mexico, where Nissan and Volkswagen were systematically modernising their productive apparatus in an attempt to answer the quality challenge which their American competitors had laid down. Between 1982 and 1992, they each invested around 1.5 billion dollars (Mortimore, 1995). Nissan relocated to Aguascalientes in the North, whilst Volkswagen, in line with the German tendency to dig deep territorial roots, remained loyal to Puebla. It did, however, modernise its immense integrated complex there. Renault would have certainly made a similar decision as the other non-American generalists, had the failure of its 'American adventure' not caused it to disengage partially from Mexico.

Industrial growth in Spain also benefited from Volkswagen's absorption of SEAT. The German group had a double objective: to penetrate the rapidly expanding Spanish market, and to take advantage of the relatively low labour costs. Still, the Catalan firm also constituted a laboratory where VW could test the Japanese principles of management which it found so difficult to force upon German employees and their unions. The construction of the Martorell complex should be analysed together with the Ford plant in Hermosillo. This was the first time that VW built a plant around the precepts of 'lean' production. The facility's architecture was designed so as to facilitate the work of multi-functional teams. It was also supposed to enable its assembly lines to receive supplies 'in real-time' from an industrial park which had been created in the immediate vicinity of the plant, and which was due to house the direct subcontractors, as well as other first-tier suppliers. This 'just-in-time' complex, the first in Europe, would serve as a model for ever more ambitious experiments, including the operations at Resende in Brazil. It would also guide the modernisation of the older, integrated sites, such as the one at Puebla (Mexico).

As for the Japanese, they showed little interest in localising in the pericentral areas. Nissan did buy a Spanish truck factory (Motor Iberica), which it wanted to reconvert to light vehicle production – but in contrast, Suzuki's interest in Santana only lasted a decade or so. The Japanese (and Korean) companies also lack any major presence in Mexico, once again with the exception of Nissan. Apparently, they fear that American protectionist measures would still apply to them, even if they were to build plants in Mexico. For this reason, they have opted in favour of US-based production. This choice will surely be modified over the medium term, now that NAFTA has been signed – as demonstrated by the activities which Honda has been building up in Mexico. It is true, however, that the 1994 peso crisis caused a freezing of several projects which had already been announced (Daewoo), and that the Asian financial crisis has put the brakes on the ambitions of the various groups involved.

REGIONAL INSERTION IS A FUNCTION OF EACH AREA'S PARTICULAR DYNAMICS

Even though each network's degree of economic and spatial integration depends on the product ranges, history, and culture of the firms involved, there has been a modicum of convergence in spatial strategies, simply as a result of rational calculation and imitative behaviour. What has now appeared is a strong degree of differentiation between the core regions, with their old automotive traditions, and the peripheral markets – the distribution of activities has been asymmetrical. However, the dynamics of integration, in and of themselves, are capable of making national industries evolve, at least with respect to their specialisation. Moreover, the logic of polarisation which has governed the spread of activities across the various spaces has also been modified. In addition, while it may be true that in Mexico and Spain similar mechanisms of integration have been matched by parallel trajectories, enormous dissimilarities remain: between the companies involved, in the countries' level of development, and in each continent's economic and institutional context. These differences have caused divergences in the integrative processes, and in each country's mode of insertion into its regional division of labour.

Similar specialisations within each continent's productive networks

Ford and GM's arrival in Spain during the 1970s would provide these companies with an opportunity to rationalise their European networks. The standardisation of product ranges across the continent made it possible for Ford and GM to define divisions of labour in which all of the internal and external industrial units which were participating in the company's productive network would find themselves linked. Little by little, Ford and GM would apply this principle in every location where they were active, and most of the other global players would soon follow suit. In this way, the integration of the Spanish and Mexican peripheries into their vertical regional divisions of labour went hand in hand with similar processes of specialisation.

The constitution of continental networks

Ford's implantation at Valencia in 1976 should be analysed within the context of the group having tried to thoroughly restructure itself so as to increase the cohesiveness of its European plants. By so doing, Ford was again affirming the bi-regional strategy that reflected its general view of the world economic situation – an outlook that soon lead to the birth of the 'global car' (Bordenave and Lung, 1988). European production was structured around an axis which was constituted by the UK, Belgium, and Germany, but another equilibrium was supposed to develop after new plants were built in Spain and in France (Bordeaux). These were early days for the principle of site specialisation, but the role attributed to the Southern pole was already quite obvious: it was to assemble both entry-level vehicles, and also engine and drive systems (motors at Valencia-Almusafes, transmissions at Bordeaux-Blanquefort). The restructuring of GM's European operation around Opel would only be finished in the mid-1980s. In Mexico as well, implantation would also be accompanied by a recomposition of productive processes and intermediary flows across the entire continent, comparable to the reshuffling which had taken place following the agreement between the United States and Canada in 1966.

When the Big Three delocalised towards the periphery, competitors who were already present in these spaces reacted by imitating some of their behaviour (that is, financially integrating local subsidiaries, narrowing product ranges). Still, each vehicle maker had its own way of integrating production across the continent, or of creating site specialisation. Renault responded almost immediately. After redefining all of its Spanish activities, the company soon put together a coherent system of production, with specialisation along both geographical and product lines. The roles which PSA attributed to its plants at Madrid–Villaverde (Peugeot) and Vigo (Citroën) were not quite as strategic – but little by little, the company did end up by limiting these sites to entry-level vehicle and light utility van production. The absorption of SEAT by VW was also accompanied by a certain degree of restructuring – the group now had a number of different marques at its disposal, and was therefore interested in a greater degree of commonalisation, and in a drastic reduction in the number of its platforms.

Nissan's and VW's networks across the North American continent were much less developed than those of their principal competitors. However, the peso crisis in 1994–1995 caused Nissan to bring forward the scheduled specialisation of the plant at Smyrna (Tennessee, USA), which soon concentrated on producing only pick-up trucks and Vanettes. The plants at Cuernavaca and at Aguascalientes also became more specialised, and began to only produce sedans (4 door saloons) and station wagons (estates). Exports rose sharply. Conversely, after shutting down its plants in the US, VW became one of the few single-site car makers on the continent: and having cost a total outlay of more than US$1 billion, today Puebla can assemble all of the vehicles which are being sold in the regional zone. Furthermore, over the past three years, the company's exports have doubled, rising from 40 per cent to 80 per cent of all units sold. Finally, Renault's attempt to limit its North American productive network to its one engine plant at Gomez Palacio should be seen as the consequence of the group's failed ambitions, as well as the closure of its assembly sites in Mexico and in the US.

At the same time as its specialisation was increasing,
the IPMs were being dominated

The new vertical regional division of labour (VRDL) which began to take shape in the 1980s, led to the pericentral zones being allocated the type of specialised production which seems to be the norm for subaltern spaces in the vehicle sector: small cars, small utility vans, and small engines.

In both Spain and in Mexico, automakers built their new, export-oriented assembly plants with the specific purpose in mind of making entry-level vehicles. To a large extent, this decision was made on the basis of the costs involved: wages represent a comparatively high percentage of the total value of small vehicles, and price is the main competitive factor for entry-level vehicles. In addition, their decision also took market considerations into account, given the over-representation of bottom-of-the-range vehicles in the Southern European and Mexican markets. In fact, legislation in Mexico encouraged this trend by subsidising the production and commercialisation of the most basic versions (described as 'austere') of these bottom-of-the-range models.

Spain and Mexico were also responsible for assembling utility vehicles, both for their internal markets, as well as for export. This activity mostly covers light utility vans derived from small vehicles, which are destined for the entire regional market – even if the production of heavy trucks continues to represent an important part of the total value produced by the sector. Spain's performance in the all-terrain (4 × 4) off-road car niche (Table 6.3) has been achieved thanks to Nissan and Santana, to whom Suzuki has sub-contracted its assembly operations.

The manufacturing of engines, a labour-intensive assembly activity, is also a speciality which the two countries share. With an annual output of more than one million motors, Spain is one of the world's leaders in this area. As for Mexico, it has often exported more engines

Table 6.3   Specialisation of production, Spain, 1984 and 1996

	1984		1996	
	Units	*%*	*Units*	*%*
Small cars	735 328	57	1 576 402	66
Small commercial vehicles	85 009	7	243 286	10
Total small vehicles	820 337	63	1 819 688	77
Compact cars	347 442	27	325 098	14
Other cars	88 553	7	67 179	3
Recreational vehicles	19 048	1	98 465	4
Others trucks	21 985	2	62 149	3
Total	1 297 365	100	2 372 579	100

Source: Author's elaboration of CCFA data.

than vehicles, and has rapidly become both the fifth largest engine producer in the world (shifting more than two million units per year), and one of the biggest exporters, with a pronounced preference for smaller engines such as the four-cylinder. In addition to its specialisation as an assembler, Mexico also produces electrical wiring and components, interior fittings, and many other low-value, labour-intensive items which are built in the *maquiladoras* along the US border. American assemblers appreciate the flexibility of labour, in all senses of the term, of these Mexican plants (job security, salary, hours, conditions of work, and so on), and this flexibility will probably not be affected by the termination, foreseen for the year 2003, of the maquiladora's special status.

Thus, the Spanish and Mexican automobile sectors, invaded by foreign firms, seem to be lacking in the higher-level functions of management and design; for the most part, high value-added products and sub-products seemed to have passed them by. However, by studying these assertions in greater detail, we will discover that they need to be relativised – even though they do correspond to expectations.

A territorial management of risk has affected the specialisation of the periphery

As we have already seen, companies have used their new implantations in the continental peripheries as working laboratories: they have seen these locations as sites where new products could be produced, and where new organisational methods could be applied. It can cost as much as US$1 billion to build or re-engineer a modern plant so that it can assemble vehicles, engines, or transmissions. This explains the sector's affinity for economies of scale, as well as the reason why vehicle makers often try to limit the number of new sites which they operate in any given space. There is also another reason why innovative products are often manufactured in neighbouring peripheral spaces: it springs from the concept of chronological convergence, which holds that new localisations will house new products. Ford long saw an implantation in Spain in parallel with its desire to penetrate the small car segment of the European market. The two projects reached fruition at about the same time – hence the company's decision to manufacture its new Fiesta in Valencia (Seidler, 1976).

However, it should be noted that a company which decides to create an implantation on the periphery can also be acting to protect its core. This can be the case if an innovative project were to fail. For example, the Fiesta already represented a considerable industrial and commercial risk for Ford–Europe. Now, one of the particularities of the 1990s was that Spain and Portugal ended up accounting for almost all of the production of vehicles which were aimed at narrow but rapidly growing niches (for example, the people carrier or the all-terrain vehicle), or else whose future was uncertain (for example, mini-city cars such as the Ka or the Twingo). This habit of establishing commercially very risky activities on the periphery altered the aforementioned logic of specialisation. In fact, the prime motivation for some of the decisions to build plants in 'virgin' territories – that is, in regions which lacked any real industrial tradition (Northern Mexico, the Ebro river valley in Spain) – had less to do with the choice of a product than with a company's desire to further the innovation of its organisation, or else to design an industrial architecture that was fully adapted to these new methods. Note that inter-company relationships are at the heart of these organisational innovations – a prime example being the 'strategic partnership', a new type of grouping between giant, oligopolistic firms. These forms of industrial co-operation tend to favour the production of niche products, that is, joint ventures which specialise in the assembly of people carriers (Ford/VW or Fiat/PSA), or badged cars (Nissan's manufacturing of the Ford Maverick). These strategic alliances are motivated by the desire to reduce commercial uncertainties, but they themselves also generate other risks: the risk of a divorce between competitors who had temporarily banded together (for example, Autolatina and AutoEuropa), and also the risk that employees will react negatively to alliances which they may consider to be unnatural. It can be advantageous to move these risky operations away from the core zones, and from employees who hold a more traditional view of what relationships between competitors should be: for example, Ford's association with Mazda went down better at Hermosillo than in Flat Rock (Babson, 1995).

Thus, the production of new products in the automotive sector's new integrated peripheral spaces has interfered with the hierarchy of specialisation which certain people had been expecting to find. The certainties of economists who can only think along the lines laid down by Vernon (1966), and who can only conceive of a one-way, unidirectional diffusion of industrial innovations (that is, from the centre to the periphery), have been thrown into question.

A parallel evolution of specialisations and localisations

The specialisation which we have just studied is not set in stone. The way in which these previously protected markets have opened and grown, and the process by which their productive apparatus has been modernised, has progressively modified companies' perceptions, of the periphery as a productive space, and of the potential of these productive units. Furthermore, this new type of industrial expansion destabilises the territories which it touches, either creating, or else destroying, localised resources.

Towards a de-specialisation of these integrated peripheral markets

Little by little, the continental division of labour which the big American companies had hoped to create by building modern productive facilities on the periphery, has been dissipated. This has resulted from the very integration of these peripheries, from wider market trends, from recurring problems, strategies, and also from the steep learning curve which the new vehicle-producing countries have been climbing rapidly.

The opening of previously protected markets has led to a supply which is more diverse and a demand which is less specific. In Spain, industrial growth also occurred at the same time as a general rise in the level of disposable income, and this considerably changed the demand structure for motor vehicles: smaller cars (less than 1500 cc), which in 1988 still represented more than half of the market, only accounted for 40 per cent of new car sales six years later (see Table 6.4). Spain had caught up with other countries' standard of living – this reduced its wage differential and ate into its price competitiveness. In addition, its flexibility advantage had been eroded, as labour relations were evolving in Europe's core regions (a phenomenon for which Spain itself was responsible) at the same time that certain areas of rapid industrialisation were starting to resist the new forms of labour (witness the recurring absenteeism and high turnover of the workforce in Northern Mexico). The process of the peripheries' economic integration thus contributed both to the destruction of the intermediary spaces which they had spawned, and also to a weakening of the factors upon which the vertical regional division of labour (as defined above) was to be founded. We can readily understand why certain assemblers and component makers tried in Eastern Europe to recreate conditions which no longer existed on the Iberian Peninsula.

Table 6.4   Motor vehicle market by engine capacity: Spain, 1988–94
(registrations)

Year	0–1000 c.c.	1000– 1500 c.c.	1500 c.c. or more	Total	Less than 1500 c.c. (%)	1500 c.c. and more (%)
1988	57128	466591	480265	1003984	52	48
1989	50882	487096	547651	1085629	50	50
1990	44329	412107	489470	945906	48	52
1991	30887	354155	447665	832707	46	54
1992	23909	356135	561136	941180	40	60
1993	22267	248343	440972	711582	38	62
1994	44109	296830	518141	859080	40	60

Source: Author's elaboration of CCFA data.

Nevertheless, growth continued in Spain and in Mexico: the attenuation of the original advantages was obviously offset by performances which were just as good as those which were achieved in other car spaces, central or otherwise.

The development of the Spanish and Mexican automotive industries was based on products, technologies, and productive organisations which were at the forefront of modernity. As such, these countries acquired, within the space of a few short years, competencies which could be partially transferred to other products. Layers of small and medium-sized local industrial sub-contractors benefited from the technological, and above all, from the organisational innovations which the assemblers were applying. The quality of the just-in-time output of the component-making industry of the Basque and Navarre regions of Northern Spain was clearly related to the fact that VW and Mercedes had built facilities in the area at the same time (Alaez et al., 1996). The performances of the Mexican industry, including its maquiladora sector, justified VW's decision to localise the production of its New Beetle at Puebla, as well as General Motors' decision to open a new engineering centre at Ciudad Juarez, a site which may have specialised in the design of less strategic components, but which nevertheless employed more than 800 Mexican engineers and technicians (Carrillo and Hualde, 1997).

The success of the generalist firms also attracted top-of-the-range specialists such as Mercedes or BMW. The vehicle makers had no qualms about choosing a peripheral location for the production of top quality products: the Mercedes V class has been assembled exclusively in Spain. From a wider perspective, even though the renewed focus on exports did at first considerably reduce the diversity of autarchic production, industrial growth was nevertheless accompanied by a certain amount of diversification, and by the manufacturing of a hierarchically superior range of products. The assembly of mid-range vehicles took off both in Spain (with the Renault Mégane, the PSA 306 and ZX, the Ford Escort) and in Mexico (with the Ford Mystique/Contour). However, the general increase in product variety, which had been perceptible since the early 1990s, was limited by the trend towards a reduced number of platforms, and towards the specialisation of sites by platform.

The productive and commercial integration of the periphery thus attenuated, in and of itself, the economic structures' particularities. It also modified the localisation of productive activities.

Towards a dispersion of productive localisations

The automotive industry's localisation within the national space of these two new automotive countries was a function of a process of polarisation/diffusion which ran in parallel with the aforementioned process of specialisation/despecialisation.

When Mexico and Spain finally opened up to the outside world, they turned to their respective continental heartland – that is, to the North. In Spain, the development of an export industry broke up the tripolar structure of the 1960s (Madrid–Barcelona–Valladolid) – benefiting the Ebro River Valley, Galicia and Catalonia (all of whom experienced greater densification) to the detriment of the region surrounding Madrid. In the new paradigm, these new industrial regions became a focal point for new implantations (Vitoria, Zaragoza, Martorell), for a further strengthening of the older assembly sites, and for a further concentration of the component-making sector (for example, around Logroño). In Mexico, the export-oriented plants which were opened during the 1980s ignored the tradition locations near Mexico City and opted for the major cities[4] in the Northern border states, at a distance of about 100km from the United States. As a result, the Mexican motor industry split up into three sectors, and three territories: the new plants of the North, which assembled vehicles and motors for export; the older sites near the capital, which only supplied the domestic market; and the maquiladoras in the border towns, which produced components for the United States (Layan and Carrillo, 1998).

We can observe that processes of integration have gone hand in hand both with spatial diffusion on a grand scale, and with a modicum of despecialisation, as studied above. In Mexico, the comparative overcrowding of the job market in Northern cities clearly explains why, from 1993 onwards, sites were being opened in the Central Northern regions, halfway between Mexico City and the US border: Nissan at Aguascalientes, GM at Silao, Honda at El Salto, Scania at San Luis Potosi, and so on. Other investments, such as Ford's complex at Mexico City – Cuautitlan, VW's at Puebla, BMW's at Toluca, or Mercedes' at Santiago de Tianguistenco, indicate, on the other hand, that these firms were renewing their marked preference for metropolitan areas. It is true that Mexico City and its surrounding metropolitan area comprise a large share of Mexico's domestic market for new motor vehicles, as well as almost all of its market for mid- and top-of-the-range segments. The region has also been a inexhaustible reservoir of skilled workers, as most industry jobs have been traditionally concentrated there. The level of training in the Federal District is much higher on average than in the rest of the country. On the other hand, economic growth in the border regions has increased the risk that the job market in these areas will become saturated. As such, the dualism of the automotive space will have only lasted 12 years or so: new or modernised plants are indifferent as to whether they produce for export or for domestic markets (Mortimore, 1995). As for Spain, despite the polarisation of the motor industry in the Ebro River Valley, the sites in Andalusia (Cadiz, Sevilla, Linarès) and in Castilla (Villaverde, Avila) have been maintained. Finally, as Pallares-Barbera (1998) pointed out, the process of geographic dispersion also affected the component-makers and subcontractors – even though they operate outside of the trend towards economic concentration.

A gradual differentiation of the integrative processes

Although we have been able to establish that Spain and Mexico both followed parallel trajectories, the two countries did not, after all, start out with the same level of development. The mechanisms of integration may have been extremely similar, but certain fundamental differences, stemming from the macro-economic environment, and from the way in which each society developed, have remained intact. Now, in the late 1990s, we can differentiate between the two processes of integration, the specialisations, and the characteristics of sectoral growth in each country. Moreover, these differences are fundamental – and involve more than the simple observation that Mexico is lagging behind Spain.

Contrasts in productive cohesiveness

Not all firms have the same motives for delocalising towards the periphery – far from it. At first, Ford and GM–Opel were interested in Spain for export assembly. It was also seen as a market with good prospects for future growth. Mexico was, at first, considered as a place where the components which are used at the beginning of the productive chain could be produced cheaply, and then exported to the United States. Vestiges of this earlier concept still remain: the relative importance of engine production; the high proportion of component-making as a proportion of total output; and the specialisation in making bottom-of-the-range components and parts such as wiring. This historical reality helps to explain why diversification in Mexico meant, paradoxically, that the country was to specialise in making hierarchically inferior products (a prime example being GM) – proof that American firms were late to focus on the needs of the domestic Mexican market.[5] In fact, the large series assembly of mid- and top-of-the-range models is a specificity which separates Spain from Mexico.

Ever since the late 1980s, Spain has been organised into a relatively coherent productive space. A priority for the country's component-making sector, and in particular, for its layers of small and medium-sized subcontractors, has been to work for Spanish and Portuguese assembly plants, even if the quality of the products being manufactured in Spain has drawn the attention of customers throughout Europe, especially the French and Germans. On the other hand, Mexican production has continued to be poorly articulated, although the signing of the NAFTA agreement holds some promise in this respect (Layan and Carrillo, 1998). For example, the component-making sector is more or less fixated on the United States. This is true for the entire *maquiladora* sector, operating as it does in the border zones. It even applies to the most modern of the *maquiladora* facilities. It is also true for a large part of the intermediary production units which are run by the vehicle makers – Ford's Chihuahua plant has never supplied a single motor to a Mexican assembly unit, not even to Hermosillo, despite its proximity. This difference between the two countries' degree of openness to the outside world can also be measured by the relative weight of exports. It may well be that in both countries, the degree of openness (as measured by the ratio export/output) is close to 80 per cent – but the ratio of output to new vehicle registrations is much greater in Mexico. The two countries' domestic markets are very dissimilar.

Dissimilar domestic markets

The Spanish market has reached a state of maturity. Like the markets in other developed countries, it can still suffer from periods of prolonged instability, as was the case during the financial crisis of 1993. Nevertheless, the importance of the demand for product replacement ensures that the upward trend will remain relatively stable over the medium term. In addition, in case of a deep recession, the country is able to implement policies which can promote a given sector's recovery. Such was the case in 1993 and 1994, with Spain's two Renove plans, similar to France's Balladur plan, wherein the State disbursed a sum of money to anyone who replaced an outdated vehicle with a newer one. This policy was legitimised by the need to rationalise the stock of domestic automobiles.

In Mexico, the vast majority of the population, including most employees in urban areas, have been excluded *de facto* from a mass car culture. The Mexican market is fragile – demand, especially for durable goods, is subject to an enormous volatility. The peso crisis was disastrous[6] for the country; new passenger car sales fell by 72 per cent in 1995 – and production for the domestic market fell to a third of its former size. Only an increased push in exports kept the drop in total output from plumbing the same depths. Moreover, in light of the dramatic effects of the 1998 financial crisis on the Mexican market, one could easily infer that the country is overly vulnerable to any downturn in the economic cycle. This will last until the increased demand for automobiles is finally accompanied by a modernisation of the road network, the adoption of qualitative regulations which can help households to purchase new vehicles, and macro-economic policies which promote a continuous and steady rise in living standards.

European community and NAFTA: two fundamentally different types of regional integration

Mexico's industrialisation was also vulnerable to problems which resulted from the existence of the very same economic growth. In the

Northern regions, the classic attributes of a crisis in industrial relations could be witnessed: absenteeism, employee turnover, and so on. Even if the gains in productivity and the improvements in quality demonstrated the remarkable ability of Mexican employees to learn and to adapt, a state-run training programme is necessary, as this is the only way to provide the automotive sector with the skilled workforce which it will need for future growth, and also to re-orient itself towards the manufacturing of higher value-added products. Spain's successful resistance against Eastern European and Turkish competition, against a background of world-wide overcapacity, demonstrates that even if a country can no longer provide overseas firms with the advantages of a lower wage structure, it can still be attractive if it is capable of providing high quality products and services. It is true that Spain benefited from the process of European integration – the Community has taken great pains to ensure the economic development of its peripheral regions by advocating a policy wherein imbalances have met with financial compensation.

NAFTA was basically integrated along trade and financial lines, and therefore does not have the same vocation. NAFTA is a loose regional association, an expression of the will of the United States, the country which dominates it. The United States reserves the right to take any measure which it deems necessary to protect itself from a commercial threat coming from its neighbour to the South – an attitude which has made several Asian and European vehicle makers reluctant to invest in Mexico. Unlike the construction of Europe, this type of regional integration has been piecemeal – it has guaranteed the free circulation of capital and of products, but it has restricted the free circulation of Mexicans. It has also relied exclusively on market forces to ensure that the national economies converge effectively, and to ensure that the region develops in a balanced manner.

CONCLUSION

An observer who compares the Spanish and Mexican motor industries may think that the two are very similar, and that the latter is simply lagging a few years behind the former. Does this mean there is only 'one best way' to a successful industrialisation – at least, in the peripheral areas of the Triad? Nothing can be less certain. There is no inevitability or permanence to the VRDL within which Mexico and Spain operate – and in any event, these structures do not constitute an optimal organisation of a productive space. VRDL's are nothing more than the consequence of decisions made by a few leading firms, including their desire to build up a continental network. They simply reflect the fact that the peripheries are only just starting off on their processes of integration. In fact, the VRDL's are only cohesive insofar as they mesh with the main objectives of the various acts of delocalisation which surround them. The irreversibility of investments can help them to stabilise, but in the end, this is only a relative stability. VRDL's are a function of the stages of macro-economic development at which the peripheries and the core countries find themselves – and they also vary to reflect the state of affairs in other, rival peripheral areas. They can be influenced by new competitive tensions within the world-wide oligopoly, as well as by the strategic turn-around of the leading firms. Moreover, the same set of parameters determines the ability of similar processes, observed in other peripheral regions, to reproduce themselves (Layan and Lung, 1997). The marked differences between the Spanish and Mexican motor industries also demonstrate that, whilst the mechanisms which control the integration of productive networks into a continental system are similar in nature, the particular characteristics of a each process of regional integration play an essential part in helping the IPMs to evolve from an initial position as a subservient member of the hierarchy into which they have been inserted (stagnant, and excessively oriented towards the needs of the outside world) to a situation in which they have been able to implement the types of economic and social structures which are the hallmarks of developed countries. It is only once this evolution has occurred that it is possible to assert that real convergence has taken place. As such, the future of Central Europe's new automotive countries depends above all on their ability to negotiate the terms of their membership in the European Union, or association with it.

Notes

*   Translation by Alan Sitkin.
1.   The use of the widespread expression 'integrated peripheral markets' should not be taken to imply either that the integration of peripheral economies is simply a result of inter-connections between markets or that these markets have been formed by institutional arrangements.
2.   The United Nations Economic Commission on Latin America.

3. According to Carrillo (1993), GM owned 18 maquiladoras, Ford 15, and Chrysler 2.
4. The notable exception to this tendency is Monterey, the only city in this region which had already been industrialised.
5. In Mexico, the Big Three's largest output concerns mid-range segments which are not greatly in demand in Mexico itself, but which are very representative of the United States car market.
6. Mexicans usually buy their vehicles on credit – and each devaluation of the peso pushed up interest rates.

Bibliography

ALAEZ, R., BILBAO, J., CAMINO, V. and LONGAS, J.C. (1996) *El Sector de Automoción: Nuevas Tendencias en la Organización Productiva – Un Analisis Cualitativo de las Relaciones Proveedores – Ensambladores en el País Vasco y Navarra.* Madrid: Editorial Civitas.
BABSON, S. (1995) 'Mazda and Ford at Flat Rock: transfer and hybridization of the Japanese model.' Paper presented to the Third GERPISA International Auto Industry Workshop, Paris, June.
BABSON, S. (1998) 'Ambiguous mandate: lean production and labor relations in the U.S.' In Babson, S. and Nunez, N. (eds), *Confronting Change: Auto Workers and Lean Production in North America.* Detroit: Wayne State University Press, pp. 23–50.
BORDENAVE, G. (1995) 'Crise et redressement de Ford Motor company: la globalisation au coeur des changements d'organisation'. Paper presented to the Third GERPISA International Auto Industry Workshop, Paris, June.
BORDENAVE, G. and LUNG, Y. (1988) 'Ford en Europe. Crises locales, crise globale du fordisme'. *Cahiers de Recherche du GIP Mutations Industrielles*, No. 17.
CARRILLO, J. (1993) 'La Ford en Mexico. Restructuración Industrial y Cambio en las Relaciones Sociales'. Doctoral Thesis. Mexico City: El Colegio de Mexico.
CARRILLO, J. and HUALDE, A. (1997) 'Maquiladoras de tercera generación. El caso de Delphi – General Motors'. *Comercio Exterior*, Vol. 47, No. 9, 747–57.
LAYAN, J.B. (1997) 'Transformación y resurgimiento de los fabricantes franceses: Renault y PSA'. *Economia Industrial*, No. 315, 139–50.
LAYAN, J.B. and CARRILLO, J. (1998) 'Intégration régionale et spécialisation des espaces: le cas de l'automobile au Mexique'. Paper presented to the 34th Colloquium of A.S.R.D.L.F., Puebla, September.
LAYAN, J.B. and LUNG, Y. (1997) 'La globalisation laisse-t-elle la place aux intégrations régionales périphériques? Le cas de l'industrie automobile'. In Lacour, C. and Célimène, F. (eds), *L'Intégration Régionale des Espaces.* Paris: Economica, pp. 255–70.
MICHELI, J. (1994) *Nueva Manufactura, Globalización y Producción de Automoviles en Mexico.* Mexico City: Universidad Autonoma Metropolitana.
MORTIMORE, M. (1995), 'Transforming sitting ducks into flying geese: the Mexican automobile industry'. *Desarollo Productivo*, No. 26.

PALLARES-BARBERA, M. (1998) 'Changing production systems: the automobile industry in Spain'. *Economic Geography*, Vol. 74, No. 4, 344–59.

RUBENSTEIN, J.M. (1992) *The Changing US Auto Industry – a Geographical Analysis*. London & New York: Routledge.

SEIDLER, E. (1976) *Opération Fiesta: Autobiographie du Projet Ford Bobcat*. Lausanne: Edita.

SHAIKEN, H. (1990) *Mexico in the Global Economy: High Technology and Work Organization in Export Industries*. San Diego: Center for U.S.–Mexican Studies, University of California.

VERNON, R. (1966) 'International investment and international trade in the product cycle'. *Quarterly Journal of Economics*, Vol. 80, No. 1, 190–207.

WOMACK, J.P. (1990) 'Perspectivas de las relaciones entre Estados Unidos y México en el sector automotriz'. In Carrillo, J. (ed.), *La Nueva Era de la Industria Automotriz en México*. Tijuana: El Colegio de la Frontera Norte, pp. 19–34.

7 Globalisation and Assembler–Supplier Relations: Brazil and India

John Humphrey and Mario Sergio Salerno

INTRODUCTION

Over the past decade, a substantial amount of FDI has been chan-nelled into the motor industries of the emerging markets. New investments in the emerging markets have become strategic not only for the assemblers but also for first-tier suppliers, and the subsidiaries of transnational companies in these markets have become more closely integrated into the global operations of their parent compa-nies. Consequently, the motor industries of these countries have been structurally transformed. In some respects, the emerging markets have been places for innovation and experimentation within the motor industry. Their weaker social institutions and regulation, combined with their convenient distance from global headquarters, have allowed experiments in assembler–supplier relations. In many respects, the assemblers are using the opportunities afforded by greenfield invest-ments and weak trade unions to introduce more advanced systems in developing countries such as Brazil, China and Thailand than might be seen in Europe or North America.[1]

Among the most interesting of these experiments have been the development of modular supply and the creation of industrial condo-miniums.[2] These are at the forefront of innovation in assembler–sup-plier relations. 'Modular mania' and 'rolling forward with modules' are examples of how specialised motor industry magazines,[3] mainly in the USA, are viewing trends in assembler–supplier relationships. Modularisation is closely associated with attempts to commonalise platforms and standardise designs at the global level and to work with the same first-tier suppliers at multiple locations around the world. These strategies are referred to as follow design (using the same design as far as possible across different markets) and follow sourcing (using one supplier for a particular part or system across all the markets where it is required). As will be shown in this chapter, there are clear signs of attempts to introduce these innovations in emerging markets.

One might imagine an 'ideal world' for a global assembler in which a new car only has to be designed once, and global suppliers would take considerable responsibility for designing various modules or systems for the car. Each module would be made available by the same supplier at every assembly plant around the world, preferably from a dedicated plant located close to the assembly site. Modular production would synchronise with the assembly process, and the modules would be delivered just-in-time to the assembly line. This service would be combined with zero defects and a highly competitive price.

In the real world of differentiated markets, economies of scale and market uncertainties, this ideal scenario will not come to pass, but companies are moving in this direction. The aim of this chapter is to examine the extent to which modular supply, industrial condominiums, follow design and follow sourcing are being implemented in two emerging markets, Brazil and India. It explores the potential and the limits of these strategies.

The next section briefly discusses recent developments in the automotive markets of the two countries. The third section considers the changing nature of the global components industry. The fourth discusses modular assembly and industrial condominiums. The fifth section examines follow design and follow sourcing. We conclude that modularisation is a strong trend in emerging markets. We also find that follow design and follow sourcing are being pursued actively by auto companies, but there are limitations to this process. The world platform is a reality but the world car is not. Markets are still too heterogeneous to make it feasible.

THE EMERGING MARKETS IN TRANSITION: BRAZIL AND INDIA IN THE 1990s

The vehicle markets of Brazil and India were both created in the context of import substitution industrialisation policies. The Brazilian industry was created in the 1950s, when the government put the auto industry at the centre of its strategy for rapid industrial development and modernisation. A virtual ban on vehicle imports, combined with incentives for companies to begin local production created a domestic vehicle industry with a high level of local content.[4] The industry grew rapidly. Production of passenger cars and light vehicles reached 374 000 units in 1970 and over 1 million units in 1980, as can be seen in Table 7.1.

The assembly sector of this industry came to be controlled by transnational companies. By the end of the 1970s, Volkswagen, Fiat, Ford and GM dominated the light vehicle sector, maintaining this domination until the late 1990s. Ownership in the components industry was more diversified. A majority of the largest component firms was foreign-owned even in the early 1970s, but some Brazilian-owned companies did occupy leading positions and were able to export to North America and Europe in the 1970s and 1980s.

In India, the motor industry developed very differently. Instead of allowing foreign companies to produce the vehicles and components demanded by the protected domestic market (as in Brazil), the Indian government placed restrictions on both ownership and output. As part

Table 7.1   Production and sales of cars and light vehicles: Brazil

Year	Sales[a] (000s)	Production (000s)	Share of 'popular cars' in car sales[b] (%)
1970	374	374	–
1980	887	1049	–
1981–89 (average)	651	862	–
1990	661	848	4.3
1991	732	888	11.5
1992	725	1018	16.0
1993	1081	1325	28.4
1994	1332	1500	45.9
1995	1652	1537	53.8
1996	1673	1738	56.3
1997	1873	1984	64.0
1998	1468	1488	72.7

Notes: [a] Includes sales of imported cars and light vehicles from ANFAVEA member companies, and sales of all vehicles imported by non-members. Non-member imports of commercial vehicles would have been extremely small. [b] Share of domestically produced cars up to 1000 c.c. in sales of domestically produced passenger cars.
Sources: 1970–97, ANFAVEA (1998); 1998, ANFAVEA (1999).

of its policy of industrial licensing, the government placed controls on the numbers and types of vehicles that could be produced and the firms that could produce them. In line with its overall industrial strategy, the government excluded foreign firms from the assembly sector and restricted foreign ownership in the components sector. Priority was given to the production of tractors and commercial vehicles, making passenger cars a scarce luxury. In 1980, only 46 000 cars and jeeps were produced, 3000 less than a decade before (Table 7.2).[5]

The industry began to change in the 1980s, when the government relaxed licensing restrictions, opened up the light commercial vehicle sector to Japanese companies and created a joint venture for car production between Suzuki and the Indian State, Maruti Udyog Ltd. The industry began to grow much more quickly, and by 1990, output had risen to 219 000 cars and jeeps (Table 7.2), half of them produced by Maruti.

Following a decade of stagnation, the vehicle industry of Brazil began to grow rapidly again in the 1990s, transformed by trade liberalisation, tax cuts, promotion of sales of 'popular' cars and regional integration through Mercosur.[6] Output of cars and light vehicles rose rapidly after 1992, reaching almost 2 million units in 1997 (Table 7.1). In India, too, the car industry experienced rapid growth after 1992. Production of cars and jeeps increased by 146 per cent between 1992

Table 7.2   Production of cars and jeeps: India, 1971–98

Year	Cars and jeeps (000s)
1971	49
1980	46
1983	67
1990	219
1991	209
1992	192
1993	244
1994	286
1995	393
1996	472
1997	486
1998	458

Source: ACMA (1999).

and 1996, as can be seen in Table 7.2. This was largely the result of stronger economic growth and the relaxation of industrial licensing laws.

The rapid growth of vehicle sales in these two markets, combined with the long-term potential for vehicle sales, led to a 'scramble for position' among car manufacturers in both markets. The auto companies were forced to meet this demand from local production. In Brazil, the government countered a surge in vehicle imports in 1994–95 by a sharp increase in vehicle tariffs and incentives for companies to produce cars locally.[7] In India, quantitative restrictions on built-up cars, local content regulations and tariffs on components of 40–60 per cent greatly restricted imports of vehicles and components. Companies could only access the domestic market through local production.

These policies stimulated foreign direct investment. In Brazil, the existing vehicle manufacturers invested heavily after 1994–95, and a number of new entrants announced investment plans. These are shown in Table 7.3. The four established light vehicle producers, Fiat, Ford, GM and VW planned open new plants by 2001, and another nine companies announced plans to build light vehicle plants in Brazil.[8] International auto companies have also rushed into India, and the extent of investment plans is documented in Table 7.4. By 1997, ten companies had announced firm plans to begin production in India. The new capacity of these plants exceeded 750 000 units per year.

Although slow growth in both Brazil and India from 1997 onwards led some companies to abandon or delay their investment plans, the construction of many plants went ahead. By mid-1999, most of the plants listed in the two tables were operating, and the cars they made were clearly visible on the roads.

Heavy investments by both new and establish producers have transformed the assembly sector in the two countries. New firms have entered the market, and model ranges have been updated and expanded. In both Brazil and India, new models have been developed to meet the specific needs of low-income countries with adverse motoring conditions (for example, the Fiat Palio and the GM Blue Macaw in Brazil, and the Ford Ikon (C195) and Tata Indica in India). These investments have also led to profound transformations in the components industry in both countries. The nature of these changes and the reasons for them are the subjects of the following sections.

154 *Brazil and India*

Table 7.3   New companies and factories for light vehicle production:
Brazil, late 1990s

Company and product	Location and anticipated start-up date	Stated investment (US$ million)	Annual capacity (000s)
Mercedes (A Class)	Juiz de Fora/1999	820	70
VW–Audi (A3, Golf)	S. José Pinhais/1999	600	120
Land Rover (Defender)	São Bernardo do Campo/1998	150	15
Renault (Scénic, Clio II)	S. José Pinhais/1999	750	110
PSA–Peugeot (206)	Porto Real/2000	600	100
Iveco (LCVs)	Sete Lagoas/1998	250	20
Fiat (pick-up)	Belo Horizonte/1999	200	100
Toyota (cars)	Indaiatuba/1999	150	15
Mitsubishi (light vehicles)	Catalão/not defined	35	8
Honda (cars)	Sumaré/1998	100	30
Chrysler (Dakota)	Campo Largo/1998	315	12
GM (Blue Macaw)	Gravataí/2000	600	120
Ford (Amazon)	Camaçari/2001	1300	250

Sources: Ministry of Industry, Commerce and Trade, ANFAVEA, Panorama Setorial, the press in general and companies. Company plans are likely to change over time.

EMERGING MARKETS AND THE RESTRUCTURING OF THE GLOBAL COMPONENTS INDUSTRY

Relationships between suppliers and assemblers in the global auto industry have changed considerably in the past decade. Three changes, in particular, are noteworthy. First, suppliers have taken more responsibility for design. The 'catalogue suppliers' who provided ready-designed parts for many different companies have moved towards greater customisation, while companies that formerly worked to the assemblers' designs have moved towards offering their own design solutions (Laigle, 1995). The assembler provides overall per-formance specifications and information about the interface with the rest of the car, but the supplier then designs a solution using its own technology.[9]

Secondly, there has been a shift towards the supply of complete functions (systems, sub-assemblies or modules) rather than individual

Table 7.4   New ventures in the Indian motor industry

Companies	Models	Capacity (000s)	Ownership
PAL/Fiat	Uno Palio Family	30–50	Fiat, 76%; PAL, 24%.
PAL–Peugeot	309		Peugeot pulled out of this venture at the end of 1997.
Daewoo	Cielo Matiz	80 70	Daewoo has a 91% stake.
Mahindra/Ford	Escort Ikon	25 100	Ford, 90%; Mahindra & Mahindra, 10%.
TELCO/Mercedes	E series	20	50:50
Birla/GM	Astra Corsa	25 –	50:50
Hyundai	Santro	100	Hyundai, 100%.
Shriram/Honda	City	30	Honda, 90%. Shriram has an option to buy back 30%.
Telco	Indica	150	Wholly owned by leading Indian conglomerate and truck manufacturer, Tata.
Kirloskar/Toyota	Kijang	–	Toyota, 70%.
HML/Mitsubishi	Lancer	30	Information not available.

Sources: Various.

components. A first-tier supplier becomes responsible not only for the assembly of parts into complete units (dashboards, brake–axle-suspension, seats, cockpit assemblies, and so on), but also for the management of the second-tier suppliers. The assembler would previously have built these modules or systems in-house, using parts supplied by many different component companies.[10]

Thirdly, assemblers are standardising their platforms across their constituent companies and divisions (see Chapter 4 by Freyssenet and Lung, in this volume). In the 1980s, regional production systems were developed for Western Europe and North America. Later, the use of common platforms was extended across regions.

These three changes, taken together, have led to considerable restructuring in the components industry. Mergers, acquisitions and the selective transfer of activities between companies have proceeded at great pace. The components industry is being increasingly concentrated in companies that can design and provide systems and sub-assemblies across many different markets. The main trends can be summarised as follows:

- The in-house component activities of the major assemblers have been given separate identities. They are encouraged to compete for business from other assemblers, and they must increasingly compete for the business of their parent companies. The most high-profile of these cases is Delphi, created out of GM's component activities, but Ford (Visteon), Fiat (Magneti Marelli) and PSA (ECIA, now fused with Bertrand Faure) have moved in the same direction.

- A wave of takeovers and mergers is affecting even the largest component manufacturers. Between January 1996 and March 1997, there were seven mergers and acquisitions in the components industry involving assets of more than $1 billion (Economist Intelligence Unit, 1997: 22). Among the top 35 component manufacturers in 1995,[11] Lucas and Varity merged in 1996 and the new company was taken over by TRW in 1999, T&N was taken over by Allied Signal, Bertrand Faure was acquired by ECIA, UTA was bought by Lear, and ITT Automotive divested large parts of its automotive businesses. In areas such as seating and braking systems, the industry has been consolidated around a few manufacturers.

- New global companies have been created through the fusion of smaller manufacturers. The case of Autoliv Inc., formed by the merger of the Swedish company, Autoliv AB, and the Automotive Safety Products Group of the US company Morton International, is one example of a merger of two smaller companies forming a new company with global aspirations.

- The development of strategic alliances between major component manufacturers in order to deliver more extensive component systems or to develop new products. An example of such an alliance was the joint venture between Lucas–Varity and TRW to develop electric steering systems, although TRW has now acquired Lucas–Varity.

These changes in the nature of global components industry have had a particularly marked and rapid effect in the emerging markets.

When motor industries were established in developing countries in the context of import substitution industrialisation, the transnational assemblers created local sourcing networks. At this time, much of the design would have been in the hands of the assemblers. Designs and drawings imported from headquarters would be used to produce parts in-house or passed on to local subcontractor suppliers. Locally based design offices might produce new models or adapt existing designs, supplying the necessary drawings to local component manufacturers.

In Brazil, for example, Ford took over the Corcel I when it bought Willys in 1968. This car, designed by Renault, was only produced in Brazil. In 1977, Ford's local design team developed a substitute model, the Corcel II, also specifically for the Brazilian market. Ford's local designers were also responsible for developing alcohol-powered engines in the 1970s. Volkswagen developed a hatchback derivative of the 'Beetle' in the 1970s, as well as a locally designed small car, the Gol, based on a Polo platform (three successive models from 1980 to 1999). The Brazilian design team was also responsible for the renewal of Santana (based on the Audi 80), a design 'exported' to VW's Chinese operations, and adaptations of German designs.

This system gave local companies a chance to enter the components industry. The story of one leading Brazilian component manufacturer, Freios Varga, is a good example. It started producing brake parts for the aftermarket in the 1950s, copying parts supplied by other companies to the domestic market. In the 1960s, it began original equipment production, working to designs supplied by Volkswagen. In 1971, it negotiated a technology tie-up with Lucas, which took a minority stake in the company. Varga began to design new products to meet the needs of the assemblers as they introduced models such as the Corcel II and VW Gol. It relied on Lucas for basic technology, but retained its own engineering capability in order adapt designs for the local market and to develop brakes for locally designed models.

This pattern of relationships between assemblers and suppliers in emerging markets has now changed. Assemblers building new plants in emerging markets begin with the objective of establishing a small base of systems suppliers, many of whom will be located at or close to the plant. In the name of commonalising platforms and reducing costs, the assembler may well adopt the 'follow design' strategy. The global 'mega' suppliers, who design modules or systems and are expected to 'follow' the assemblers to new markets, and not only supply the parts and systems required but also organise the rest of the supply chain to meet the assembler's standards. The designs for components are no longer the property of the assembler, to be supplied to locally owned component manufacturers, but rather the property of the first-tier component supplier, which will most probably arrange for production at a wholly owned or joint-venture subsidiary. Insofar as follow sourcing is the assembler's preference, contracts in emerging markets are awarded to those component manufacturers who develop and supply the part or module in Europe, Japan or North America. It follows that suppliers without global coverage will find it increasingly difficult to maintain their positions as first-tier suppliers. The requirements for the first tier include not only design capabilities and manufacturing excellence but also the ability to make and deliver products across many markets. This requires the financial and managerial resources that only the largest companies can mobilise. The position of locally owned companies in emerging markets is undermined.

This view of trends in the global automotive industry is an abstraction based on tendencies visible in emerging markets in the mid-1990s. While these tendencies were very real, it remains to be seen how the practices of modular supply, industrial condominiums, follow design and follow sourcing are implemented and what the limits to the application of the new supplier paradigm might be.

MODULAR ASSEMBLY AND INDUSTRIAL CONDOMINIUMS

In both Brazil and India, assemblers are developing the industrial condominium and modular assembly concepts. This involves not only physical proximity but also the development of new relations between assemblers and suppliers based on the transfer of activities to the supplier and an increased service content in the relationship. Proximity is about the service the supplier provides the client: technical assistance, solutions to quality problems and so on (Salerno *et al.*, 1999).

An industrial condominium is formed when the assembler organises the facilities of key suppliers around its plant. The assembler defines which parts/modules will be produced, selects the suppliers, and specifies that they must build dedicated plants. In the new condominium concept, all the supplier facilities are planned by the assembler as part of the plant development strategy. This is very different from market driven (locational advantages for the supplier) or policy driven (state aid for location at given sites) proximity.

Clearly, the components most likely to be supplied from plants in condominiums are items that previously would have been produced or assembled in-house by the assembler. The work is merely transferred from the assembler's plant to the co-located supplier plant. Examples might be seats and exhausts. Typically, these parts present logistics problems, either because the transport of bulky items is expensive, or because the components and sub-assemblies have to be produced to match the model mix at the assembler. Proximity reduces transport costs and enables the supplier's and assembler's production schedules to be synchronised.

The industrial condominium concept was first developed in Japan, and it was introduced into India in the mid-1980s by Maruti. It was designed to create a supplier base that could meet Japanese supply requirements. The new company brokered joint ventures between Indian companies and transnational companies (most of which were suppliers to Suzuki in Japan). These included companies to produce seats, fuel tanks, instrument panels, sheet metal parts, radiators and steering. Some of these joint ventures located their plants at the perimeter of the Maruti plant, and Maruti played a leading role in establishing infrastructure facilities for suppliers on the site. For example, Maruti built its own combined cycle gas turbine generating facility to supply power to its suppliers (Gulyani, 1997). Not all of the new joint ventures brokered by Maruti were willing to locate their new operations at Gorgaon. Major companies such as Asahi Glass and Climate Systems India (a joint venture between Ford and Maruti) located elsewhere in Northern India.

These concepts have now become the norm for new assembly plants in Brazil and India. All the new mid- and large-scale plants in Brazil have created industrial condominiums around them. The extent of these condominiums is shown in Table 7.5. Seats, exhausts, axles, dashboards, wheel/tyre assemblies, cooling systems and fuel systems were the items most commonly produced in the seven condominiums listed. A number of new entrants to the Indian car market are also setting up similar arrangements. Companies such as Ford and Hyundai are not only bringing many new suppliers to India, but also encouraging them to locate close to their new assembly plants. Ford, for example, is building a condominium at its new plant in Chennai (Madras) and suppliers of internal trim, seats, exhausts, suspension, instrument panel clusters, wiring harnesses and wheel/tyre assemblies will be located there. Industrial condominiums are frequently associated with

Table 7.5   Products delivered by the suppliers located in the industrial condominium: Brazil

Plant	Mercedes (A Class)	VW/ Audi	GM (Blue Macaw)	Ford (Amazon)	Renault	Chrysler	VW Taubaté
Seats	•	•	•	•	•		•
Exhausts	•	•	•	•	•		
Wheel and tyre	•	•	•	•	•	a	
Cooling system		•	•	•	•		•
Fuel tank		•	•	•		a	•
Fuel system	•	•	•	•			
Glass/windscreen	•	•	•				
Trim			•	•	•		•
Brake system		•	•	•		a	b
Plastic parts	•	•					
Wiring harness	•		•				•
Dashboards	•		•	•			
Pressed parts			•		•		•
Suspension			•	•		a	b
Lighting		•	•				
Axles		•			•	a	b
Bumpers			•	•			•
Injected plastic			•				•
Paint			•	•			
Fastenings			•	•			
Engine assembly						•	
Body assembly			•				

Notes: [a] These items are provided as part of a complete chassis, with steering, springs, driveshaft, and so on, by Dana. [b] These items are provided in a single module.
Sources: Interviews, company documents, newspapers (*Gazeta Mercantil, Autodata*) and information organised by Ana Valéria Carneiro Dias.

modular supply. While early condominiums produced items such as seats and exhausts, more recently, they have been the sites for complex modules, such as complete cockpits and front corners (springs, shock absorbers axles and brakes), and also basic processes such as stamping, body construction and painting.

In new plants in emerging markets, many basic vehicle production activities are transferred to the suppliers. The development of modular production has three main aims: to reduce costs, to increase the efficiency of low-scale assembly, and to minimise the assemblers' investment requirements in new plants. The second and third of these aims are particularly important in emerging markets, which are characterised by limited scale and inherent market volatility (see Chapter 2 by Lung and Chapter 3 by Humphrey and Oeter, in this volume).

A shift towards modular supply was evident in both India and Brazil. Until recently, tiering of suppliers was unheard of in India. It was one of the 'Japanese' practices not used by Maruti. In 1996, Maruti had a supplier base of 400 companies that mostly supplied discrete components rather than modules and systems. However, with the entry of new competitors, supply systems have begun to change rapidly in India. Ford has created a first-tier supplier base of under 80 companies, and Fiat planned to hand over stamping and body construction at its Mumbai (Bombay) plant to an independent company in November 1999. Engine casting and machining will also be outsourced.

Modular supply has been more extensively developed in Brazil. One of the most advanced examples is the 'rolling chassis' supplied by Dana to the Chrysler plant at Campo Largo. This consists of a frame, front and rear axles, driveshaft, suspension, steering systems, brakes, fuel tank, electrical circuits and tyres. This chassis accounts for 33 per cent of the cost of the vehicle, and this might be raised to 45 per cent of the vehicle cost later.[12] GM's new plant for the Blue Macaw model in Southern Brazil will rely heavily on modular supply. It is claimed that this reduces the size of the plant and GM's investment by two thirds, clearly reducing the risks for GM.

How far will component manufacture be shifted towards plants close to the assembler? The basic reasons for proximity remain transport costs and synchronisation of production. Modular supply greatly increases the importance of these factors. For example, many brake/suspension modules are possible (left- and right-hand drive, size of brake disk, size and type of wheel and tyre assembly, suspension type and type of friction material allowed in for brake pads in the market where the vehicle will be sold). The number of possible combinations is so high that the module must be put together close to the assembler's plant. Frequently, the supplier of the module will only received 40–80 minutes notice of the model mix being assembled. In that time, the module must be assembled and shipped to the line. Clearly, proximity is vital for such an operation.

Nevertheless, this in no way implies that all production of components must be located close to the assembler. Some components vary little between vehicles and can be produced at a centralised locations. Just-in-time delivery can be managed from decentralised warehouses. For parts with scale economies greater than can be achieved by one plant or customer, centralized production still makes sense.

Further, the demands of synchronised JIT delivery of modules can be met through centralised production of parts combined with final assembly close to the customer. The range of variation in each particular element of the module is much more limited than the final module itself. Therefore, it is common practice for items such as brakes, springs, etc. to be produced in plants some distance away from the assembler and then stocked at the module assembly plant.

It is worth noting that total imports of components into Brazil increased from the US$1.1 billion in 1990 to US$4.8 billion in 1997 (Queiroz and Carvalho, 1999). Lower tariffs and export–import balancing schemes have encouraged greater international division of labour in components production. High-value items such as gearboxes and electronics are increasingly sourced from the Triad economies. Increased use of local components in Brazil and ASEAN (see Chapter 9 by Guiheux and Lecler, in this volume) in the late 1990s was driven by cost factors following the currency devaluations of 1997–99 rather than a need for proximity.

Modular supply appears to have particular advantages for assemblers trying to cope with small scale and market uncertainty in emerging markets. However, it also has more general applications. GM and Ford are pursuing modularisation in North America and Europe in order to reduce the costs of building small cars. For these reasons, some of the lessons learnt from modular supply experiments in emerging markets are being extended to the Triad markets. In 1998, GM's top management declared that it would introduce 'the Brazilian model' into North America. The 'Yellowstone' project will establish two modular assembly plants in the US for initial production in 2001.[13] Ford's new small car, the Amazon, consisting of 17 modules constituting 80 per cent of the car's value, will be produced in Europe as well as Brazil. Fiat remodelled the Melfi plant on modular lines for the launch of the new Punto.[14] Some adaptations may be required for the Triad markets, particularly because of the differing union situations in the Triad economies. In mid-1999 GM was still negotiating with the UAW over the organisation of the Yellowstone plants, and Ford had decided that some of the Amazon modules made by suppliers in Brazil would be produced in-house in Europe. This would not only enable existing facilities to be used, but also limit redundancies.

FOLLOW DESIGN AND FOLLOW SOURCING

How extensive are follow design and follow sourcing in India and Brazil, and in what way are the two strategies related? Six assemblers in Brazil (three new entrants and three established producers) and two assemblers in India were interviewed about design and sourcing policies. In addition, suppliers were interviewed in both countries.

All seven cases showed the impact of designs taken from Europe. Recent models were all based on platforms taken from Europe or North America. In some cases, such as Mercedes, Renault and Ford in Brazil, clear instructions were given to limit design modifications to the absolute minimum, and new entrants to the Brazilian car market, such as Mercedes and Renault, carried out design changes at headquarters, not in Brazil. Even VW, which had a well-developed design centre in Brazil and a long history of designing local cars, had begun to shift to world platforms, centralizing the design process and the choice of suppliers in Germany.

In spite of the attempt to standardise design, design modifications were needed in both Brazil and India. These fall into five main categories. Firstly, minor changes are required to meet the preferences of local customers. Many European designs use door mirrors and horns different from those favoured in Brazil. In India, the widespread use of chauffeurs means that even small cars require electric windows in the back, where the owner sits. Secondly, changes arise from differences in road and usage conditions in both Brazil and India. The General Motors Omega/Carlton, for example, required chassis reinforcement, a more powerful engine, a revised fuel system, and modifications to the suspension system. Vehicles for the Indian market also require modifications to steering and suspension. In some cases, such modifications have a cascade effect, since suspension changes may have consequences for the brakes and steering. Thirdly, design adaptations may also be made because the characteristics of local materials are different, or because different production processes are more efficient at low volumes.[15]

Fourthly, much more substantial changes may be required to meet local market needs. In Brazil, a number of assemblers introduced new model variants to meet the demands of the local markets. This was generalised practice in Brazil. Small pickups, based on the Corsa, the Fiesta, the Gol and the Uno were introduced by GM, Ford, VW and Fiat respectively. Three-box small cars and estate versions of small cars are also popular in Latin America and have been developed by the assemblers. In India, attention has focused on other issues, such as rear passenger space and roof height. The Indica small car produced by India's leading truck manufacturer, Telco, created a rear seat space substantially wider and longer than common in Europe because of the widespread use of chauffeurs in cars of all sizes in India. Similarly, Ford stretched the Fiesta platform by 40 mm in order to increase rear seat space for the Ikon model (known as the C195 within the company). In the rush to put products onto the Indian market in 1997–98, the new entrants offered models which were unsuited to Indian conditions, needs and purchasing power. The later range of small cars launched in 1999 began to address this problem.

Fifthly, follow design usually leads to over specification and costs in relation to local rules on security, pollution, and so on.[16] Therefore, local adaptations frequently aim to reduce costs. Ford in India did extensive redesign work on the Fiesta platform in order to keep costs down. Various design changes were made in order to achieve the target price, and suppliers were involved in redesigning parts. A number of base-level small cars in India sell for under US$7000, and European-specification models cannot match this price. Even the Palio, a car specifically designed for emerging markets, is too expensive for India and will have to be modified to reduce costs. Similar strategies are evident in Brazil. GM, for example, designed the 'Blue Macaw', based on the Corsa platform but with a target price 20 per cent below the standard Corsa.

Design changes are necessary to meet market requirements in Brazil and India, but where will the design work be done? The assemblers appear to have different strategies in this respect. Some are centralising design as far as possible, even when they produce designs specifically for emerging markets. This was Ford's strategy for its Ikon model in India. Virtually all the work was carried out in Europe. Even in the case of the Fiat Palio, most of the design work was carried out in Europe (Balcet and Enrietti, 1999), with engineers from Brazilian subsidiaries and suppliers spending time in Turin.[17] However, one possible consequence of the development of vehicles specifically for emerging markets would be an increase in the regional dispersion of design. This might be driven by both supply factors (the quantity and quality of design staff and their cost) and demand factors (the possible need to be close to the markets for which design changes are required). In Brazil, contradictory trends were evident at the end of the 1990s. While GM and Fiat were expanding their Brazilian design operations, Ford and VW were reducing them.[18]

If designs have to be adapted for the local market, what are the consequences for follow sourcing? If designs are unchanged, follow sourcing provides considerable advantages. The follow source firm has the design readily available and this allows more cost effective and speedy introduction of new models. The savings on homologation tests and tooling can be significant. If, on the other hand, design changes are made and quite distinct 'unique parts' are created, then the advantages held by the follow source firm are lost.

Various assemblers in Brazil and India expressed a fairly clear hierarchy of sourcing preferences: globally preferred supplier for the part (wholly owned or in a joint venture); alternative transnational supplier; locally owned company using licensed technology from one of the globally preferred suppliers; and least of all, a local company using its own technology. In practice, sourcing strategies focused almost entirely on the first two options, as is illustrated by the cases of the Mercedes A car in Brazil and the Euro Motors[19] car in Brazil and India.

The sourcing for the Mercedes A Car in Brazil is shown in Table 7.6. Follow sourcing was extensive, and this was facilitated by the large number of European and North American component manufacturers in Brazil. However, some important components were not being made by follow sources; in some cases, the follow source was not available, while in others the follow source had facilities in Brazil, but a different supplier was preferred. Most of these non-follow sources were transnational companies, as can be seen in the middle column of Table 7.6.

The extent of follow sourcing at Euro Motors in Brazil and India is seen clearly in Table 7.7. This provides information on 31 components. It can be seen that few components were imported. Some parts were imported into Brazil because the European follow source would not build a local plant. In the case of India, key high-value parts (engines and gear boxes) were imported from Europe because the scale of productions planned for India at that time did not justify local production. Follow sourcing was extensive in Brazil. Follow sources supplied 20 of the 31 items listed in the table. In India, follow sourcing was more restricted, with just 13 items being supplied by follow sources. In part, this reflects the different nature of the components industries in the two countries. The leading European assemblers had been building European-style cars in Brazil for over 20 years, and most of the leading European and American component manufacturers had plants in Brazil. In contrast, production of European models of passenger cars only began in India in the 1990s. Almost all of Euro Motors' follow sources in India were formed by new joint

Table 7.6   Mercedes 'A' car sourcing in Brazil

Supplied by company supplying in Germany	Supplied by other transnational company	Supplied by locally controlled company
Engine mounting	Seats	Petrol tank
Rear door assembly	Exhaust	Taillghts
Wiring harness	Dashboard	Wheels
Wheel and tyre assembly	Starter motor	Aluminium wheels
Windscreen/glass	Headlights	Plastic parts set
Heating/cooling system	Torsion bars	Mirrors
Dashboard	Springs	
Shock absorbers	Plastic parts	
Distributor	Steering system	
Clutch	Brakes	
Electrical components		
Air bags		
Trim		
Relays		
ABS		
Sensors		
Rear axles (Mercedes truck plant)		

Source: Adapted from Zilbovicius and Arbix (1997: 36).

ventures between its globally preferred suppliers and Indian companies. These component manufacturers were under considerable pressure to follow their customers. As well as the need to maintain good relations with powerful customers, follow sourcing also excludes potential competitors. If a supplier does not follow the customer, then the customer may develop an alternative supplier that might later compete in other markets.

Nevertheless, follow sourcing is far from universal. When an agreement on prices, volumes and location cannot be reached, the assembler will seek an alternative supplier. In most cases, this will be another transnational company, rather than a local supplier, as can be seen clearly in Tables 7.6 and 7.7. In many cases, the non-follow source for a particular model will supply the same part for other models produced by the assembler. Therefore, the assembler knows the supplier and has confidence (sometimes misplaced) that international standards will be met by the local plant.

The complexities of negotiations on sourcing in emerging markets can be demonstrated in the case of one particular component system.

Table 7.7   Sourcing in Brazil and India by 'Euro Motors'

Source[a]	Brazil	India
Imported[b]	Steering gear, steering column	Engine, gearbox, engine management system, constant velocity joints
Follow source	Engine, gearbox, engine management system, steering wheel, clutch, front and rear brake, rear suspension, rear axle, shock absorbers, paint, glass, starter motor, alternator, taillight, instrument panel, radio/ CD, seats, door boards, wheels	Steering gear, steering wheel, rear axle, rear brake, paint, starter motor, wiring harness, front and rear seatbelts, instrument panel, seats, headliner, exhaust
Other transnational company	Constant velocity joints, fuel tank, brake actuation, headlamp, wiring harness, headliner, exhaust	Clutch, steering column, brake actuation, front brake, rear suspension, fuel tank, alternator, headlamp, taillight, radio/CD, door boards, wheels
Locally owned company	Front and rear seatbelts	Shock absorbers, glass

Notes: [a] Joint ventures between original source and local company counted as follow sources. [b] Excludes products made in Argentina.
Source: Interviews with managers in Brazil, India and Europe.

This system, which cannot be identified for reasons of confidentiality, contain three basic parts that can be supplied by a single company, or two or three separate companies. Table 7.8 shows the sourcing for this part for nine passenger cars made in Brazil and/or India. The seven models made in Brazil were also made in Europe, and the main European suppliers of this component all had plants in Brazil. Consequently, follow sourcing was adopted in six of the seven models. Even in the seventh case, two of the three elements of the system were supplied by the follow sources. According to one of the suppliers of

Table 7.8   Use of follow sourcing for a particular component system in
Brazil and India

Company	Brazil	India
Model 1	Not produced in Brazil	Currently, imported. Future local production will be split between follow source (80%), which is in the process of setting up operations in India, and one other long-established producer in India (20%).
Model 2	Follow sourcing.	Partly imported, partly produced by a transnational non-follow source.
Model 3	System produced by two of the three companies producing in Europe. Partial follow sourcing.	One of the two companies making this part in Brazil did not have a factory in India. The other company refused to use a design supplied by a competitor, and now designs and supplies the whole system.
Model 4	Follow sourcing.	Produced by a transnational non-follow source.
Model 5	Follow sourcing.	Not produced in India.
Model 6	Follow sourcing.	Follow sourcing.
Model 7	Follow sourcing.	Not produced in India.
Model 8	Not produced in Brazil.	Assembler tried to negotiate a joint venture between follow source and Indian company, but failing this, used a transnational non-follow source.
Model 9	Follow sourcing.	After failing to persuade transnational company in India to use follow source's licensed design, used design of transnational non-follow source

Source: Interviews with component manufacturers in both countries.

this part, open bidding for contracts was quite normal, but it was basically a 'game with marked cards', undertaken solely to drive down the follow source's price. In India, follow sourcing was less extensive, as can be seen in Table 7.8. All of the seven models in the table were being produced by new entrants, and these included companies from

Europe, Japan and Korea. It was not always possible or cost-effective to rely on the follow source, and this led to complex negotiations. While some of the assemblers made (mainly unsuccessful) attempts to broker joint ventures or licensing agreements between their established suppliers and component manufacturers with plants already operating in India, they frequently ended up buying the part from the latter. Once joint venture plants were ruled out, it frequently proved difficult to come an agreement on licensing the original design, and the non-follow source then provided its own design.

The follow sources are in a strong position to win the contract, but their success is not guaranteed. What other factors influence supplier selection? Quality is essential, although assemblers in both countries complained about the failure of subsidiaries of transnational companies to attain European quality standards, and a supplier must have access to the engineering resources needed to make the adaptations required for the Brazilian and Indian markets (see above). In the final analysis, however, price is critical in the emerging markets. Both assemblers interviewed in India said that their small car target price was lower than in Europe, and this translated into a 'European price less x per cent formula' for Indian components. In Brazil, the European or North American FOB price was usually the starting point for negotiations. If an agreement with the follow source on price could not be reached, then alternative sources would be investigated.

Some follow source suppliers interviewed in Brazil admitted to offering components at a loss in order not to endanger their contracts in Europe. One company chairman said that his company sometimes agreed a price with the assembler and then had to develop programmes to try to reduce costs to meet it. This could mean pressuring second tier suppliers and its own staff to reduce costs or redesigning the component in order to meet the target price.

Follow design and follow sourcing provided economies in design and production when vehicle manufacturers integrated their European operations. The extension of these principles to emerging markets is clearly more problematic. First, essential design changes reduce the advantages of follow sourcing. Secondly, follow design can lead to cars that are over-engineered and too sophisticated for emerging markets. Thirdly, new assemblers in emerging markets cannot provide sufficient business to justify new component plants. Follow sourcing may, in fact, exacerbate the problems of lack of scale in emerging markets (see the papers by Lung and by Humphrey and

Oeter in this volume). For the component discussed in Table 7.8, a rigid application of follow sourcing would have produced at least five suppliers in India for a market of considerably less than one million light vehicles. This compares with three main suppliers in Europe for a market of 13–14 million passenger cars.

Not surprisingly, assemblers have used non-follow sources to a much greater extent than they had planned. Euro Motors originally planned only to use follow sources in Brazil, but it was forced to modify this strategy. When it expanded into India, it adopted a much more flexible policy with regard to follow sourcing. It might well be the case that the high point of follow design and follow sourcing strategies was reached in the new investments made between 1995 and 1997. While the trend towards global platforms will continue, local realities will force substantial deviations from strict follow design and follow sourcing policies. In the final analysis, follow design and sourcing were meant to reduce costs. If, in fact, they create unsuitable, over-engineered and expensive products, then changes will be made.

These limitations to the follow design and follow sourcing strategies do not open up opportunities for locally owned companies. Tables 7.6 and 7.7 show that non-follow sources were almost always global suppliers. The use of locally owned companies was extremely limited. The consequences for locally owned companies in both Brazil and India have been serious and direct. In the 1980s, a small number of the largest Brazilian firms attempted to expand into North America and Europe, following up their success in exporting to these markets. However, they remained small by global standards: the largest Brazilian component manufacturer had a turnover of less than US$1 billion in 1996. Unable to achieve global coverage, these firms found their position in the domestic market undermined by the follow sourcing trend. Recognising this, some of the largest Brazilian component manufacturers have sold out to transnational companies. In 1995, 12 of the top 25 Brazilian component manufacturers[20] were wholly or majority, local-owned. By the end of 1998, seven of these twelve had been taken over by transnational companies.[21] The options open to locally owned companies are narrowing. They do not have the global coverage to offer their own technological solutions. Joint ventures with leading global component manufacturers have been an option, but these manufacturers now appear to want full control. Similarly, licensing international technology has become more difficult. The leading companies are more reluctant to offer licences now that the emerging markets have become more integrated into the global production strategies of the assemblers. Is this the end of the locally owned first-tier supplier?

In India, the restructuring of the industry is at an earlier stage, but the same tendencies are visible. There are clear signs that minority foreign partners in long-established joint ventures are eager to take control, even when the Indian partner is reluctant. The latter frequently lacks the resources to finance expansion, and this gives the foreign partner an opportunity to increase its stake. Many Indian suppliers are looking for niches outside the car sector, tie-ups with smaller transnational companies, which have technology but not international resources, or comfortable niches in the second tier. It is becoming increasingly difficult, even for the largest Indian companies in the components sector, to sustain wholly owned operations or even majority stakes in joint ventures.

CONCLUSIONS

The motor industries of Brazil and India were both transformed in the 1990s. The transnational automotive companies were extremely optimistic about growth prospects, and major investments were made. The assemblers introduced industrial condominiums and modular supply, and sought to standardise designs and use follow sources. In many respects, these policies have become the standard international 'best practice'. The combination of investments in new plants in emerging markets and weak labour institutions has allowed companies to experiment with these practices in emerging markets.

Modular supply is being adopted quite extensively in both Brazil and India. This certainly helps assemblers to reduce their investment costs and risks. It may also provide assemblers with a partial solution to the problem of assembling vehicles efficiently at low volumes, although with the exception of the Chrysler–Dana rolling chassis case, most plants using modular supply are projected to assembler vehicles in volumes exceeding 100000 units per year. Industrial condominiums have also become a standard feature at new plants, although a variety of means need to be found to make proximity compatible with scale and efficiency. Follow design and follow sourcing are more problematic. Standardised cars at the world level offer the prospects of reduced design costs, greater economies of scale and greater flexibility in matching production and markets at different locations. However, the need to adapt products, prices and cost to local conditions (road conditions, physical environment, income levels, idiosyncratic local preferences, availability of material, and so on) is reflected in the continuing need for platforms to be adapted and design work to be carried out. The world platform is a reality, but the world car is not. A trade-off exists between flexible global sourcing and the design of cars adapted to heterogeneous markets.[22] The latest casualty in the battle to produce the 'world car' is the Ford Amazon project. After two years of trying to design a new small car that would be identical in Europe and Mercosur, Ford's designers finally came to the conclusion that a car that met European handling and safety requirements would be too expensive for the Brazilian market.

If such global standardisation remained unattainable, then the relationship between Triad markets and emerging markets remains open. In the area of design, auto companies are still looking for viable solutions. While some companies increase the degree of centralisation and control of design activity, others appear to be moving towards a 'sun and planets' model, in which a global design headquarters has local design offices linked to it. A more radical solution would arise if companies viewed emerging market consumers as having particular and distinct needs that were best served by designers located close to them. For example, the development of Third World cars and low-cost pickups might eventually be centred on countries such as Brazil and Thailand.

It is clear that the greater the size and sophistication of the supplier base in any particular market, the greater will be the tendency for follow sourcing to develop. This is the conclusion to be drawn from the comparison between Brazil and India. However, the increased commonalisation of designs across countries, combined with the transfer of design activities to suppliers, increases follow sourcing in all markets and undermines the position of locally owned component companies in both Brazil/Mercosur and India. On current trends, the first-tier of the components industry will soon become entirely populated by transnational firms. Even when locally owned firms have the necessary technological capability, they lack the international coverage, scale and finance resources needed to compete in the first tier.

This chapter has focused on assembler–supplier relationships and sourcing strategies in two large markets, Brazil and India. Some of the findings are applicable more widely. The first point to note is that modular supply and industrial condominiums are likely to be found in all markets, including new plants in Triad economies. Secondly, design adaptations seem inevitable in the larger PAMs and in the ERMs.[23] If these markets share common features, then broader, trans-regional markets might develop for vehicles which meet their common needs. This is the basis of Fiat's intention to assemble the Palio in a range of countries (such as Poland, Turkey, South Africa and India). GM may adopt a similar strategy for the Blue Macaw model.

The IPMs might be included in such a strategy, but only to a limited extent. Insofar as the auto industry in these markets is integrated into the respective Triad economies, this will favour the production of models that suit Triad markets. As Chapter 6 by Layan, in this volume, points out, several models produced in Mexico are 100 per cent exported to the US and Canada. Nevertheless, 'Third World' cars, such as the Fiat Palio, may be produced in and for the enlarged Triad regions. Assembly of the Palio in Poland and sales of the Palio Weekend in Italy show that markets need not be completely seg-mented. The extent of this inter-regional trade will depend very much on how trade policies and trade agreements structure the global auto industry.

Notes

1. This observation on the pace of change in developing countries is based on presentations by various motor-component manufacturers and the statement by Harold Kutner of Mannesmann VDO in *FT Automotive Components Analyst*, May 1999.

2. The term 'industrial condominium' is used to denote an area adjacent to an assembly plant created for suppliers. The use of this area is defined by the assembler, which chooses the products and the companies to place within it.

3. For instance, *Automotive Industries*, November 1998, p. 43; *Automotive News*, 29 March 1999, p. 24j.

4. An analysis of the policies used to promote the domestic auto industry can be found in Shapiro (1994).

5. For further information on the development of the Indian auto indus-try, see Mukherjee (1997).

6. Mercosur is the regional trade zone formed by Argentina, Brazil, Paraguay and Uruguay.

7. For a discussion of automotive industry policy in Brazil and India, see Chapter 3 by Humphrey and Oeter, in this volume.

8. Significant further investments were made in Argentina, and in truck and engine plants.

9. The use of a supplier proprietary design does not entail single sourc-ing. With a standard interface, an assembler can use the products of several black box suppliers in the same model.

10.   The language of modules, systems and sub-assemblies is sometimes vague. However, Sturgeon and Florida (1999: 68) observe that 'Some automakers refer to contiguous sub-assemblies as "modules" and functionally related non-contiguous parts as "systems".'
11.   Based on 1994–95 sales, and excluding tyre manufacturers.
12.   Information about the 'rolling chassis' is taken from *Auto Asia*, Jan./Feb. 1999, p. 49.
13.   *Automotive News*, 17 May 1999, p. 6.; *Automotive Industries*, May 1999. This plan was confirmed in interviews with suppliers in Brazil.
14.   This information comes from discussions with researchers at University of Calabria in Rende, Italy, June 1999.
15.   The materials and processes used to make hundreds of thousands of components in Europe may not be suitable for production of a few tens of thousands in Brazil or India.
16.   See Chapter 8 by Sugiyama and Fujimoto, in this volume.
17.   For further discussion of the Fiat Palio project, see Volpato (1998).
18.   This information is taken from a presentation by Ruy Quadros of the University of Campinas at the 7th GERPISA International Auto Industry Colloquium in Paris, June 1999.
19.   This company has been given a pseudonym in order to maintain confidentiality.
20.   Turnover exceeding US$100 million, excluding tyre companies *Os Melhores e Maiores, 1996*, and *Gazeta Mercantil* (1997).
21.   The competitive pressures on Brazilian component manufacturers were greatly increased by the Automotive Regime introduced in 1995. This temporarily reduced component tariffs to under 5 per cent at a time where exchange rates overvalued the Brazilian currency by 30 per cent.
22.   See Chapter 8 by Sugiyama and Fujimoto, in this volume, for a more developed discussion of this contradiction.
23.   These categories are explained in the introduction of the book.

References

ACMA (1999) *Automotive Industry of India: Facts and Figures, 1998–99*. New Delhi: Automotive Component Manufacturers Association of India.
ANFAVEA (1998) 'Anuário Estatístico 1998, ANFAVEA – Associação Nacional dos Fabricantes de Veículos Automotores'. Web Site – www.anfavea.com.br, accessed January 1999.
ANFAVEA (1999) Carta da ANFAVEA, January 1999, 'ANFAVEA – Associação Nacional dos Fabricantes de Veículos Automotores'. Web Site – www.anfavea.com.br, accessed February 1999.
BALCET, G. and ENRIETTI, A. (1999) 'La mondialisation ciblée de Fiat et la filière automobilie Italienne: l'impact dans les pays de Mercosur'. *Actes du GERISPA*, No. 25, 23–39.
Economist Intelligence Unit (1997) *European Automotive Components 1998: Part 1, The Industry*. London: The Economist Intelligence Unit.
GULYANI, S. (1997) 'Transforming the Infrastructure Constraint into an

Asset: Maruti and the Auto Industry in India'. Mimeo. Cambridge MA: MIT.

LAIGLE, L. (1995) 'De la sous-traitance classique au co-developpement'. *Actes du GERPISA*, No. 14, 23–40.

MUKHERJEE, A. (1997) 'The Indian automobile industry: speeding into the future'. Paper presented to the 5th GERPISA International Auto Industry Colloquium, Paris, June.

QUEIROZ, S. and CARVALHO, R. (1999) 'Recent developments in Brazilian autovehicle and components trade: building the space of production in Mercosul'. *Actes du GERPISA*, No. 25, 65–75.

SALERNO, M.S., DIAS, A.V.C. and ZILBOVICIUS, M. (1999) 'Industrial condominiums and modular consortiums: criteria for global sourcing or suppliers' proximity in new auto plants in Brazil'. Paper presented to the 6th International Conference of the European Operations Management Association, Venice.

SHAPIRO, H. (1994) *Engines of Growth*. Cambridge: Cambridge University Press.

STURGEON, T. and FLORIDA, R. (1999) 'The World that changed the machine: globalization and jobs in the automotive industry'. *Final Report to the Alfred P. Sloan Foundation*. Cambridge MA: MIT.

VOLPATO, G. (1998) 'Fiat Auto and Magneti Marelli: towards globalization'. *Actes du Gerpisa*, No. 22, 69–97.

ZILBOVICIUS, M. and ARBIX, G. (1997) 'O Novo Panorama de Relacionamento entre Montadoras e Autopeças no Brasil'. Mimeo. São Paulo: University of São Paulo.

8 Product Development Strategy in Indonesia: a Dynamic View on Global Strategy

Yasuo Sugiyama and Takahiro Fujimoto*

INTRODUCTION

The purpose of this chapter is to explore dynamic aspects of strategy formation in global product development. By describing and analysing the design and organisational choices of some Japanese vehicle makers for products targeting the South East Asian markets, particularly in Indonesia, we aim to better understand how international manufacturing firms try to balance goals that often contradict: to adapt their products and activities to local requirements, and to enjoy scale or scope economies through standardised global operations and resources. We pay special attention to the dynamic nature of a firm's capability building or organisational learning, through which its product design strategies, organisational capabilities, and its environments co-evolve over time.

Practitioners and researchers in international management have long discussed how a multinational manufacturing firm balances the benefits and costs of global standardisation and local adaptation. Product design and development for emerging markets (for example, Asian developing countries) has been an area where this trade-off problem was particularly difficult to solve. Globally standardised designs, exemplified by the 'World Car', often failed to attract local consumers (Sinclair, 1983), whereas so-called 'low cost vehicles' (that is, simplified models specifically designed for such local requirements) seldom prevailed as dominant products in the emerging markets. Based on these past lessons, today's multinational vehicle firms tend to choose more subtle and sophisticated approaches in making trade-offs between local-specific and global-standard designs. One such design strategy is to use old platforms that may have already been discontinued in the home market, but to develop new derivative models that are optimised to various local conditions. We may call this approach the 'Old Platform Derivative'. We see some examples in Japanese models for Indonesia, which we will analyse in detail later on.

Research on the global–local trade-off in product development is by no means new. In the field of international marketing, for example, the product design choice between global standardisation and adaptation to local needs has been a central issue (Levitt, 1983; Douglas and Wind, 1987). Further, the role of global integration and local responsiveness has been emphasised in the literature on international management (Prahalad and Doz, 1987; Bartlett and Ghoshal, 1989). However, most of the existing analyses tend to treat this global–local issue as one of static optimisation under given constraints. In other words, there has been an implicit assumption that managers of multinational firms can make deliberate and optimal strategic choices, given their environmental and resource capability conditions in both home countries and local markets at a certain point in time.

This assumption is not necessarily appropriate in real-life settings, however. Considering the bounded rationality of managers, the uncertainty of the local environmental conditions, and the cumulative nature of firms' organisational capabilities and managerial resources, it would be more realistic to assume that global firms find effective solutions through trial and error, and that their product design strategies are formed in a more or less path dependent way.[1] Further, such strategies may be realised in a way that managers neither foresee nor intend in advance – an 'emergent strategy' (Mintzberg and Waters, 1985). What the company needs for effective strategy formation in such unpredictable situations is a certain dynamic capability for not only intentional learning but also for opportunistic (ex-post) learning (Fujimoto, 1999).

When environments change unpredictably, what used to be an optimal design solution may turn out to be a sub-optimal one in the following period, and the company may not be able to adjust its strategies and resources instantly. In addition, the strategic choices, once implemented, affect environments and capabilities: a dynamic process which results in cumulative interactions, generating a gap between the actual and optimal choices. Thus, over adaptation or mis-adaptation may be the rule rather than the exception, at least in the short run.

The importance of organisational capability in global strategy implementation has been emphasised in a number of past researches (Prahalad and Doz, 1987; Bartlett and Ghoshal, 1989). Nevertheless, this was not well connected to the notion of dynamic interaction between strategy, capability and environment.

In this chapter, taking into account the above possibilities of path dependence, emergent strategies, over adaptation and so on, we apply a dynamic view of strategy formation and capability building to the case of international product development in the Indonesian vehicle industry. More specifically, we try to answer the following questions about the international product development strategies of Japanese automobile makers for Indonesian markets:

1. *Context:* What was the situation that the automobile firms were facing in Asia (Indonesia), including market size and needs, government regulations, manufacturing/design capabilities of local operations, supplier systems, and so on?

2. *Strategy Formation:* How did the firms choose a particular strategy in terms of product design choices? How did they choose locations for development organisations and product development processes for Asia (Indonesia)?

3. *Competitive Results:* How did the above strategic choices affect the competitive performance of their products in Asia (Indonesia)?

4. *Co-evolution:* How did the strategic choices affect local market needs and local manufacturing capabilities, as well as their evolution?

5. *Over-adaptation:* Did the companies suffer from the problem of over adapting their product designs to the local environment? If so, how and why?

These issues will be discussed for the case of the product development strategy of Japanese vehicle firms for Indonesian markets. We pay special attention to this case, partly because the dynamic process of path dependent strategy formation and over adaptation was particularly obvious in this country. In the second section, we elaborate our framework for analysing the dynamic aspects of international product development. In the third section, this framework will be applied to explain the strategy of the Japanese vehicle makers' product development for country specific vehicles in Indonesia. Then we will sum up the discussion in the fourth section.

INTERNATIONAL STRATEGY OF PRODUCT DEVELOPMENT: A DYNAMIC VIEW

The types of international product design strategy and their competitive effect

In this section, based on the research questions mentioned above, the framework for analysing international product development strategy in newly emerging markets, such as South East Asia, will be presented.

In general, strategic decision making regarding international product development can be divided into two parts: (1) strategies for product design itself, and (2) strategies regarding the configuration of product development organization. The brief explanation of each is given below.

Figure 8.1 represents a framework for understanding product design strategy in the global context. In this framework, we first classify the design strategy for the product in terms of the width of its target market (Takeuchi and Porter, 1986). A global design is one whose physical structure is basically the same in the home and foreign

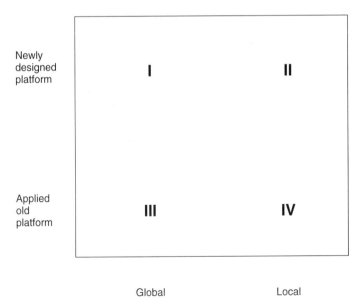

Figure 8.1   Product design strategy for local market

markets. This strategy tends to be chosen when demand condition in emergent markets are relatively similar to those in other markets. On the other hand, a local design is one whose physical structure varies somewhat between the home market and markets in other countries. This strategy tends be chosen when demand in the local market is different and independent from that of other countries. These choices reflect the similarity of markets among countries.

Secondly, we also classify strategies according to the linkage between new product development and the existing platform (or core component) of the product. We include this classification because it reflects the applicability of new designs, and the cost of development and manufacturing the product. When a new product is based on a newly developed platform, the development cost is higher, but the scope for adoption of new designs might be wider. On the other hand, in the case of an applied old platform, a relatively smaller tolerance for the application of a new design is allowed in new product development. While the degree of freedom for design changes is smaller, the cost of producing a new model is reduced.

On the basis of the above classification, four typical types can be defined, whose functional characteristics are summarised below.

1. Global design product using a newly developed platform

This is the typical example of global standardisation (Levitt, 1983). The major advantage of this strategy is savings on development costs. The investment cost for production equipment can also be shared for imported parts, but this is not the case for locally produced parts, which require double tooling anyway. Another advantage is that the model can incorporate state-of-the-art technologies, but this often means over specification and cost increases. At the same time, manufacturing quality is high due to the supply of products whose functionality has already been proven.

2. Local design product using a newly developed platform

In this type, either the platform is developed solely for the local market, or platforms from current models are quickly made available. In the case of a rapidly transferred platform, the main advantage is a balance between design adaptation and scale economy. Although additional investment is needed for product development, cost savings are still significant, particularly when the original project and the derivative projects overlap (Cusumano and Nobeoka, 1998). Investment costs can also be reduced for those parts produced centrally and imported for local assembly. These models can also incorporate the latest technologies, but this often means over specification from the emerging markets' point of view. Investment cost savings may also be limited for those parts produced locally, since this usually means double tooling.

On the other hand, in the case of platforms developed solely for the local market, design adaptation to local markets and design simplification for local production base are emphasised for achieving cost and quality competitiveness simultaneously. Savings on development and investment costs are not pursued.

3. Global design product using an old platform

This strategy calls attention to Vernon's concept of the product cycle. Vernon (1971) predicted that the market and production site would shift from developed to developing countries as the product becomes matured and standardised. The main advantage of this strategy is cost saving both in product development and capital expenditure for production equipment. This is particularly the case when the old equipment can be transferred to local production facilities. Another potential advantage is that the old product designs tend to be simpler and thus easier for the local producers/suppliers to handle. Further, the technology is proven, which is less risky from the point of view of manufacturing quality. Its major disadvantage, however, is the very fact that the design is old. In the information age, consumers in emerging markets know what products are sold in other countries. Simply, old designs do not attract such customers, even with extremely low prices.

4. Local design product using an old platform (old platform derivative)

This is also a strategy aimed at balancing design adaptation and scale economy, but there may be more significant cost reductions in this case. As for the carried over parts and platform, most of the tools and equipment may be transferred to the local facilities without much additional cost. Development costs can also be reduced. The design is also less subject to the problem of excessive quality that the new platform may suffer from, but the overall design of such models may be still attractive to the local customers. This enhances the likelihood of such products being accepted as new models by the middle-class customers in emerging markets. This approach, however, may need a high level of product development capability, because using an old platform often means more constraints for the engineers of the derivative products than in the case of new platforms. In this chapter, we refer to this strategy as the 'old platform derivative'.

In a static analysis, it is recommended that global enterprises select the most appropriate strategy taking into account various conditions such as market characteristics, market size, and nationalisation policies in each country.

Types of international configuration in
product development organisation

The configuration of activity is one of the critical issues that global strategy has to address (Porter, 1986), since it is related to the utilisation of locational advantage (Dunning, 1981). For product development strategy, the choice of location (the deployment or allocation of resources) for product development organisation is the focal issue.[2] Product development organisation consists of various functional activities such as product planning, designing, prototyping, testing, process engineering, and so on (Clark and Fujimoto, 1991). Each activity can be located in the home country or the local country. In the case of Asian models, there is a strong tendency to concentrate these activities in the home country, as will be seen later. The decision about configuration depends mainly on the stickiness of information (von Hippel, 1994), and the scale effect for development activities (Ghoshal, 1987).

In the case of models produced and sold locally, which part of the activities is to be transferred to the local site and which part is to be left in the home country will be decided according to the stickiness of the problem solving information exchanged between the local market, local production facilities and the development organisation of the home country. This in turn will decide the locational distribution of international product development activities.

Although product development is essentially a production of information assets as opposed to physical products (Clark and Fujimoto, 1991), its performance may still be affected by certain scale factors in terms of the number of projects executed at each unit. For example, a number of projects may be needed for the efficient use of such developmental tools as prototyping equipment, supercomputers for simulations, and testing facilities. When only one project is executed for local product development, it may have to use the central facilities in the home country.

The path-dependent selection of product design strategy (emergent strategy)

Companies do not necessarily make a rational and *ex-ante* selection of a product development strategy described above. Rather, it seems more appropriate to think that the choice was attained emergently through successive rounds of decision-making.

If global product strategy is determined by the cumulative decision-making of the past and environmental constraints, the explanation found in existing static global strategy theory, which is based on an implicit assumption that managers of multinational firms can make deliberate and optimal strategic choices, is not sufficient. In order to explain path-dependent decision-making in global strategy, a framework that includes dynamic capability building and the co-evolution of strategy, capability and environment is indispensable.

As the selection of strategy is restricted by the condition of accumulated capabilities, strategy selection consequently becomes dependent on the path of the strategy selected in the past. For example, the above 'old platform derivative' strategy might possibly be achieved through two different paths.

The first path comes from the classical transfer strategy in which an old model no longer produced in the home country is transferred without any change. This, however, overlooks the fact that local needs also do progress and advance at their own pace. The old model gradually loses customers in the local market as they learn more about products, often comparing local models with more advanced models sold in the home country. Faced with sluggish sales of the old model, vehicle makers typically try to overcome this crisis by introducing a derivative and locally adapted model. As a result, a derivative model based on the old platform is developed, which is the ex-post, rationalised selection made possible by learning, rather than a strategic selection intended from the start.

The second path occurs when the local model, which had been planned as a derivative model from the current platform in the home country, later becomes a derivative model based on the old platform as a result of a model change in the home country. This happens because of the time lag between model changes in the home country and the local market, which can be attributed to differences in production volumes and the degree of competition. In cases where the local production was imposed by local content regulations, the intervals of model changes tend to be prolonged in order to generate adequate returns on the local capital investment in production equipment. In the home country, on the other hand, severe market competition tends to lead to frequent model changes and the swift introduction of models in which new technology is applied. As a result, the local models are left behind as old platform based models. Thus, the local model based on the old platform can be a strategic choice or an unintended consequence.

The co-evolution of strategy, capability and environment

Strategy is not only determined by the environment and organisational capability, but also influences the market environment and organisational capability in the long run. Strategy, environment and capability co-evolution evolve through mutual influence. Figure 8.2 briefly summarises how strategic choices are affected by past experi-

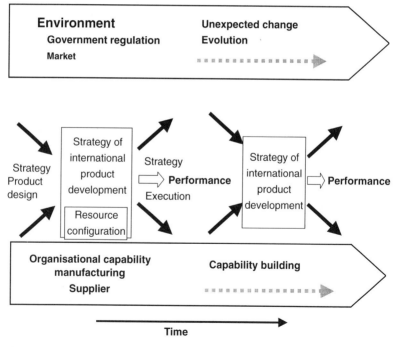

Figure 8.2   Dynamic view of strategy

ences and how they affect the future. Irrespective of whether it is intentional or not, enterprises are entities which accumulate capability through the execution of strategy. The trajectory of resource accumulation and the evolutionary path of the environment, both of which affect decision-making, do not necessarily match, and there is also a possibility that the strategy appropriate at one time may become inappropriate as the environment and resources change (Leonard-Barton, 1992).

Both mis-adaptation and excessive adaptation may occur. For instance, although the 'old platform derivative' does appear to fit local conditions, resolving to some extent the dilemma of cost reduction and meeting local needs, it does not address the evolution of customers and production capability in the local market. The 'old platform derivative' may, in fact, freeze local needs, and accelerate the fragmentation of demand and production system by nation. In other words, the introduction of this model might possibly hinder the movement towards the homogeneity of market needs and local production capability. It is possible that flexible development generates inflexible models. Two concrete examples of such a dynamic follow:

1. Adaptation to local production capability. Even globally standard designs sometime require modification in the local market due to lower local capability and differences in production volume. This modification enables the production of a model that fits the local production capability, while, on the other hand, this adaptation eliminates the pressure on the local production system to improve its capability.

2. Adaptation to local market conditions. Although the introduction of a locally adapted model through local design based on the local platform boosts local sales, this consequently isolates local customer taste from the international market, which adversely affects the competitiveness of the local product. In addition, low export potential limits overall production volumes, which in turn restricts the possibility of upgrading production technologies and hinders the improvement of manufacturing capabilities.

In other words, the 'old platform derivative' strategy is adopted in a path dependent manner, and price and non-price competitiveness will be enhanced in the local market. In this respect, this strategy excels in balancing the pursuit of scale economies and the adaptation of designs to local needs. When looked at dynamically, from the perspective of the evolution of organisational capability and market needs, however, the local adaptation of products lessens the pressure for global homogeneity, including the improvement of capabilities and the advancement of market needs in line with global trends. This may be called the 'over adaptation' condition of product development strategy.

In fact, for the Japanese makers which introduced models suitable for the local market in South East Asia, the paradox of 'flexible organisational capability generates inflexible products' became manifest with the economic crisis in the region. The merit of local adaptation is naturally emphasised when the local market is growing, but when it is shrinking, the standardisation of design which enables exports to other regions becomes a priority. At this point, over adaptation to the local market becomes problematic. The Asian Crisis after 1997 dramatically revealed this problem.

On the other hand, strategy and corporate environment also develop through reciprocal influence. The co-evolution of company and customer needs clearly indicates this relationship. Companies adopt a product strategy to adapt to customer needs, and in using their products, customers learn about them. As a result, customers come to have new needs, demanding new adaptations from their products. The products which had been adapted to the customer needs then become obsolete, and companies cannot survive without introducing products that satisfy the new needs. Customer needs and products, having gone through such a process of co-evolution, become oriented towards finer differentiation (Clark, 1985). The adoption of a strategy for local adaptation lowers the pressure for the advancement of market needs from a global perspective, developing instead the needs specific to the local market. This consequently isolates these needs from the global market, reducing the efficacy of the strategy which had once been effective. This may in turn undermine global competitiveness.

Thus, from a dynamic perspective, companies engage in cumulative decision-making while repeating the failures of under adaptation and over adaptation, which is paralleled by the evolution of market needs and local production capability. Through the experiences of recurrent adaptation over time, learning organisations may accumulate certain dynamic capabilities in the long run, through which the firm can readjust their product strategies quickly to the environmental changes

(Teece *et al.*, 1997). Such a dynamic point of view would be crucial in looking at global strategy.

In the next section, we will focus on this particular design strategy from a dynamic point of view. That is, we will analyse not only how this strategy achieved the competitiveness of the product in the local market at a certain point in time, but also how this strategy was chosen through a certain path dependent sequence of decisions, and how such strategic choices affected the companies' capabilities and environments over time.

A CASE STUDY: THE DEVELOPMENT OF COUNTRY-SPECIFIC MODELS FOR INDONESIA

In this section, we apply the framework proposed in the last section to the case of vehicle-product development for ASEAN markets. In particular, we analyse the case of the development of Indonesia-specific vehicles by Japanese vehicle makers, because Japanese firms have a very strong position in Indonesia, maintaining a market share greater than 95 per cent. We discuss the product design strategy for adapting to the local environment, the formation of organisational capability to realise it and the organisational inertia formed by that capability. First, we overview the specific conditions and history of the Indonesian car industry, as well as the Japanese vehicle makers' product development strategies as a response to such conditions. Then we will discuss the dynamic aspects of this issue analysing the development processes for two Indonesian models and the capability building of the firms. Finally, we discuss the environmental change caused by recent economic crisis, and the apparent vulnerability arising from over adaptation against it.

Context and conditions: the Indonesian car industry

First, we analyse the environmental conditions for product development for the Indonesian market. We describe the situation that the vehicle firms were facing in Indonesia, including government regulations, market size and needs and dominant strategy in the past.

Government regulation and its consequences

Since the late 1960s, many of the governments of Asian developing countries adopted import substitution policies for their motor industries, protecting local production operations from imports. The Indonesian government adopted a localisation policy in 1969, prohibiting all import of built-up cars, obliging foreign vehicle makers to employ locally capitalised makers for CKD assembly, and restraining the entry of foreign assemblers. This was followed by a policy of promoting the localisation of commercial vehicles in 1976, increased tariffs on the import of commercial vehicle CKD kits, while concurrently encouraging domestic parts procurement.

Such local content policies, however, meant government protection of local assembly and parts manufacturing operations, which lacked international competitiveness because of the limitations of their manufacturing capabilities, production scale, material availability, technologies, and so on. Compared with Japanese domestic operations, which are known for their world class competitiveness in both quality and productivity, the operations in ASEAN countries tended to lack the competitiveness required for exporting vehicles and components. Their low wage rates could not compensate for their low productivity.

The above mentioned disadvantages of local operations *vis-à-vis* their Japanese counterparts have been particularly serious in the case of parts manufacturing, which tends to be more capital intensive and scale sensitive than vehicle assembly. As a result, the cost competitiveness of locally produced vehicles tended to decrease as the local content ratio increased. The manufacturing quality of local parts was also low in many cases. This often meant that the vehicle makers had to modify parts designs in order to match them to local manufacturing conditions.

The New Automotive Policy, which came into effect in 1994, was aimed at strengthening the competitiveness of domestic vehicle makers. It liberalised the import of built up vehicles and lowered the tariffs imposed on components. This effort nevertheless eventually marked a considerable setback as a result of the contraction of the domestic market. Although the governments of Asian developing countries have, in recent years, attempted to shift from import-substitution to export-promotion policies in some sectors, such a transition was difficult in the automotive sector, in which the above mentioned vicious cycle of increasing localisation and decreasing competitiveness was quite common.

Since the 1970s, as an alternative strategy, some developing countries have attempted to promote increased exports and imports of

Table 8.1   Vehicle production in Indonesia,
1980–95

Year	Passenger cars	Commercial vehicles	Total
1980	21776	150211	171987
1981	25813	181991	207804
1982	30096	158675	188771
1983	23050	128808	151858
1984	23729	128602	152331
1985	25267	119047	144314
1986	33687	128342	162029
1987	28893	130819	159712
1988	32663	125757	158420
1989	31906	146247	178153
1990	56510	218093	274603
1991	45774	215570	261344
1992	30006	139527	169533
1993	32230	178231	210461
1994	40219	281451	321670
1995	37835	340861	378696

Sources: LTCBR (1997: 5), Nikkan Jidosya
Shinbunsya (1999: 229) and *Asia Pulse*, 16 March
1999 and 17 March 1999.

components or vehicles inside a given regional community such as
ASEAN, aiming at increased production scale for each local operation. Typical examples include the so called BBC scheme in ASEAN
vehicle-producing countries, which actually facilitated intra-firm trade
of certain components among the Japanese vehicle makers' component factories in the region. The impacts of such regional complementation policies on competitiveness of their products have been
limited, however.[3]

Market conditions

In terms of sales, the Indonesian market has expanded considerably
since the beginning of the 1990s (Table 8.2), However, the demand
took an acute downturn during the economic crisis, falling sharply
from 387000 vehicles in 1997 to 58000 in 1998.[4] Moreover, the 1997
crisis resulted in a dramatic shrinkage of the combined ASEAN
market to about 400000 units, or less than one-third of its peak

Table 8.2   Vehicle sales in the ASEAN-4 region, 1980–95

Year	Thailand	Indonesia	Malaysia	Philippines	Total
1980	89201	171987	101199	55574	417961
1981	89236	207804	100926	50815	448781
1982	91076	188771	102161	53629	435637
1983	118280	151858	122052	48954	441144
1984	113502	152331	127090	12141	405064
1985	86178	144314	106988	6935	344415
1986	78467	162029	74591	4335	319422
1987	101651	159712	54304	8580	324247
1988	142014	158420	68710	19629	388773
1989	208233	178153	122704	46993	556083
1990	304056	274603	186390	57865	822914
1991	268540	261344	199637	47949	777470
1992	362987	169533	145084	60360	737964
1993	456461	210461	154401	83811	905134
1994	485678	321670	200435	103471	1111254
1995	571580	378696	285792	128162	1364230

Source: LTCBR (1997: 5).

volume. Prior to the Asian economic crisis, however, the vehicle makers had been predicting a rapid market growth in this region based on the robust market performance from late 1980s to the mid 1990s (Table 8.2). In response to such market expectations, as well as continued government policies for local production, the Japanese vehicle makers and parts suppliers had continued to invest in local assembly and parts production, as well as the development of models specific to the local market.[5]

Low per capita incomes naturally result in a relatively low rate of vehicle ownership, which is below 3 per cent in Indonesia. The per capita GNP of Indonesia amounted only to US$980 in 1995, which was one twenty-seventh of the level in the USA, and one-quarter of Brazilian GNP. Even in the 1990s, the average monthly salary for a senior manager of a major company was approximately US$130.[6] In terms of price, therefore, low priced cars have been in most demand, with the exception of the small market for luxury high-class passenger cars. In the areas outside of cities and suburbs, in particular, poor road conditions have enhanced the demand for specifications usually required for trucks, such as waterproofing quality, especially for low priced passenger cars. On the other hand, meeting the Japanese

Table 8.3　Diversified vehicle markets in the ASEAN-4 region
(sales in units)

	Passenger cars		Commercial vehicles	
	Sales (units)	Share of domestic market (%)	Sales (units)	Share of domestic market (%)
Thailand	163 371	28.6	408 209	71.4
Indonesia	37 835	10.0	340 861	90.0
Malaysia	224 991	78.7	60 801	21.3
Philippines	71 195	55.6	56 967	44.4

Source:　LTCBR (1997: 5).

quality standard for mass-produced vehicles has not been a necessity for product development for this particular market.

Despite the efforts of ASEAN countries to build an integrated regional market, patterns of user needs have varied considerably from country to country. As indicated in Table 8.3, the difference in consumer choices of vehicle types across the ASEAN countries is remarkable. While nearly 80 per cent of total sales is derived from passenger car sales in Malaysia, the corresponding figure in Thailand is less than 30 per cent, and in Indonesia only 10 per cent. Differences are also seen within the commercial vehicle category. Whereas pick-up trucks comprise the major segment in Thailand, van (or mini-bus) type vehicles are the main commercial vehicles sold in Indonesia. Such a diversified demand structure prevented automakers from pursuing scale-economies through the introduction of a single product design for all the ASEAN countries.

Consumer needs in Indonesia centre on commercial vehicles, as was mentioned above. Above all, consumers show a strong preference for van-type commercial vehicles. There are several reasons for this. First of all, the tax structure favours commercial vehicles, as was mentioned above. This has led to the substitution of the major portion of the demand for passenger cars by commercial vehicles. In Indonesia, the purchaser class of passenger cars has always been limited to a small portion of the high income bracket, while buyers of commercial vehicles have mostly been small to medium-sized transportation companies. With the rise of a middle-income class, however, a demand for low-priced passenger vehicles was generated. This group tended

to buy van type commercial vehicles because of the tax system, purchasing vehicles that came in the form of a cab chassis only. Local
servicing manufacturers would then attach the rear body using pri-
mitive sheet metal processing. The technique used was quite rough
and ready, with low precision matching of the rear body and cab
chassis and putty applied to fill gaps.

The typical customers for these van-type vehicles were people who
could employ drivers and maids. These customers required that the
driver, maids, and baby sitter (if they had children), could get into the
same vehicle as family members. This created a demand for passenger vehicles that could accommodate more than seven people. Under
these circumstances, van-type commercial vehicles were developed as
a substitute for passenger cars.

The dominant strategy in product development

The above mentioned environmental conditions, including the small
size of the market, diversified user needs, relatively low incomes, and
the limited capabilities of local factories and suppliers, creates difficult and complex design requirements. While several firms tried to
develop a country specific vehicle for Indonesia, Toyota had most
success in bringing such a vehicle to the market. Toyota started investing in Indonesia in 1971 through a joint venture with Astra International, a local conglomerate. This was almost four years after the
government of Indonesia had first approached the vehicle makers.

The Toyota Kijang is the most popular vehicle in Indonesia. It is
defined as an Indonesian car, fully designed especially for Indonesia.
In 1977, six years after the establishment of the joint venture between
Toyota and Astra, the first Kijang was introduced in Indonesia. It was
designed to meet the local needs of the Indonesian domestic market,
for use in transporting agricultural products and building materials in
rural areas. The Kijang had no doors. Although this feature was
beyond the imagination of Japanese engineers in Toyota, they were
able to adopt this design thanks to the input from local stuff. The
Kijang did not even have a rear (upper) body, and the part covered
by the upper body included only the front seats. The rear body was
produced by local body makers as was mentioned above. The first
Kijang was the most popular vehicle in the Indonesian market, and
its successor, the second Kijang, remained cost competitive and very
popular, while introducing a slightly more stylish design. In 1989, the

basic grade of Kijang was sold for only US$5700, which was less than one third of the price of Toyota's main passenger car, the Corolla.[7]

Product design strategy: the 'old platform derivative'

Country-specific vehicle as a concept of product design

Following the conditions mentioned above, Japanese makers have introduced products developed for Indonesia with the concept of the country-specific vehicle. This concept signifies models developed in order to adapt to demand in a particular country and to sell free of tax by satisfying local content requirements fixed by the government for commercial vehicles. The tasks involved in the product design for these vehicles were to develop a low-cost model suited to the local production environment that met local needs. This fitted ideas advocated in the 1970s such as 'appropriate technology' (Jequier, 1976).

One instance is Model X, a product that Firm A developed especially for the Indonesian market. This is produced in the local factory of a joint venture with local capital.[8] Six-sevenths of output of Model X is in the form of an MPV (Multi Purpose Vehicle) types, with the remainder in pick-up form. The present model is the third generation, with the last model change carried out in 1997.

Firm B's Model Y is also a product planned as a country specific vehicle for Indonesia.[9] Its development was initiated in 1992 as 'the car to change the scene in Indonesia', and production started three years later, in 1995. Although this vehicle was later produced in Malaysia, China and Vietnam, it was initially planned as a country-specific model. There are three variants of this vehicle, produced in roughly the same proportions: a built-up van-type vehicle, a semi-complete vehicle shipped for local parts servicing, and a pick-up.

Parts sharing: the application of old platforms from the home country

The product design strategy for these vehicles was local design using an old platform, that is the 'old platform derivative' in our terminology. Equipment costs were reduced by using the core parts and components of outdated Japanese models for new local models, and it was unusual to find cases where current Japanese and local models shared the same parts. Using designs from current Japanese models would not have been cheaper. The quality of many of the parts would have exceeded customer needs, which would have cancelled out the effects of the reduction in development costs.

In the development of Model X, the suspension and transmission were applied unchanged from the first generation, although the frame was remodelled. When the first generation of the model was introduced, core components such as the engine were imported from Japan, sharing their design with the home country model at that time. Later, although the production site was transferred from Japan to Indonesia, the production facilities remained unchanged. For example, the engine plant had originally been transferred from Japan to Australia and was then transferred to Indonesia. By transferring facilities, the company minimised its investment.

Firm A tries to utilise old facilities as much as possible, even if some design change are inevitable. The current engine for Model X is an expanded version of one that was used for the first generation. The original 1100 cc overhead-valve-style engine was expanded to 1500 cc, and later to 1800 cc for use in the current Model X.

In the case of Model Y, the 'Old Platform Derivative' was applied through the classical transfer strategy. Firm B originally produced the transferred model without any modifications. Then, Model Y was developed using the old platform. Therefore, despite a press release explaining that it was a wider version of a model made in Japan, the model sold in Japan was actually totally different in its physical structure. Overall, the company succeeded in halving equipment costs and greatly reducing development costs by applying the platform from an old model.

*The fit between the trajectory of strategy and
the progress of local technology*

Firms have to adapt their strategy to fit the local environment. For Model X, the quality standard in the evaluation of design was substantially relaxed. From a need to develop a low cost product that suited the local environment, chief engineers were more flexible in their judgments and occasionally approved designs that did not meet Firm A's standards. Local production capabilities, for example, may be sufficient to manufacture stamped parts, but may present problems for matching parts together. The rigid application of standards is,

Table 8.4   Cases of design adaptation to local production capability

Instrument panel	Due to the low capacity of resin injection casts, steel was partly applied. Although the total injection required a 2000-ton machine, local makers only possessed 1300-ton ones. In 1997, the problem had already been resolved as one of Firm A's suppliers had acquired a 3000-ton machine.
Seat cover	Local products of low technological level are used. Leather is weak, and the fabric is prone to yield to pressure and to whiten. They do not meet the quality standards of Firm A proper. Although the starch used is not of good quality and easily cracks, Firm A agreed to use it because imported materials cost more.
Steel sheet	In Japan, steel strips (rolls) are used and the yield is high at 70%. Locally, sheet material is used, and the yield is only 64.5%. As the local steel is made partly from scrap steel, zinc plated steel sheet cannot be used. Therefore, the warranty against rust and holes is shortened to 3 years and 5 years, respectively, from 5 years and 10 years, respectively, applied in Japan.

Source: Field interviews.

therefore, not practical. Table 8.4 contains a list of cases in which designs were adapted to local production capabilities.

As a result, the level of quality for Model X was very low, far from the level that could be exported to Japan. For the time being, possible export destinations remain limited to the South Pacific countries outside the ASEAN region. Export to the Middle East is possible in terms of quality, but this is precluded by temperature problems. While the temperature occasionally reaches 50 degrees centigrade in the Middle East, Model X is likely to have problems in temperatures exceeding 35 degrees centigrade. Moreover, there are practically no emission controls or safety standards in Indonesia, and the safety features are on a totally different level from those in Japan. As the addition of emission controls costs more than US$100, it was excluded on cost grounds. Although air conditioning is fitted, the model is not equipped to function in cold climates, as it lacks a heater or demister. Thus, the priority placed on reducing costs to meet market requirements in Indonesia largely precludes sales in export markets.

On the other hand, local technology and production capabilities, which are the targets of adaptation efforts, have been improving, resulting in a corresponding, gradual upgrading of parts design. In Model X, several improvements have been made from the previous model, in line with improving local capabilities. First of all, a major change in styling took place. This was to meet changes in demand in Indonesia, as well as to adapt to the more advanced parts production technology of local suppliers. For instance, an improvement in styling was made possible by improved glass technology at the local supplier – specifically, the use of three-dimensional curved surface glass. Glass was always locally sourced from the first generation of Model X. While it was initially one dimensional, it gradually shift to two-dimensional and three-dimensional curved surfaces as supplier capabilities improved.

Highly advanced production technology also became feasible with the expansion in production scale. Welding is one example. With the first model (monthly production of 500 to 1000 units), double sheet welding was frequently used to minimise fixed cost. With the current model, more advanced techniques such as single sheet welding and closed sections were applied, which resulted in a lighter body and higher rigidity. This enabled a reduction in the number of parts as well as a 30 per cent cut in unit costs through decreasing the weight by 30 kg.

The effect of product development capabilities on product design

According to Clark and Fujimoto (1991), the Japanese vehicle makers during the 1980s tended to outperform their Western counterparts in lead times and productivity in product development. The performance of the Japanese vehicle makers was supported by a set of organisational capabilities for early and integrated problem solving, including parts suppliers' ability to take part in component design (Asanuma, 1989), manufacturing capabilities to support the development process (for example, prototyping and die making), overlapping problem solving between product and process engineering, strong project management, and so on. Due to the lower development cost of Japanese firms and their ability to implement the 'old platform derivative' strategy, it became possible for them to develop models specific for countries with low volume production. In fact, Japanese makers announced the development of Asia specific cars in the mid-1990s, taking advan-

tage of these characteristics, and some models were actually introduced to the Asian market. The characteristics of these models are
that each model has a specific target country. While the Honda City
and Toyota Soluna are mainly aimed at Thai market, the Toyota
Kijang and Daihatsu Espass were originally targetted at the Indonesian market.

International configuration in development activities

The choice of configuration

As was mentioned above, Japanese firms tend to concentrate their
product development organisations for the ASEAN market in the
home country. This, coupled with the small number of local suppliers
with sufficient technology and prototyping capability in Indonesia,
means that local development is not feasible. Looking at the actual
configuration of activities in the case of Model X, everything up to
design prototyping was done in Japan, and then the local site took
over from the stage of trial production in the plant. Locally, it was the
technology department that engaged in development. Their central
responsibility was the inspection of locally procured parts. The only
exception was the deck of the pick-up truck, which was designed
locally.

There was a similar division – product development in Japan and
process engineering locally – in the case of Model Y, although the local
staff in charge of process engineering did make visits to Japan. Out of
two stages of design prototyping, the first one was done with almost
all the parts from Japanese suppliers, but the second aimed at nearly
100 per cent local parts procurement. In practice, approximately 60
per cent of the total parts used were local in the second design prototyping. Among the Japanese suppliers who participated in the first
prototyping, those who maintained a local affiliation (about 60 per
cent of the total) were asked to start local mass production of their
parts under their own initiative. While both prototypes were tested
entirely in Japan, everything from trial production in facilities was
done locally.

As for process engineering, press dies and outer sheet metal are
sourced from Japan, while interiors are procured locally. The press
dies for the exterior, which must be finished to a high standard, have
to be procured in Japan. In this case, any modification to the dies is

done by staff visiting from Japan. As for injection dies, larger ones (such as instrumental panels) are transferred from Japan or Taiwan, and smaller ones (such as bumpers) are procured locally.

*The effect of product development capabilities on
international configuration*

The centralisation of development organisation permits the active use of capabilities accumulated in the development department in the home country. In the case of Model Y, development was carried out within the same organisation as domestic models, without the establishment of a specialised project team. This organisational structure was adopted because it was believed that having the overseas department as a separate organisation would hamper the acquisition of cooperative assistance from each functional department. It was reported that even without a special project team for Model Y, there were some delays in the schedule in the areas of design and process engineering attributed to the tendency seen in each department to neglect overseas operations. It is presumed that it would have been even more difficult to gain cooperation from the domestic side of the operation if the design department had been organisationally separate.

The effect of the accumulated capabilities in the process engineering department based on the past experiences in development is also noteworthy. As Model Y was the first overseas specific model to be developed, the process engineering department for overseas operations was not familiar with overlapping problem solving. The role of this department had previously been limited to the overseas exploitation of the existing models produced in Japan, which only required replicating the established manufacturing process of a vehicle whose design had already been finalised. This time, however, they could not effectively handle the changes made in design and in the process. Consequently, the effect of having development in Japan was that the process engineering department accumulated capability in development pertaining to overseas production.

Capability building in the 'old platform derivative' strategy

For the development of locally adapted products, the maintenance and further innovation of a rapid and highly flexible development process that takes advantage of the high 'integrated problem-solving capability' in Japan is indispensable. The existing capabilities were not enough in some respects, and further capability building was sometime necessary for firms to realise their intended strategy.

Reduction of development costs through organisational innovation

If product development costs are high, the development of locally specific vehicles is futile. While Japanese makers maintained low-cost product development, they also created a low-cost development process for the development of specific models for overseas. In the development of Model Y, for instance, dies and tools for prototyping were not manufactured so as to cut down development costs. As the policy was not to use prototype dies, the design process proceeded with the utmost caution in an attempt to concentrate design changes in the early stages of development. This type of managerial strategy is often called the 'front-loading' of problem solving in product development (Thomke and Fujimoto, 1998). From the second design prototyping, the manufacturing of the prototype parts was carried out in mass production facilities. As a consequence, the second prototyping practically became trial production, and the total lead time was shortened. Although the lead time for Model Y was 3 months longer than for other models in the domestic market, the fact that it was the first locally specific vehicle needs to be taken into account.

Following the success of the new development process that minimised the use of prototyping facilities, it has been transferred back to the development of vehicles for the domestic market. The chief engineer for the development of Model Y was later engaged in the development of models for the domestic market.

Capability transfer: handling the relation with joint venture suppliers

As a result of maintaining an organisational pattern that supported the product development capability of Japanese companies, meeting local content requirements and adopting a design strategy which entails the development of the local specific parts have been difficult. In particular, the fact that the vehicle makers have been dependent on the capabilities of suppliers has created some problems in developing parts specifically for the local market.

In cases in which there are joint venture parts suppliers in the local market, this does not seem to present a major problem. In developing Model Y, the company attempted to maximise technology transfer, even in the cases of Black Box Parts, in order to promote local production. When local suppliers with Japanese partners were available (such as the suppliers of shock absorbers, springs, and tyres), Firm B let its local subsidiary select a local Japanese supplier. Firm B also asked their Japanese suppliers to send their engineers to the local sites and actually make drawings there.

*Capability rebuilding: handling the relation with
technologically affiliated partners*

However, when there are no local joint ventures but only technologically affiliated partners available in the local market, there is a need to transform Black Box Parts into Detail Controlled Parts when localising parts production. In the case of Model X, although Firm A holds a simplified drawing, all the other information not present in the drawing, as well as the detailed drawings required for production, are retained by the parts suppliers. Therefore, Firm A did not have the know-how and knowledge to design these particular parts. In the case of exterior mirrors, for example, Firm A transferred a drawing made by its supplier since there was no designer in Firm A who could draw it. In addition, there are cases when firms ask their parts suppliers to give technological assistance to local component firms. This sometimes becomes problematic. For instance, a Black Box Parts supplier conducted technological assistance to a local supplier for the development of silencers. The mere transfer of the drawing, however, failed to transfer the latent know-how, which resulted in the poor quality of the final product.

In such cases of technological assistance, parts suppliers cannot recover their cost by parts sales after full-scale production is started. Therefore, their incentive to engage in technological assistance is small, and this has tended to produce relatively low local capabilities compared to the cases in which parts are produced in joint ventures. Thus, technology transfer is difficult for Black Box Parts, often calling for confirmation and modification at the stage of trial production. In developing locally specific parts, organisational patterns that involve the supplier's involvement in development presented obstacles to meeting local content requirements.

Even with Detail Controlled Parts, there are cases in which the knowledge pertaining to design was accumulated in both parts and die suppliers, which occasionally led to problems in localising production. When Detail Controlled Parts are developed, parts suppliers also occasionally make modifications to design, taking into account the manufacturability at the trial production stage in Japan. After localisation, the know-how of the suppliers is no longer available. Furthermore, when die suppliers are localised, problems are likely to arise in the manufacturing process, as the local suppliers will only produce what is drawn in the designs supplied. This also results from die suppliers solving problems in manufacturing by themselves in Japan. In the case of Model Y, there were many instances in which drawings and products did not match in practice, and this necessitated some alteration in facilities in order to match the tools and facilities to the drawings. While the suppliers and die makers' own accumulation of knowledge constituted a strength in the home country, which was facilitated by the established organisational pattern of integrated problem solving, it was an obstacle to local production overseas.

The Asian crisis and the manifestation of 'over adaptation'

The Asian crisis and problems with the Asian car

Despite some fluctuations, the vehicle market in Indonesia showed sustained growth, and by the mid-1990s the demand for cars and light vehicles had started to penetrate into the middle class. Model X and model Y were sold to the middle class as vehicles that met specific local needs at a relatively low cost. In this sense, these models can be seen as a product design strategy with a relatively good balance between the adaptation to the local demand pattern and the achievement of scope and scale economies through the international sharing of parts and platforms.

However, the acute fall of Rupiah in September 1997 following the outbreak of the Asian currency crisis, coupled with the domestic political crisis that started in May 1998, drastically cut back demand for vehicles, forcing many of the local vehicle makers and parts makers to suspend production. Many dealers' outlets were destroyed in the May 1998 riots, and with many overseas Chinese leaving the country for safety, local business became paralysed. The demand from the middle class, which had been driving the vehicle market, almost ceased to exist, resulting in demand falling to 60 000 thousand units per annum (less than one-sixth of the previous year). The political confusion continued in 1999, and no sign of recovery in vehicle demand was observed, except for the relatively stable demand from the upper class. Indonesia displayed a sharp contrast to the Thai market, which was back on a growth curve in 1999.

Following the drastic contraction of the local market, the problems inherent in Models X and Y, which are low cost cars based on the old platform, suited to local needs in Indonesia, became manifest. These include, first of all, the limited possibility of improving price competitiveness by currency depreciation, because of the models' low local content (less than 50 per cent for model X) compared to their Thai and Malaysian counterparts.

The second problem is that the adaptation of designs for the Indonesian market (or South East Asia) in the cases of model X and model Y precludes export to other regions (such as Europe, North America, the Middle East and Oceania). These vehicles can be regarded as cases of 'over adaptation' to the local market (Fujimoto, 1999). In the case of model X, for example, export of built-up cars has been sluggish, and so declining domestic demand led directly to a drastic fall in domestic production. This is in contrast to the pick-up trucks produced in Thailand by Toyota, Mitsubishi Motors, Isuzu, Nissan and Mazda and Honda's passenger car, the 'Accord'. These vehicles have had the characteristics of 'global models' that are valued in different regions.

The 'Old Platform Derivative' strategy, represented by Models X and Y, had been the most appropriate strategic selection in the Indonesian market prior to the Asian Crisis. This was reflected in their market performance. Moreover, in developing such models, the Japanese vehicle companies seem to have adopted a flexible development process, free from the development routine and design standards of products for home market. Ironically, this flexibility in international product development appears to have resulted in the generation of models overly adapted to local demands. It can be said that the dilemma of flexible development processes generating inflexible (marketability) models became manifest during the Asian Crisis.

At present, some Japanese companies, including Company A, seem to be aiming at the development of models with design and technology content that can be successful in other regions (such as Japan) for the next generation of Asian models. This is undoubtedly the result of the experience of the current models.

It is nevertheless misdirected to dismiss the problem of over adaptation manifest in the Asian Crisis as a simple mis-judgement of strategy. As long as the 'bounded rationality' of companies is assumed, it is unrealistic to assume that the present situation had been predictable prior to 1997 when the Asian markets were booming. It is not until they fell into the condition of 'over adaptation' as a result of the Asian

Crisis that they began to change strategy in order to achieve greater compatibility between global marketability and local adaptation.

As seen above, companies that face an uncertain environment with radical changes experience numerous situations of 'under adaptation' and 'over adaptation' in the short term. In the long term, they gradually become more capable of balancing local adaptation and global efficiency by transforming their design strategy in a path-dependent manner and accumulating the dynamic capabilities through such transformation, learning from their experiences. At the same time, customer needs in each country also become more sophisticated, which leads to global convergence in some aspects, while retaining notable regional difference in others. Thus, the essence of global product development in the automotive industry cannot be grasped correctly unless the dynamic strategic model is applied, which explains that the strategic selection, environment, and organisational capability co-evolve and influence each other.

CONCLUSIONS

In this chapter, we have indicated the importance of a dynamic perspective for considering global strategy. By looking at the Indonesian case, in particular, the significance of a path-dependent organisational capability in adapting to the local environment as well as the vulnerability of over-adaptation against environmental change have been clarified. The following summarises the discussion in this chapter.

1. The ASEAN automobile markets are relatively small, diversified, and constrained by the relatively low income levels of customers. Their supplier base is also different from that of the home country.
2. Such conditions create a trade-off between local adaptation and international standardisation that the product developers of the auto firms have to balance.
3. One commonly used product design strategy is to design a derivative product from an old platform. It requires a sophisticated product development organisation and capabilities, but may achieve a good balance between the two forces.
4. The resource configuration strategy of the Japanese vehicle makers in Asia, even when compared with their North American and European operations, shows that product development for Asian cars tends to be centralised in the technological centres in

Japan. However, certain problem solving capabilities are moved to the local facilities, where local information is 'sticky'.

5. Such choices of product design strategies may be formed through a series of path dependent (or emergent) strategic choices, rather than a deliberate decision-making based on foresight.

6. These strategic choices, once they are made, may then affect the patterns of evolution of both market needs and organisational capabilities. While the derivative approach based on the old platform requires sophisticated product development capabilities, the strategic choice forms new capabilities suitable for its execution.

7. Sometimes, the cumulative effects of strategic formation and market evolution, together with unexpected market changes such as the Asian economic crisis, may result in the problem of 'over adaptation'. It is difficult for the firms to avoid this kind of problem.

8. Through the experiences of adaptation, over adaptation and lack of adaptation over a long period, learning organisations may accumulate certain dynamic capabilities in the long run, through which they can re-adjust product strategies quickly to the environmental changes.

These findings show the necessity of using a dynamic framework to grasp the global–local trade-off. In a dynamic perspective, firms select the product strategy cumulatively, with repeating the failures of under adaptation and over adaptation, which is paralleled by the evolution of market needs and local production capability. Such a dynamic point of view might be crucial in looking at global strategy.

Notes

*   We are grateful for the helpful comments and suggestion provided by Mario Sergio Salerno, Annalee Saxenian and Yoshikazu Takahashi on an earlier draft. All responsibility for remaining errors belongs to the authors. This research was supported by Japan Society for Promotion of Science and the Globalization Research Programme of the International Motor Vehicle Programme at MIT.

1.   The concept of path dependency tends to be applied to depict situations in which a later outcome depends on small events at an earlier stage because of positive feedback (Arthur, 1989). The concept of path dependency used here means that the capability accumulated by learning from past activities and decision making plays a key role in decision-making in the present.

2. Needless to say, product design strategy and location strategy have reciprocal influence on each other. This line of argument, however, is omitted in this chapter.
3. A more extensive discussion of these schemes can be found in chapter 9 by Guiheux and Lecler, in this volume.
4. *Asia Pulse*, 16 March, 1999, 17 March 1999.
5. Doner (1991) described the historical dominance of Japanese firms in South East Asia. As success factors, he pointed to their long-term orientation and flexibility both in strategy and production.
6. According to an interview with the manager engaged in the Indonesian operation.
7. The description here is based on *Fortune*, 2 January, 1989, p. 16, and *Institutional Investor*, November 1991, p. 105.
8. The data on the development of Model X in this section was collected mainly through interviews with several managers of Firm A in June 1997.
9. The data on the development of Model Y in this section was collected mainly by an interview with the Chief Engineer of Firm B in October 1997.

References

ARTHUR, B. (1989) 'Competing technologies, increasing returns, and lock-in by historical events'. *Economic Journal*, Vol. 99, March, 116–31.

ASANUMA, B. (1989) 'Manufacturer–supplier relationships in Japan and the concept of relation-specific skill'. *Journal of Japanese and International Economics*, Vol. 3, 1–30.

BARTLETT, C.A. and GHOSHAL, S. (1989) *Managing Across Borders: the Transnational Solution*. Boston. MA: Harvard Business School Press.

CLARK, K.B. (1985) 'The interaction of design hierarchies and market concepts in technological evolution'. *Research Policy*, Vol. 14, 235–51.

CLARK, K.B. and FUJIMOTO, T. (1991) *Product Development Performance: Strategy, Organization, and Performance in the World Auto Industry*. Boston, MA: Harvard Business School Press.

CUSUMANO, M. and NOBEOKA, K. (1998) *Thinking Beyond Lean*. New York, NY: The Free Press.

DONER, R.F. (1991) *Driving A Bargain: Automobile Industrialization and Japanese Firms in Southeast Asia*. Berkeley and Los Angeles, CA: University of California Press.

DOUGLAS, S.P. and WIND, Y. (1987) 'The myth of globalization'. *Columbia Journal of World Business*, Vol. 22, Winter, 19–29.

DUNNING, J.H. (1981) *International Production and the Multinational Enterprise*. London and Boston: Allen & Unwin.

FUJIMOTO, T. (1999) *The Evolution of a Manufacturing System at Toyota*. New York: Oxford University Press.

GHOSHAL, S. (1987) 'Global strategy: an organizing framework'. *Strategic Management Journal*, Vol. 8, 425–40.

JEQUIER, N. (ed.) (1976) *Appropriate Technology*. Paris: OECD.

LEONARD-BARTON, D. (1992) 'Core capabilities and core rigidity; a paradox in managing new product development'. *Strategic Management Journal*, Vol. 13, 111–25.

LEVITT, T. (1983) 'The globalization of markets'. *Harvard Business Review*, Vol. 61, May–June, 92–102.

LTCBR (1997) 'ASEAN jidousha sangyo: buhin sangyo no kyosoryoku to nikkei buhin meika no sinshutsu. (ASEAN automobile industry: the competitiveness of the components industry and expansion of Japanese suppliers)'. *Sokenchosa*, No. 72.

MINTZBERG, H. and WATERS, J.A. (1985) 'Of strategies, deliberate and emergent'. *Strategic Management Journal*, Vol. 6, 257–72.

NIKKAN JIDOSHA SHINBUNSHA (1999) *Jidosha Sangyo Handobukku- (Auto industry handbook)*. Tokyo, Japan: Nikkan Jidosha Shinbunsha.

PORTER, M.E. (1986) *Competition in Global Industries*. Boston, MA: Harvard Business School Press.

PRAHALAD, C.K. and DOZ, Y. (1987) *The Multinational Mission*. New York: The Free Press.

SINCLAIR, S. (1983) *The World Car: the Future of the Automobile Industry*. New York: Facts on File Inc.

TAKEUCHI, H. and PORTER, M.E. (1986) 'Three roles of international marketing'. In Porter, M.E. (ed.), *Competition in Global Industries*. Boston, MA: Harvard Business School Press.

TEECE, D.J., PISANO, G. and SHUEN, A. (1997) 'Dynamic capabilities and strategic management'. *Strategic Management Journal*, Vol. 18, 509–33.

THOMKE, S. and FUJIMOTO, T. (1998) *The Effect of 'Front-loading' Problem-solving on Product Development Performance*. Harvard Business School Working Paper, No. 98–10. Cambridge, MA: Harvard Business School.

VERNON, R. (1971) *Sovereignty at Bay: The Multinational Spread of U.S. Enterprise*. New York, NY: Basic Books.

VON HIPPEL, E. (1994) 'Sticky information and the locus of problem solving: implications for innovation'. *Management Science*, 429–39.

9 Japanese Car Manufacturers and Component Makers in the ASEAN Region: a Case of Expatriation under Duress – or a Strategy of Regionally Integrated Production?

Gilles Guiheux and Yveline Lecler

INTRODUCTION

Until the 1960s, vehicles sold in the ASEAN countries came exclusively from Western manufacturers. These were designed and produced in Western countries and exported to the region. Toyota, followed by other Japanese makers, entered these markets in the 1960s by opening assembly plants for CKD vehicles. Then, during the 1970s, as the ASEAN countries began to adopt policies that favoured localisation (see Chapter 3 by Humphrey and Oeter, in this volume), the Japanese vehicle makers began to outsell their Western rivals, and this in turn attracted Japanese component manufacturers who also began to set up operations in the region.

Due to the way in which 'national' vehicle manufacturers were being protected, and because the only customers in the local market came from the wealthiest socioeconomic classes, vehicle makers were able to charge high prices for the vehicles they offered. Thus, despite their small size, and their high production costs, the ASEAN markets were profitable for Japanese firms.

Two factors began to change this situation between 1985 and 1995. First, the region's growth potential attracted new competitors, who challenged the Japanese domination of local markets. Secondly, attempts were made to increase economic efficiency through regional integration. The initial impact of these schemes was insignificant, but recent initiatives (AICO–AFTA)[1] could have a greater effect, particularly because of changing conditions following the Asian crisis.

The present chapter examines the responses of Japanese firms to these changes: the regional integration of components sourcing; the development of an 'Asian car'; and changing relations between assemblers and suppliers. It also delves into the consequences of these responses, not only as they pertain to the relationships between Japanese firms located within the ASEAN region, but also with respect to inter-firm relations within Japan itself.

MARKETS WITH GREAT GROWTH POTENTIAL BUT LIMITED IN SIZE

In 1996, most observers estimated that future demand for new vehicles in the ASEAN-4[2] countries would reach the 2 million mark by the year 2000 and that these markets would eventually act as a catalyst for a restructuring of the global automotive industry. Living standards, and thus potential consumption, were on the rise almost everywhere. The per capita GNP of two countries, Thailand[3] and Malaysia, had already surpassed US$3000 (Table 9.1), the level considered essential for the development of mass motorisation, and the other two countries' proximity to this threshold augured well for the future.

However, these countries are characterised by enormous socioeconomic and regional disparities. For this reason, average per capita Gross National Product (GNP) is an unreliable indicator of potential motorisation. The evolution of vehicle sales in the ASEAN-4 countries from 1991 onwards (Table 9.2) demonstrates that increased motorisation was not only limited to those countries whose per capita GNP had surpassed the US$3000 mark.

The annual sales volumes of the four ASEAN markets combined in the mid-1990s would, by themselves, have amply justified mass production. However, because of consumer attitudes (often influenced by national regulations, including tax exemptions that can create a highly diversified demand structure), and because of government policies aimed at the development of national motor industries, the situation was more complex. Demand and markets were fragmented, as can be

Table 9.1   Market potential in terms of each country's stage
of motorisation

	Indonesia	Philippines	Thailand	Malaysia
Per capita GNP 1996 (US$)	1119	1165	3007	4656
Vehicles per thousand inhabitants 1996	17	24	49	155
Stage of motorisation	Initial spread	Initial spread	Mass motorisation	Mass motorisation
Source of demand for vehicles	Governments, firms, institutional demand	Governments, firms, institutional demand	Middle classes	Middle classes

Sources: LTCBR (1997: 8); TED (1998: 2) and Sakura sogo kenkyujo (1998: 15).

Table 9.2   Annual vehicle sales in the ASEAN-4 countries

	1991	1992	1993	1994	1995	1996	1997
Thailand	268 560	362 987	456 461	485 678	571 580	589 126	363 156
Malaysia	181 877	145 084	167 928	200 435	285 792	364 788	404 469
Indonesia	261 307	169 533	210 769	321 760	378 684	332 035	386 691
Philippines	47 949	60 360	83 361	103 471	128 162	162 011	144 435
ASEAN 4	761 684	739 956	920 512	1 113 338	1 366 213	1 449 956	1 300 748

Source: Fourin (1999: 3).

illustrated by the cases of Toyota and Honda. Toyota's top-selling
product in Thailand in 1995 was the Hilux, a one-ton pickup; in
Indonesia, its multipurpose Kijang model came out on top; in the
Philippines, its best selling model was the Corolla, a small sedan. In
addition to three Daihatsu models it also distributed, Toyota offered
ten different models in the ASEAN-4 countries in 1995 (the number
dropped to seven in 1999). With the exception of the Corolla in
Thailand, the Kijang in Indonesia, and the Hilux pickup in Thailand
(whose output was in part exported towards extra-zonal markets),
output for each of these models was less than 30 000 units (Automotive Industries, 1999). Similarly, Honda assembled its Civic, City, and
Accord models on four different sites in 1997, with cumulative annual

volumes of 36 000, 32 000, and 12 000 units, respectively (Fourin, 1999: 24). As long as prices were high enough to ensure profitability, market size was not the crucial factor. The priority was to satisfy customers, all of whom belonged to the wealthiest socioeconomic groups. Models were being sold for twice the price charged in Japan. The component suppliers were also being paid one and a half or two times as much as in Japan. Moreover, the locally produced models were usually outdated, enabling vehicle makers to keep their local investments to a minimum. These factors allowed companies to make profits in the local market.

The Japanese vehicle makers, for a long time the only vehicle manufacturers to have established operations within the region, adapted their production systems to the attempts by governments to promote motor industries within their countries. The history of the Japanese vehicle makers' ASEAN-4 sites explains why these companies continue to this day to offer a product variety that is greater than that warranted by the size of local markets.

LOCAL CONSTRAINTS AND INCENTIVES IN THE ASEAN AREA

Up to the 1990s, Japanese penetration of the ASEAN-4 zone had, to a certain extent, been dictated by governmental policies in the host countries, and, for Japanese component manufacturers at least, by local content requirements. Attempts to overcome the problems of restricted market size through regional integration were largely frustrated up to the mid-1990s.

The role of local content policies

The introduction of local content requirements was the driving force behind local sourcing. In the 1960s, a few Japanese suppliers had already set up operations in the zone in order to satisfy aftermarket demand, but the local supply of original equipment parts was not on their agenda. However, during the 1970s, the ASEAN countries adopted measures to promote local sourcing. For example, local content legislation was introduced in Thailand in 1972, with locally assembled vehicles having to source 15–25 per cent of their content locally if they were to remain exempt from import tariffs. This requirement rose progressively, reaching 54 per cent for high-volume vehicles such as pickups and passenger cars (see Chapter 3 by Humphrey and Oeter, in this volume).

Given the shortcomings of the local industrial base, it would have been impossible to meet the required local content by sourcing solely from locally owned firms. Therefore, local supply was achieved through new investments by Japanese component manufacturers and technology transfer agreements that often turned into joint ventures. Even without local content requirements, it is probable that the Japanese vehicle makers and their suppliers would in any event have turned to local sourcing from the mid-1980s onwards. They would have wanted to benefit from the lower production costs, after the appreciating yen had made Japanese goods more expensive. However, this would have been linked to parts with a low value-added, requiring no significant transfer of technology.

Many technology transfer agreements were signed in the 1980s, and this trend has accelerated since. For example, in Thailand, 70 per cent of Toyota's locally sourced parts in 1996 came from the local plants of Japanese suppliers, and 20 per cent from companies that were benefiting from technological assistance provided by a Japanese partner. In other words, pure Thai companies only accounted for 10 per cent of total sourcing.[4] The strategy achieved its goal. By the early 1990s, Toyota achieved a 50 per cent local content ratio in Thailand and Indonesia.[5]

Although raising the ratio beyond this level was considered difficult, Toyota continued to raise its local content ratio. In 1995, the firm's Thai vehicles achieved a 60 per cent local content ratio, 6 per cent higher than was legally required. The company felt at the time that it would be difficult to move beyond this level.[6]

The effectiveness of schemes of mutual complementation

To overcome the handicap that the domestic markets' small size represented for local sourcing, and to enable supporting industries to develop, there was much talk from 1969 onwards about the feasibility of establishing a regional system of complementation in the ASEAN area.

Despite much discussion, it was not until 1981 that the first scheme, AIC (ASEAN Industrial Co-operation), was born. This scheme was limited to a small number of components and required that trade occur on a strictly reciprocal basis. Covering less than 1 per cent of intra-ASEAN trade, the scheme's impact was also limited by the fact that the Japanese vehicle makers were reluctant to accept it (Legewie, 1998). The Japanese vehicle makers considered that their own competitiveness had to a large extent been predicated on the efficiency of their existing sourcing relationships, and thus preferred to continue to rely upon this network for the components they needed in their ASEAN assembly operations. In addition, in the early 1980s, Malaysia announced a national car programme, thus destroying hopes for an ASEAN-wide integration of the local motor industries.

It was not until 1988, after many rounds of negotiation, that a real scheme of complementation was enacted, replacing the AIC. This was the BBC scheme, whose objective was to allow firms with operations in more than one of the ASEAN-4 countries to trade parts and specialise, thereby attaining economies of scale and cheaper sourcing. Once each country had given its agreement, the BBC scheme, which only covered the motor industry, reduced tariffs by half on parts traded on a mutual, inter-zonal basis between companies with the same brand. The components traded within the scheme were counted as 'local' for the purposes of local content requirements. Mitsubishi (1988), Toyota (1989), Nissan (1990), and later Honda (1995), all adopted this programme.

This scheme had clear limitations. Indonesia only ratified the agreement in 1995, once it had added conditions involving the application of local content ratios, and opinions have continued to diverge amongst the various ASEAN member states. Moreover, the scheme did not apply to suppliers: only parts produced in the vehicle makers' own plants were included. Another barrier to integration lay in the scheme's procedural complexities: new authorisation had to be given for any model change, and companies had to provide proof that the trades were made on a strictly reciprocal basis. Although the BBC certainly reflected progress in the division of labour between ASEAN countries, it excluded the supplier segment, which could have had the greatest impact on the development of a local supporting industry. The scheme had limited impact, and export flows between the participating countries remained limited (Table 9.3). As late as 1995, component exports from the ASEAN-4 countries were predominantly directed to countries outside the region. Honda, for example, had structured a system for sourcing parts within the ASEAN zone, but even though the Thai Civic incorporated some 'local' parts, made outside of Thailand, of the 70 per cent that were

Table 9.3   Components exports from the ASEAN-4 countries by destination (1995, % of total component exports)

	Exports from			
Exports to	Thailand	Indonesia	Malaysia[a]	Philippines
Thailand	×	1.2	2.9	9.2
Indonesia	1.1	×	1.9	1.8
Malaysia	3.5	2.1	×	0.7
Philippines	1.4	3.0	1.9	×
Singapore	19.5	31.2	17.4	0.4
Vietnam	0.9	0.8	0.1	0.2
Japan	15.7	11.7	8.4	31.8
Others	57.9	50.1	67.5	55.9
Total	100	100	100	100

Note: [a] Data refers to 1994.
Source: LTCBR (1997: 70–3).

considered to be 'local' in nature, only 9 per cent were, in fact, manufactured outside of Thailand.

Looking to the future: from the BBC to the AICO and the Common Effective Preferential Tariff Scheme

A further attempt to encourage regional integration in the auto industry was adopted at the December 1995 meeting of ASEAN economics ministers. The AICO scheme, which began to function in November 1996, was broader in scope than the BBC. It was not restricted to vehicle industry, thus allowing component manufacturers as well as assemblers to use it. In a move towards the Common Effective Preferential Tariff Scheme (CEPT), due to take effect in 2003, tariffs on products traded within AICO were lowered to between zero and 5 per cent. At least 30 per cent of the capital of any firm participating in the AICO had to be owned locally (a condition that will disappear with CEPT), but the local manufacturing ratio for the whole of the ASEAN region could drop to 40 per cent, compared to 50 per cent for BBC. However, no single local content requirement prevailed throughout the entire zone, as each member state remained free to make its own decisions in this area. Procedural complexity remains, as trade reciprocity must still be proven. Nevertheless, the first agreements within an AICO framework were signed in 1998, between such vehicle makers as Volvo, Toyota, Isuzu, and parts makers such as Sanden, Denso, and Nihon Cable (Fourin, 1999: 14).

This regime may become more extensive as time goes on. In the past, Japanese manufacturers opposed government pressures to localise production because they wished to minimise their commitments in the region. Nowadays, they are demanding procedural simplifications and greater liberalisation, so that the division of labour can be extended not only within the ASEAN zone, but also with respect to Japan and other neighbouring countries. This change in attitudes dates from the mid-1990s, when Japanese vehicle makers established in the ASEAN region were confronted by fierce competition from new entrants.

NEW CHALLENGES FOR ASEAN CAR MANUFACTURERS AND COMPONENT MANUFACTURERS

In the mid-1990s, as a result of increased competition, especially from Korean makers, and a loss of competitiveness following the appreciation of the yen, Japanese vehicle and component manufacturers were forced to redefine their strategies within the ASEAN area.

Increased competition and the strong yen

In the early 1990s, Japanese companies experienced a small but noticeable decline in their domination of ASEAN markets (Table 9.4). Although the situation was not yet too serious across the industry and ASEAN as a whole, there were already enough concerns about the passenger car business[7] to provoke a response by Japanese car makers, especially in the light of the damage caused to their competitiveness by the continued appreciation of the yen.

In spite of the ending of the bubble economy in Japan, the yen continued to rise in 1994–95, reaching a level that undermined the competitiveness of Japanese vehicles. Toyota raised the prices of its Corona and Corolla models on the Thai market in February 1995 and then again in June of the same year. Even in Malaysia, where the government controlled the selling prices of motor vehicles, increases could not be avoided, and 11 car makers sought official permission to

Table 9.4   Japanese makers' market share in the ASEAN-4 countries
(% of units sold)

	Passenger cars		Commercial vehicles		Total	
	1991	*1994*	*1991*	*1994*	*1991*	*1994*
Thailand	83.2	69.2	99.1	99.1	95.2	89.5
Malaysia[a]	26.1	16.2	84.6	88.2	45.9	32.2
Indonesia	80.7	73.7	99.5	98.4	96.2	95.4
Philippines	84.6	87.0	99.1	99.7	90.9	92.5

Note: [a] Figures for Malaysia exclude Proton models.
Source: Ishizaki (1996: 20).

raise prices (Ishizaki, 1996: 20). At a time of increased intra-zonal competition, a strategy based on increasing prices had clear limits. Further, it was impossible to offset the yen's rise by rationalising production and cutting labour costs. Given the cheapness of labour, and the small proportion it represented in total costs, the savings that could be expected were minute.

According to the spring manufacturer, Chuo Spring, interviewed in July 1996, given that materials accounted for 60 to 70 per cent of total costs, if local procurement could replace imports from Japan this would lead to a sharp fall in costs. Loss of competitiveness was basically due to the prohibitive cost of parts and raw materials imported from Japan. The solution was to become less dependent on these imports.

A new strategy with cost-cutting at its core

Cost-cutting required increased local sourcing even beyond the ratios specified in national regulations. This resulted in all the Japanese car-makers attempting to develop a product innovation, the 'Asian car'. Japanese parts makers were very involved in this strategic reorientation, as it required substituting imports from Japan with locally produced parts. Even if extending local production remained a response to pressures from the car makers, it would become increasingly the result of the dynamics of a production system integrated on a regional, or even international, basis.

The Asian car: a new concept for localising production within the ASEAN region

The Asian car was specially designed for the Asian countries, satisfying a number of criteria: local consumer preferences, driving and climatic conditions, and above all, a low retail price. Based on a previous model generation, it incorporated various essential modifications: removal of the heating system, extra air-conditioning, and increased component durability. Above all, the Asian car had to be manufactured in the host countries, taking their technological capabilities into account.[8] All of these factors would serve to enhance the competitiveness of this car against its low-cost Korean rivals.

By the late 1990s, various Japanese manufacturers were launching, or had announced plans to launch, their 'Asian cars'. In May 1996, Honda launched the City, a 1300 c.c. four-door car that sold for 20 per cent less than previous similar models. In 1997, Toyota, which was already selling the updated Kijang[9] model in Indonesia, launched the Soluna, a 1500 c.c. four-door, five-seat variant of the Tercel model. Even though the Asian strategies followed by the various Japanese vehicle makers differed in some respects, most of them had begun to market a low-priced Asian vehicle by early 1997. The main objective of this strategy was to increase the manufacturability of vehicles within the ASEAN region: that is, to redesign them so that most of the parts and components could be produced locally. This was the starting point for the deliberate implementation of a regional division of labour based on mutual intra-zonal trade.

Increasing local sourcing: the challenge for supporting industries

In an effort to reduce their vulnerability to the fluctuations in the value of the yen, the Japanese vehicle makers all announced that they would be increasing their local procurement ratios. For example, Siam Nissan Automobile Co. and Siam Motor Company, two Thai subsidiaries of the Nissan group, both announced in 1995 that their local sourcing ratios for passenger cars and for one-ton pickups would rise to 80 to 85 per cent, respectively by 1998, compared to 50 and 60 per cent in 1995. Even Isuzu Motors, which had already reached an 80 per cent local sourcing ratio with its Thai pickup truck, aimed to attain 85 per cent by 1998 (Ishizaki, 1996: 21).

However, if these components were themselves produced from materials and parts that were imported from Japan, there was no guarantee that the targeted cost savings would be achieved. Therefore, the relocated Japanese suppliers were also strongly encouraged to increase their own local procurement ratios. What is at stake is the development of a supporting industry that could supply both parts and materials. Although this orientation gave local industries a foothold in the rapidly growing market for automotive supplies, they urgently needed help from their Japanese vehicle manufacturer and component making partners in order to improve their technological capabilities. Much work was done in this area, and it was reinforced by government actions aimed at providing help both to supporting industries and to other small and medium-sized local companies. Even so, such a strategy can only be long term, and the substitution of locally produced parts for imported components served above all to persuade a new wave of Japanese suppliers to move to the ASEAN region, and especially to Thailand, between 1994 and 1996. The Japanese component manufacturers intended to use this new wave as a basis for increasing the local content of the parts that were being manufactured in the ASEAN region. According to a February 1996 survey by the Sakura Research Institute (Center for Pacific Business Studies), many of the Japanese parts makers in the ASEAN-4 countries (from 25 to 60 per cent, depending on the parts) intended to extend their list of ASEAN-made parts over the following two or three years – even though the manufacturing capacities for the new items did not even exist at the time of the survey (Mori, 1999: 18).

The capability-building process had already begun even before the Asian crisis erupted. However, given that this process was largely confined to transplants and joint ventures with Japanese firms, it is not certain that it will contribute to the development of a locally owned supporting industry.

ECONOMIES OF SCALE: ORGANISATIONAL INNOVATIONS AND THE RESTRUCTURING OF NETWORKS

Given that investments in the ASEAN region could no longer be made profitable by charging high prices for vehicles and components, the need to achieve economies of scale became evident for all companies in the sector – vehicle manufacturers, their component making subsidiaries, Japanese component manufacturers and local suppliers. Several strategies were developed towards this end, including mutual supply and joint-production agreements between manufacturers and suppliers and specialization by country for parts production. At the same time, changes were made to the *keiretsu*-type relations that had previously prevailed between suppliers and assemblers.

Mutual sourcing and joint production

In order to increase scale, manufacturers and suppliers made two major organisational innovations within the ASEAN framework. Assemblers began joint sourcing of parts and suppliers started to diversify their customer base. Both trends represented a break with the *modus operandi* of the Japanese *keiretsu*.

Mutual sourcing by the assemblers

To increase scale and cut unit costs, the assemblers began to conclude two novel types of agreements: mutual sourcing and the joint construction of new plants that were destined to assemble several different types of vehicles at once. In Thailand, for example, Nissan, Isuzu, and Toyota signed a mutual sourcing agreement for diesel engine pickups in February 1995. Each manufacturer would specialise in a specific part, with Siam Toyota Manufacturing (Toyota) producing cylinder head blocks, Siam Nissan Casting (Nissan) cylinder head gaskets, and IT Forging (Isuzu) crankshafts. The participation of other Thai firms in this project made it possible to increase the local content ratio (Fourin, 1996: 61). Manufacturers set up networks that allowed them to exchange not only parts but also services as well. In March 1996, Honda and Isuzu signed an agreement in Thailand in which the former supplied pickup parts to the latter, whereupon Isuzu would assemble engines for the Honda Civic. Isuzu's local dealer network would also distribute Honda vehicles (Fourin, 1996: 61).

Joint vehicle assembly

A second type of co-operation involved the creation and/or joint utilisation of an assembly unit by several manufacturers at the same time. Some of these agreements brought together firms that belonged to the same industrial grouping. In Malaysia, UMW Toyota assembled vehicles for Daihatsu (Fourin, 1996: 97). In return, Thai Hino Industry assembled vehicles for Toyota. Similarly, Siam Motors (Nissan) assembled trucks for Nissan Diesel (Fourin, 1996: 56). However, total production was still too low to be profitable, and in order to achieve economies of scale, manufacturers not only had to maximise the synergies within their own group (Nissan–Nissan Diesel,Toyota–Hino–Daihatsu), but they also had to try to benefit from the synergies that existed between companies which belonged to different groups. This led to the sharing of assembly plants amongst several manufacturers. Given the competition between industrial groups in Japan, this was a major innovation. In Thailand, Bangchan General Assembly (a member of the Honda group) assembled pickups for Daihatsu (a member of the Toyota group). In the Philippines, Columbian Motors (Nissan Diesel) assembled vehicles for Daihatsu. In Malaysia, Automotive Manufacturers (Isuzu) produced Citroën's AX model in co-operation with Proton, the national assembler with which Mitsubishi was also associated (unlike Citroën, Mitsubishi had taken a capital stake in Proton). The establishment of these networks for exchanges of components and services (imports, distribution), and the joint production of different brands of vehicles at a single site, constituted major innovations for industrial companies that competed ferociously with each other in other markets.

Country specialisation by product for components exports

One result of the search for economies of scale was that the production of parts and components, both for the local market (ASEAN) and for the whole region, including Japan, became concentrated in those countries with comparative advantages. This was leading to an increased specialisation by country and by product: engine parts in Thailand and Indonesia, steering parts in Malaysia and transmission parts in the Philippines (Table 9.5). There was a significant rise in trade in components throughout the ASEAN region, especially for Toyota, the company that seems to have made the greatest strides toward a regional division of labour. The value of Toyota's intra-ASEAN trade increased by a factor of 10 between 1992 and 1996. At first, the export of parts towards Japan had been motivated by desire to increase scale and underpin the profitability of ASEAN production sites. More recently, this flow was integrated into a deliberate strategy of producing the most labour-intensive parts in the ASEAN region. This was the dawn of a new division of labour, not only on an ASEAN scale but also on a much wider regional scale that also integrated Japan, Taiwan, and even China.[10]

In 1996, a survey of the Toyota suppliers that had set up operations

Table 9.5 Division of labour for parts of Japanese vehicle makers in the ASEAN-4 countries

	Toyota	Mitsubishi	Honda	Nissan
Thailand	Diesel engines stamping parts	Casting parts suspensions	Stamping parts	Engine parts stamping parts
Malaysia	Steering gear suspensions	Steering gear stamping parts	Plastic products suspensions	Steering gear stamping parts
Indonesia	Petrol engines cylinder blocks	Engine parts	Cylinder heads cylinder blocks	Petrol engines[a]
Philippines	Transmissions transm. parts	Transmissions	Casting parts	Transmissions stamping parts
Intra-ASEAN trade volume (billion yen)				
1992	<2	<0.5	<0.5	<0.2
1996	20	3	4	1
2002[b]	90	>20	>20	20

Notes: [a] Operations due to start in 2000. [b] The figures date from mid-1997. They were scaled back significantly following the Asian crisis.
Source: Legewie (1998: 10).

in the ASEAN region revealed that the processes of integration between this zone and Japan was restricted to labour-intensive parts, the only ones for which the ASEAN countries had a comparative advantage (Guiheux, 1998). It can be hypothesised that the regional division of labour will increase as the ASEAN countries' parts industries increase their competitiveness in terms of both price and quality (as a result of a higher output, increased local sourcing, and a continuation of technology transfers). Parts requiring simpler production processes will be produced outside of Japan, and products requiring more complex processes in Japan itself. The first-tier suppliers have also been involved in the creation of regional trading networks, and none more so than Denso, a component manufacturer which has organised a complex flow of products between its various establishments in the ASEAN zone. Denso's Indonesia site has specialised in the production of compressors for air conditioning systems and spark plugs; alternators and starters are produced in Thailand; condensers and evaporators are produced in Malaysia, and so forth. These products are not only traded with the ASEAN zone but also exported to Japan, Taiwan, and even Australia and New Zealand (see Figure 9.1).

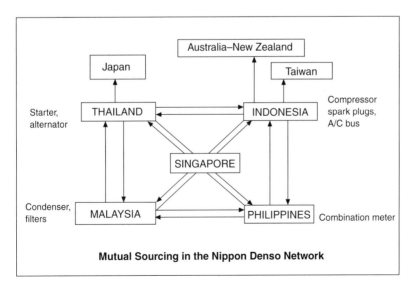

Figure 9.1   Denso's trade flows in Asia
Source: Elaborated from Fourin (1996: 28).

That such a network has been put together demonstrates the extent to which things have changed compared to the first three decades of Japanese presence in the ASEAN region. Operating under the double constraint of market diversity and government regulation, Japanese makers and suppliers followed a strategy that focused on establishing overseas production and assembly capabilities within a framework that was essentially national in scope. Nowadays, strategies are regional, and they integrate the ASEAN-4 zone into a wider Far Eastern and Pacific space.

New relations between vehicle makers and component manufacturers: the industrial *keiretsu* revisited?

The ASEAN space has also been a site for a number of innovations in the area of assembler–supplier relations. Given that each assembler produces few vehicles, it is in the suppliers' interest to diversify their client base. This policy has consequences which are difficult to measure for a suppliers' degree of dependence on their principal customers (expressed by the percentage of sales with these clients). Some suppliers that are very dependent upon a single assembler in Japan rely less on this client in the ASEAN region. Others find themselves in a similar situation in both spaces. The process is still evolving.

Component manufacturers setting up operations in an ASEAN country attempt to increase their total output and reduce unit costs by increasing the number of companies with which they do business. Even if the component firm is affiliated with a specific automaker, the latter will sometimes encourage this diversification strategy. Some Japanese companies have even tried to do business with non-Japanese car makers (as they were already doing in the USA and in Europe). In this way, the ASEAN markets have given the Japanese component manufacturers opportunities to build new customer relationships.

If a car assembler has no *keiretsu* supplier in a given country, it may do business with another supplier – even one with which it does not trade back in Japan. This also holds for independent manufacturers. For example, in Thailand, a rubber and plastics manufacturer called Fukoku has been trading directly with Honda, Nissan, and Toyota, although this would never have occurred back in Japan, where the vehicle makers deal with their existing *keiretsu* suppliers. In Thailand, a company that is a member of the Toyota group (Toyota Gosei) has been supplying Nissan, a relationship that does not exist back in Japan. In these overseas markets, the *keiretsu* pyramid seems somehow to have been turned upside down: there are many assemblers, and reliable suppliers are few and far between.

In Japan, the existence of a co-operation club supposedly indicates that a parts maker and a vehicle manufacturer are affiliated. In Thailand, however, over 50 per cent of the components firms that belonged to a given Japanese assembler's co-operation club were members of more than one such club (Higashi, 1995). This is different from the Japanese *keiretsu* system, in which the car maker presides over a vertical division of labour. Here, one components firm will deal with a number of assemblers. So even if some exceptions can be found, the level of dependence of component manufacturers on their Japanese *keiretsu* customer is often weaker in the ASEAN area than in Japan. For example, in 1995, Koito, a lighting equipment and parts manufacturer and a member of the Toyota group, sold 47 per cent of its Japanese production to Toyota, whereas in Thailand, it only sold 35 per cent of its local production to TMC (Koito data, 1996).

Over the years, Japanese companies' decision-making processes for overseas investment have evolved in ways that reflect changes in assembler–supplier relationships. In the 1970s, the suppliers moved into Asian countries because the vehicle makers asked them to do so. In the 1990s, the situation has become less straightforward. Assemblers have long encouraged parts makers to move into these new spaces, and they apparently used to offer substantial guaranteed business in return. However, such guarantees have become much less evident as of late (Ozeki Akito, JAPIA, 6.8.96). Increasingly, suppliers' overseas investment decisions are being made autonomously. This may vary from one country to another, and from one assembler to another, but the trend is clear, and undoubtedly reflects the increased uncertainty of the Asian markets, as well as a new strategy in which assemblers and suppliers will be obliged to share risks.

Japanese vehicle makers and suppliers adopted a certain number of ASEAN strategies in the mid-1990s which were aimed at allowing them to adjust to changing conditions in these markets. Faced with growing competition, the new priority was to cut production costs through organisational innovations including co-operation between vehicle makers, between suppliers, and specialisation by country and by product. As part of these strategies, there was some revision of the *keiretsu* relationship. To spread their risks, vehicle makers encouraged suppliers to diversify their client base in the ASEAN region – in essence, forcing them to assume an unprecedented degree of autonomy, and therefore liability. The revision of the traditional relationship between suppliers and assemblers was at first a reflection of the difficulty of ensuring an adequate return in such a small market. Now, it has become a conscious and deliberate strategy.

This strategy has been implemented not only in the ASEAN region but also in Japan itself. Faced with plunging volumes in their main market, and forced to find savings, suppliers have tried to diversify their Japanese client base and sought additional customers, sometimes even searching outside of the automobile sector. Ichikoh Industries, for instance, a member of the Nissan group, supplied Toyota for its Rav 4 vehicles, having offered production costs that were 25 per cent lower than an offer by Koito Manufacturing, which is a member of the Toyota group. Similarly, Aisin Industries (Toyota group), supplies Mitsubishi with regulators for its exhaust system (Fourin, 1996). Moreover, in order to reduce their own production costs, vehicle makers now started to share certain parts in Japan itself. For example, Koyo Seiko supplies both Mitsubishi and Suzuki with power steering parts. Aisin W. supplies these same two automakers with identical parts for their gearboxes (Fourin, 1996: 74). In sum, things have also changed in Japan itself – nowadays, a single supplier will belong to a variety of assemblers' clubs, and will even sometimes work together with suppliers belonging to different groups in joint production activities.

For the moment, it would appear that this customer base diversification has not caused the break up of any of the traditional affiliations. However, the situation may change. A whole new set of relations have been built up with other assemblers' suppliers, and between suppliers and assemblers, both in the ASEAN region, and in the other spaces into which the Japanese firms have moved (North America, Europe and China) – and all of these factors have contributed to the change of the traditional *keiretsu* relationship.

CHANGING CIRCUMSTANCES FOLLOWING THE ASIAN CRISIS AND THE MARKET'S CONTRACTION

Japanese manufacturers and parts makers, having established plants in the ASEAN zone, were busy launching the Asian car, re-shuffling their networks to increase output and experimenting with new systems of mutual sourcing by 1997. At this point, the Asian crisis profoundly modified the environment. It appears that the crisis may have actually served as a catalyst for further and faster change. For example, the schemes of regional co-operation promoted by ASEAN governments have been enhanced. Some analysts may end up attributing the difficulties being experienced by the countries that are particularly committed to co-operation-based schemes to this very orientation – arguing that a co-operative approach is a handicap, and that a system based on pure competition is a better option. However, the trade liberalisation that is at the heart of the IMF's plans could paradoxically end up by strengthening these co-operation-oriented reforms. Plummeting sales will surely reinforce the trend towards the concentration of production, especially given how far output has already sunk. The move towards a specialisation by country and/or by product has not always been well-received, but this could very possibly change now that the very survival of overseas sites is at stake. Far from abandoning the zone, the Japanese firms are getting ready for its recovery, and they believe that this will be accompanied by an increase in competition as a growing number of non-Japanese vehicle makers, particularly GM and Ford, enter these markets. In 1995, the outlook for vehicle sales in the ASEAN-4 countries was very encouraging. However, when sales forecasts for the year 2000 were reviewed in March 1998, they were lowered from 2 million vehicles to 625 000 units. Despite this substantial drop, the automakers seem to have remained relatively (possibly overly) optimistic with regard to the outlook for long-term growth. The March 1998 forecasts have suggested that the sales expected in 2000 will not be achieved until 2005 (Table 9.6).

Japanese vehicle makers and suppliers have been putting together a variety of strategies allowing them to survive the recession. As markets have collapsed, automakers have all been faced with large surplus capacities. Their immediate reaction has been to study the feasibility of vehicle exports, especially from Thailand. This strategy enabled Toyota to start up production of the Hilux again, albeit with single shift working, after having ceased production in November 1997. Mitsubishi has concentrated its production of pickups at its new plant in Laemchaebang, Thailand, and it has already exported 40 000 pickups to Europe. In fact, the firm's future plans are to cease production of pickups in Japan, and to supply Central and South American markets from its Thai plant, which is now forecast to export 80 000 vehicles in the year 2000.

According to the JAMA (Japan Manufacturers' Association, 1998),

Table 9.6   The evolution of demand in the ASEAN-4 countries
(number of vehicles)

Year[a]	Thailand	Indonesia	Philippines	Malaysia	Total for the ASEAN-4
1997	363 156	386 691	144 435	404 837	1 299 119
1998	144 065	58 261	80 231	163 851	394 008
1999	170 000	68 000	88 000	160 000	832 000
2000	200 000	105 000	120 000	200 000	625 000
2001	270 000	180 000	140 000	240 000	830 000
2002	340 000	202 000	160 000	300 000	1 002 000
2003	450 000	300 000	185 000	340 000	1 275 000
2004	690 000	400 000	250 000	502 000	1 842 000
2005	740 000	425 000	245 000	510 000	1 920 000
1995 forecast for 2000	800 000	600 000	200 000	400 000	2 000 000

Note: [a] 1997 and 1998, actual outcome. 1999–2005, forecasts made in 1998,
with the exception of the 1995 forecast for the year 2000.
Sources: 1997 and 1998: Fourin (1999); 1999 to 2003: Fourin (1998); 2004
and 2005: Sakura sogo kenkyusho (1998); 1995 forecast: TED (1998).

between January and June 1998, exports from Thailand towards
Central and South America rose by 29.8 per cent over the previous
year, while exports towards the Near and Middle East increased by
20.5 per cent. Even though these volumes are relatively small and
might never be substantially increased, there is no doubt that real
efforts have been made to support production in the ASEAN assembly units.

Taken together, the export targets announced by the various Japanese automakers for their Thai plants exceeded 150 000 vehicles in 1999
– with pickups comprising the majority of these exports. As the Thai
market starts to grow again, another 150 000 to 200 000 vehicles should
be sold domestically, and total output was expected to reach 300 000
to 350 000 vehicles in 1999 (Kato, 1999), a strong recovery from 1998
levels, and almost back to the 1997 performance. Although an export
boom is quite implausible, it is nevertheless evident that the addition
of these export markets will provide great support for local production. However, it is not clear how long the effects of this new strategy
will last. A distinction must be made between pickups and passenger
cars. Mitsubishi's experience would make it appear that the exporta-

tion of trucks and pickups from an ASEAN production base, to various markets, including Triad markets, may remain a key strategic option. On the other hand, the long-term priority for passenger cars remains the local markets (Toyama, 1999).

Nevertheless, the Asian crisis has made it clear that redirection of output towards other markets should remain an option, and the Asian car concept goes against this thinking. The Asian car strategy is about designing vehicles that are geared towards the conditions in the country or region in which they are made and sold. Whether because of their quality standards, level of sophistication, or climatic attributes (for instance, the lack of a heating system), it is difficult to adapt such vehicles to other markets.

For reasons of price competitiveness, the total abandonment of the Asian car is not on the agenda, but upcoming models might be redesigned so as to incorporate, from the very outset, modifications which will enable them to be sold onto markets other than those for which they were initially destined. The idea is both to dispense with everything that is not absolutely indispensable for the target market, and also, through flexible design, to modify certain attributes without incurring excessive costs – for example, moving the steering wheel from the left to the right, so as to be able to sell into the Australian market. The same flexibility could also applied to the heating system, or to the anti-corrosive characteristics – with an eye to the Latin American markets. Of course, this degree of flexibility has not yet been attained, although Toyota does appear to consider moving in this direction (IIES interviews, June 1999).

In sum, although the export of passenger cars towards non-ASEAN markets[11] is clearly a survival strategy rather than a new paradigm, makers will probably incorporate export possibilities into their future thinking in their efforts to minimise the risks of market uncertainty.

The greatest rise in exports has probably taken place in the area of components, where efforts to improve quality have started to take effect, and where potential growth is greatest. In 1995, these items already represented a significant proportion of the ASEAN-4 countries' exports, even though the volumes and values were low in absolute terms. It is probable that the ASEAN countries, including Malaysia (which adopted a strategy based on the development of a national automobile industry), will in the future be integrated into the international division of labour that Japanese vehicle makers, at least, are trying to put together. Of course, locally produced parts will need to become more competitive internationally, and production will need to shift from parts manufacturing to subsystem assembly. Nevertheless, whether in Thailand, where the components industry has made great progress over the last few years as a result of the Japanese suppliers' increased concentration, or in Malaysia, where the development of an electronics industry has created the basis for specialisation, this orientation appears to be feasible in the long term.

For the moment, increasing exports of parts since the outbreak of the Asian crisis has primarily reflected imports into Japan, and the main purpose of this activity has been to keep the overseas sites in business. The exportation of parts towards Japan had already risen between 1990 and 1994, when the value of ASEAN-4 exports rose from 15.3 to 37.1 billion yen, but since late 1997 there have been daily stories in the Japanese press in which automakers or suppliers have announced their intention to increase imports from the ASEAN region, or else, to begin sourcing a given component from an ASEAN subsidiary rather than from Japan.

From a Japanese point of view, it is true that the sums involved are still of marginal importance, but for the ASEAN countries, they are already quite significant. The dynamics of export of parts to Japan has been accompanied by an accentuation of the trend towards a specialisation by country and by product. In the future, it is conceivable that a growing proportion of components will be concentrated in those countries that provide advantages in terms of quality/price/capability, and that they will then be exported not only towards the other ASEAN countries, but also towards Taiwan, or Japan. Thailand, which has become the principal base for the Japanese automobile industry in the ASEAN region, is probably the country where the final assembly will occur before export to the other ASEAN countries and to other countries on the periphery of the zone.

CONCLUSION

The economic growth that the ASEAN countries experienced during the 1990s caused household incomes to rise rapidly. This in turn engendered rapid growth in the regional automobile markets. For a long time, these markets constituted a sort of private hunting ground for the Japanese vehicle makers. They were small in size, and the presence of a large number of vehicle makers accentuated the fragmentation of production across a large number of models. However, because of the particular characteristics of the regional clientele, profit rates were high.

Until the 1980s, this strategy had provided the Japanese vehicle makers with a cushion of profitability. It then ran into the double constraint of higher local content requirements and the stronger yen. Needing to react to the situation, manufacturers and component manufacturers redefined their strategies. They increased local sourcing, and at the same time sought economies of scale in the belief that this would help them to cut their unit costs. In the mid-1990s, these changes were accentuated by the sharply rising yen, and by the entry of new competitors into these markets. Cost-cutting suddenly became the number one priority. Large-scale innovations were attempted in a variety of areas. With respect to the product lines, new vehicles were designed especially to be manufactured locally, and to satisfy the specific demands of the Asian markets. In the area of production management, local sourcing was increased even beyond regulatory thresholds, and parts and components production was concentrated in a few sites to facilitate economies of scale. This shift from national production to a regional division of labour was partially supported by mutual trading programmes that were set up within the ASEAN framework. The clear objective was to raise output, particularly in the production of components; to cut costs; and to improve price competitiveness in the face of increasing competition. Although exports flow between ASEAN countries were still limited, Japanese makers began to put an Asian division of labour, in the form of specialisation by country and by product, on their strategic agenda.

In 1997–98, the ASEAN markets and currencies collapsed, and the crisis gave birth to new parameters for the Japanese firms. Once again, manufacturers and parts makers were forced to revise their zonal strategy. Above and beyond their short-term adjustments, and notwithstanding variations between firms and countries, firms sought salvation in export markets. In order to reduce excess capacity as far as possible, and to keep at least part of their existing sites in business, it became imperative that at least part of production be sold outside of the ASEAN region. Parts manufacturers, and to lesser degree assemblers, were both involved in this trend.

The systematic organisation of an intra-ASEAN trade in parts had preceded the crisis, but the process was considerably accelerated by the new economic situation. Previously, intra-zonal exchanges had been limited, because its various governments had been cautious about specialisation by country and product. However, they were no longer in a position to resist. The vehicle makers, whose previous focus on national markets had caused them to be indifferent or even hostile to regional integration measures, now called for the immediate adoption of these mechanisms.

The long-term outlook remains very uncertain. Because of their lack of competitiveness in terms of price and quality, no one envisages a lasting integration of the ASEAN assembly sites into the Triad market systems (with the notable exception of pickups and trucks). On the other hand, it is conceivable that there will be a continuous flow of passenger car exports towards markets on the zone's periphery: Australia, New Zealand, the Middle-East, and even South America. Toyota, for example, has expressed its desire to adapt its 'Asian car' so as to be able to sell it on the South American market. Strategies have certainly changed since the crisis erupted. The ASEAN markets themselves are still the prime target, but in order to protect themselves against local risks, firms now target some of their products towards external markets.

As for components, the adjustments necessitated by the recent changes in circumstances could give birth to a new system, especially if the ever greater transfer of technology enables supporting industries and local suppliers to become more competitive. For the moment, only labour-intensive ASEAN parts are exported to Japan. However, Japanese firms may choose in the future to relocate an increasing share of their components production outside of Japan.

In sum, the policies that the ASEAN countries have been following with a view to the development of national motor industries seem to have been partial failures. The domestic markets would have had to absorb greater production volumes, and supporting industries would have had to be in a position to satisfy local sourcing requirements. Neither of these conditions was fulfilled – hence the decision to adopt solutions that have revolved around a regional organisation of the ASEAN economic space. As a result of the product and information flows that they generate, Japanese firms have been the protagonists of this regional division of labour. Yet, this strategy also has its shortcomings: output is still well below profitable levels, and procurement still depends to a large extent on Japanese sources. The crisis simply aggravated a situation that had existed since the mid-1990s. Hence the search for panaceas such as the partial integration of the ASEAN region into the mainland Japanese economic space; the export of parts, but not vehicles, into other peripheral spaces; and the export of parts and vehicles towards markets in the Mid-East, Australia, or New Zealand.

Alongside the implantation processes that have characterised the history of Japanese vehicle makers in the ASEAN region, new forms of productive organisation have emerged, including co-operative relations between assemblers and/or between suppliers, and a revision of the vertical links between firms and their suppliers. Seen in this light, the effects of the organisational innovations carried out by Japanese firms in the ASEAN region will probably be felt in Japan itself. The ASEAN region has become a space in which new practices can be learned. Firms have been induced by the internationalisation of their activities to construct new management systems that will enable them to better cope with the uncertainty of the marketplace.

Notes

1. AICO, ASEAN Industrial Co-operation Organization. AFTA, ASEAN Free Trade Area.
2. Thailand, Indonesia, Malaysia and Philippines. Singapore, considered as a New Industrialising Economy, is excluded from the present study. The almost complete absence of an automotive industry in the other ASEAN member states also precludes their inclusion.
3. In 1998, following the Asian crisis, per capita GNP in Thailand fell below the US$3000 mark.
4. TMC's Purchasing Division: Interview 29 July 1999.
5. Interview with Yukitoshi Funo, Deputy General Manager, Toyota Planning Division (Gipouloux, 1994: 211).
6. These figures have to be considered with care, because what is denominated as a local product often includes a significant imported element. However, the figures do reveal increasing local content over time, as the basis for calculating local content remained constant.
7. For example, the opening of a Hyundai plant in Thailand was considered responsible for the 14 per cent decrease in Japanese passenger car sales.
8. See Chapter 8 by Sugiyama and Fujimoto, in this volume with respect to the consequences of this strategy for vehicle design.
9. The Toyota Kijang has been in development since the 1970s (see Chapter 8 by Sugiyama and Fujimoto, in this volume). The shape of the first Kijang had few curved body panels and no windows in the doors. It was a truly basic car. Later, the model was transformed until it became the epitome of the 'popular car' in Indonesia. In 1994, 60 000 Kijangs were sold in this country – 20 per cent of the entire market.
10. Taiwan, for example, specialised in the production of plastic parts.

11.   The Triad markets will not be target for exports of passenger cars produced in the ASEAN region for many years to come. This is due to these
vehicles' relative lack of sophistication, and to the fact that consumers in
a mature market would consider their quality to be unacceptable.

References

AUTOMOTIVE INDUSTRIES (1999) '1997 Worldwide production data,
automotive industries'. Website – www.ai-online.com/stats/, accessed Feb-
ruary 1999.
FOURIN (1996) 'Ajia jidosha sangyo 1995/1996 (Asian Car Industry
1995/1996)'. *Sekai jidosha sangyo,* Vol. 6, No. 3. Nagoya: Fourin Inc.
FOURIN (1998) *Fourin's Automotive Forecast.* Nagoya: Fourin Inc.
FOURIN (1999) 'Ajia jidosha sangyo (The Asian Car Industry)'. *Sekai jidosha
sangyo* Vol. 9, No. 1. Nagoya: Fourin Inc.
GIPOULOUX, F. (ed.) (1994) *Regional Economic Strategies in East Asia: a
Comparative Perspective.* Tokyo: Maison Franco-Japonaise.
GUIHEUX, G. (1998) 'A survey on the current investments of Japanese auto
parts industry in Asia: the example of Toyota's first tier suppliers'. Paper
presented to the 6th GERPISA International Auto Industry Colloquium,
Paris, June.
HIGASHI, SHIGEKI (1995) 'The automotive industry in Thailand: from pro-
tective promotion to liberalization'. In Institute of Developing Economies
(ed.), *The Automotive Industry in Asia: the Great Leap Forward?.* Tokyo:
Institute of Developing Economies, pp. 16–25.
ISHIZAKI, YUKIKO (1996) 'New phase in Asia strategies of Japanese-
affiliated automobile and parts manufacturers'. *RIM Pacific Business and
Industries,* Vol. 1, No. 31, 17–32.
JAMA (ed.) (1998) *1998, the Motor Industry of Japan.* Tokyo: Japan Auto-
mobiles Manufacturers' Association Inc.
KATO, MASHU (1999) 'Kozokaikaku ni idomu asean jidosha sangyo'
(ASEAN car industry facing structural Changes). *Nissei kiso kenkyujo,
shoho,* Vol. 9, 56–84.
LEGEWIE, J. (1998) 'Driving industrial integration: Japanese firms and the
automobile industry in Southeast Asia'. Paper presented at the DIJ-
Conference, Regional Co-operation in Asia 'Will Japan Stand up to a Leadership Role?', Tokyo, October.
LTCBR (ed.) (1997) 'Asean jidosha sangyo – buhinsangyo no kyosoryoku to
nikkei buhinmeka no shinshutsu – (The ASEAN car industry – the competitiveness of the parts industry and the penetration of the Japanese transplants' parts makers)'. *Sokenchosa,* No. 72.
MORI, MINAKO (1999) 'New trends in ASEAN strategies of Japanese-
affiliated automobile parts manufacturers – the role of exporting and
priorities for the future'. *RIM Pacific Business and Industries,* Vol. 1, No. 43,
12–27.
SAKURA SOGO KENKYUJO (ed.) (1998) 'Tai jidosha sangyo [masuta
puran] kanrenshiryoshu' (Documents relating to the Thai Automobile
Industry [master plan]). Mimeo.

TED SEMINAR (ed.) (1998) *ASEAN jidosha sangyo no saishindoko oyobi kongo no ichizuke to senzaiteki seichoryoku* (New orientations for the ASEAN auto industry: future positioning and potential growth). Mimeo. Jidosha mondai kenkyu semina dai 153 kai (153rd Research Seminar on the Problems of the Automotive Industry), TED semina No 8343 tekisuto. Tokyo: Mitsubishi jidosha kogyo Inc.

TOYAMA, ATSUKO (1999) 'Asian business development of the world's major automobile assemblers through strategic alliance'. *RIM Pacific Business and Industries*, Vol. 1, No. 43, 2–11.

10 Changing Patterns of Inter- and Intra-Regional Division of Labour: Central Europe's Long and Winding Road

Attila Havas

INTRODUCTION

Central Europe's unique history together with its geographical location provide an excellent opportunity to analyse the dynamics of inter- and intra-regional division of labour, the role and scope of global and regional patterns, national policies and firms' strategies. Central European countries have long-established, but somewhat different automotive traditions, shaped by the three distinct socio-economic systems occurring in the space of 90 years. These traditions continue to shape the auto industry even today.

The following section describes the development of the motor industry in the period up to the collapse of the Soviet Union. This is followed by an analysis of major current developments, in particular FDI projects, as well as production and sales prospects. Then Central Europe's role in the European division of labour is discussed, and finally the impacts of re-integration and FDI on the structure of the local supplier industry are considered.

MOTOR-INDUSTRY TRADITIONS IN CENTRAL EUROPE

The motor industry in Central Europe dates back to beginning of the 20th century. In Bohemia, now in the Czech Republic, Václav Laurin and Václav Klement produced their first genuine car in 1905. By the 1920s lorries, buses, aircraft engines and agricultural equipment had been added to the L&K product lines, and the company merged with the large engineering firm, Škoda, in 1925. In Hungary, cars were first assembled from imported kits in 1903, and the first Hungarian designed and built car was produced in 1905. While the motor industry was ravaged by war and depression, there was some recovery in the 1930s, and Ford models were produced under a licence agreement. All the major car parts – engines, gears and chassis – were produced in Hungary until the mid-1940s. In other words, Hungary's vehicle manufacturers had accumulated skills in automotive engineering, building upon a long tradition in mechanical engineering, even though no major indigenous car maker had emerged. Finally, in Poland Fiat established its first joint venture, Polski Fiat, as early as 1920 to import vehicles. Healthy sales figures soon prompted the idea of setting up local assembly, but the Great Depression delayed the investment programme.

Prior to the end of World War II, the Central European motor industry was to a large extent based on Western technologies. It was mainly a 'one-way street': assembled cars, kits and technologies were imported from the West. The only exception was Škoda, the Czech car maker, with its own strong design capabilities. There was no deep division of labour between the Western and Central European regions, nor a significant division of labour within Central Europe.

After World War II, the countries of Central and Eastern European were forced to join the Council for Mutual Economic Assistance (CMEA), the trading bloc of the Soviet empire. The CMEA, controlled from Moscow, granted mandates for its member countries to produce and exchange certain goods. This ambitious plan to organise an international division of labour on a large scale and in a fairly detailed way did not follow any economic rationale, and its intention was not to promote mutually beneficial development and economic growth. On the contrary, its main aim was to centralise resources and exploit them for strengthening the Soviet empire. All the major industries were co-ordinated centrally by CMEA headquarters, and thus the motor industry was also organised at this level: who could produce what vehicles and what products would be traded within the CMEA and with other countries/regions was centrally controlled.

For cars and for almost all other consumer goods, a very strict import restriction regime was introduced and maintained for decades. Western makes were only imported for use by politicians, except during certain short periods in some countries. In the early 1970s in Hungary, for example, a small number of Western cars were 'rationed' for ordinary people. There was no competition between car makers – on the contrary, given severe shortages buyers were 'competing' for new cars – and hence no incentives to innovate. Cars made in the CMEA countries, even the previously successful Škoda models, became increasingly obsolete, and less and less marketable in Western Europe. Trade in cars with Western Europe was minimal. It was in line with the overall principle of the CMEA to maintain a self-sufficient economic system based on natural resources and import substitution. Technology imports, however, did play an important role in building car plants in various CMEA countries, including the Soviet Union. Fiat was a leading licensor in the region with its Soviet and Polish agreements, while Renault was active in Romania and (the former) Yugoslavia.[1] Usually these were one-off projects, and hence technological upgrading and continuous improvement did not take place.

Degrading Škoda

Škoda, along with all major private firms in Central Europe, was nationalized after World War II. It continued to develop its own models, although new models were introduced from time to time, their quality and performance increasingly lagged behind Western makes. Its cars became increasingly uncompetitive in advanced countries, in spite of their low price.[2] However, Škoda cars were the most popular ones in the CMEA region, especially in Central Europe, because they were still superior to other CMEA cars. Given the very nature of central planning, no other car makers were allowed to operate in Czechoslovakia, and imports, either from Western Europe or other CMEA countries, were insignificant. Hence Škoda practically enjoyed a monopoly in the domestic market. In short, central planning maintained Škoda's design capacity, but did not maintain its former technological performance. By the end of the 1980s it was no longer viable as independent company, and a technologically and financially strong partner was needed to re-vitalise it.

The heritage of the CMEA in Hungary

Although automotive production facilities in Hungary were ruined during the war, manufacturing of motorcycles, buses, lorries and other commercial vehicles resumed relatively soon after. Car production, however, was abandoned under the new industrial policy shaping Hungary's industrial structure within a CMEA-wide division of labour. The new policy first was influenced informally by Soviet advisors working in Hungary and then by a formal Soviet–Hungarian specialisation agreement signed in 1964. The accord co-ordinated the two countries' industrial development projects, including vehicle manufacturing, in the wider context of CMEA. It stipulated that Hungary would specialise in producing buses for the entire CMEA. Ikarus, Hungary's bus manufacturing firm, became one of the largest in Europe, turning out some 14 000 units a year in the 1980s.[3]

Bus manufacturing provided an excellent opportunity to make use of the considerable assets and skills accumulated in auto parts manufacturing companies, in spite of the lack of car manufacturing after the late 1940s. Hungarian suppliers began to ship car parts to other CMEA countries in the 1960s.[4] Certain components, such as engines, axles, undercarriages and tyres for commercial vehicles, as well as bulbs, batteries and dashboards for cars, were also exported for hard currency (to Western Europe, the USA and India). Cars were mainly imported from the Soviet Union, East Germany, Czechoslovakia, Romania and Poland – Lada, Trabant, Wartburg, Škoda, Dacia and Polski Fiat models accounted for 90 per cent of the Hungarian car park in 1989.

Fiat in Central Europe: Poland

Fiat renewed its licence agreement with the Polish authorities in 1948, and hence, Fabryka Samochodow Osobowyh (FSO) was established with the intention of starting manufacturing Fiat models from 1950.[5] Politics interrupted this planned collaboration again, but in December 1965 a new contract was signed allowing FSO to produce the Fiat 125, a compact model, with a capacity of 70 000 units a year. The first Polski Fiat 125 rolled off the line in November 1967.

A few years later, in October 1971, a further licensing agreement was concluded with Fiat to produce its new sub-compact model, called the 126. Manufacture of the Polski Fiat 126 model started in July 1973 at FSM, the Fabryka Samochodow Malolitrazowych, in Bielsko Biala. This agreement included the promotion of local components manufacturing, too, at a nearby plant in Tichy. Unlike in other cases, technological development was part of the agreement, and thus in 1972 FSM opened a research centre with Fiat's assistance. In 1979 the contract was extended both in terms of its time span and coverage. The parties agreed for the following 10 years to export Polski Fiat 126 models to Fiat's other markets (production in Italy was stopped in 1980) and to source automotive production equipment to be used at Polish plants as well as larger Fiat models to serve the Polish market. The co-operation was continued in the same vein in 1987, when the Polski Fiat 126 was to be replaced by a newly developed small car, called the Cinquecento.[6] This stage of the long-established collaboration, however, can be regarded as a smooth transition to a new economic era since the production of this new model only started at the Tichy plant in 1991, after the transition to the market economy.

To conclude, this period – in a sharp contrast with the earlier one – was characterised by a strong regional division of labour, both between Eastern and Central Europe as well within Central Europe. This was based on the shipping (not really trading) vehicles and components. Central Europe was tied to Eastern Europe, but the whole CMEA remained dependent on Western technology. Yet, trade in automotive products with Western Europe was limited, with the exception of Fiat's exports from Poland and component exports from Hungary.

DEVELOPMENTS IN THE 1990s:
FDI, CAR PRODUCTION AND SALES

The ever weakening – and eventually collapsing – Soviet Union was unable to glue together its wider Central and Eastern European empire towards the end of the 1980s, and hence the transition towards the market economy and multi-party political democracy started in 1989–90 in Central Europe. Formerly nationalised industries have been privatized in various different ways and at different time, private enterprise is being promoted, and economic and political ties with Western European countries have been strengthened or re-established. The three Central European countries analysed here in more detail had become associate members of the EU by the early 1990s, and they joined the North Atlantic Treaty Organisation (NATO) in 1999. Their socioeconomic systems – and hence the overall business environment for local and foreign firms – had changed yet again.

The motor industry has been in the forefront of the radical economic developments seen in the region. New, foreign players have taken the lead, raising both production and sales considerably.

Foreign Direct Investment

The single most important development in the motor industry has been FDI in the form of acquisition of existing production facilities (brownfield investment) and the construction of new plants (greenfield investment). In just a few years all the major Czech, Hungarian and Polish automotive firms were privatised and sold to foreign investors, the existing car assembly and components manufacturing capacity was substantially modernised and extended, and new firms were established. As a result of these FDI projects, the products, processes, management techniques and markets of the Central European motor industry were radically restructured in a short period of time. The region has become integrated into the Western European automotive space through ownership links, production, procurement and sales networks.

It should be stressed, however, that the first major investment decisions by foreign companies had been made before the Central European countries became associate members of the EU. Economic integration preceded the start of the lengthy and cumbersome process of political integration. However, it is likely that both the managers of Western automotive firms and Central European government officials anticipated potential EU membership in their medium-term scenarios.[7]

The list of principal investors in Central Europe includes VW (with production facilities in all the three countries plus Slovakia, Bosnia, Belarus and Russia), Fiat (currently active only in its traditional Central European 'home country', Poland but with major plans in Russia again), Daewoo (with assembly and components plants in Central Europe, as well as Romania and in the former Soviet republics of Ukraine and Uzbekistan), GM Opel (with operations in Poland and Hungary), Ford (with car assembly and components plants in Central Europe as well as Belarus and Russia), Suzuki (car production in Hungary) and Isuzu (engine manufacturing in Poland).

FDI projects have reinforced pre-existing production patterns: the Czech Republic and Poland are specialising in car production, while components manufacturing has remained the core activity in the Hungarian automotive industry. FDI, however, has also resulted in rather spectacular changes in Hungary. Two foreign car companies, looking for favourable new locations and market opportunities, 'resurrected' the Hungarian car industry in the early 1990s after a 50-year interval. Both Opel Hungary and Magyar Suzuki started producing cars in 1992. A third manufacturer, Audi, started assembling cars in 1998.[8] It is also worth noting that Škoda, in contrast to earlier periods, is no long relying exclusively on its own technological capabilities. Following its acquisition by Volkswagen, new models based on platforms developed for the whole VW group are being introduced.

A common feature in Central Europe is that the new players, both assemblers and suppliers, in most cases replace – more precisely restructure and revitalise – formerly state-owned firms, as opposed to, for example, the Mercosur countries, where major transnational firms have had a long-established and strong presence.

The main motives inducing foreign investors to penetrate the Central European economies relate to international competitive conditions in the auto industry. Vehicle companies face strong competition and mature markets in their traditional area of operation. Moreover, they are not – and in the foreseeable future most likely they will not be – in a position to expect a technological breakthrough to solve their problems. Among the various strategies they have devised and implemented to cope with their difficulties, three are relevant for Central Europe:

- finding new markets with new customers and ideally less intense competition;
- cutting costs in order to keep existing markets by offering lower prices;
- introducing organisational innovations to improve flexibility and shorten lead and delivery times.

The above list can be read as a summary of 'push factors' forcing car makers and their suppliers to seek new locations. Central Europe offers promising opportunities to face these challenges. In other words, the region can be characterised by a number of 'pull factors'. Thus the motivations of the foreign investors can be understood as a combination of push and pull factors.

First, vehicle companies wanted to secure access to these new, emerging markets. Indeed, in 1990–91, when most projects were started or planned, the 'new democracies' seemed to offer excellent opportunities. Severe general shortages had induced sizeable forced savings in the previous decades, and most observers believed that people would rush to buy previously unavailable Western goods, especially cars, to replace their outdated and boring Ladas, Polski Fiats and Škodas. Equally important, Western consumer goods were new status symbols. The 65 million potential Central European consumers offered a powerful argument for setting up assembly capacity in any one of these countries to serve the whole region. In the beginning the geographical proximity to the potentially huge Russian market must have been even more significant. The 1990s, however, have seen general instability in Russia, and all the big motor industry projects announced so far have been postponed.

Secondly, wage differences between Western and Central European countries are considerable. German wages, for example, are still seven or eight times higher than Czech or Hungarian ones, and the productivity gap has almost been closed. In addition, trade unions are weak in Central Europe, for a number of reasons. In general, they have been discredited because of their close ties with the former political system. Further, rocketing unemployment – for decades an unknown phenomenon in these countries – has put employers into a favourable bargaining position, especially in the case of greenfield investment projects, in areas where no tradition of trade unions exists at all.[9] So when Western European car manufacturers had to face up to increasing Japanese competition, Central Europe seemed to be the right place to find low-cost and flexible production sites. Of course low wages alone would have not have been sufficient to attract foreign investors; they wanted skilled workers, too. Western managers unanimously and constantly express satisfaction with the skills and experience of Central European workers and engineers (interviews in Hungary, *The Economist*, 22 November 1997; *FT Auto*, 1 March 1999). With the profit margins on the production of small cars being really squeezed, it is hardly surprising that Fiat has located the entire production of its small cars, first the Cinquecento and then its successor, the Seicento, in Poland, and Suzuki also serves Western European markets from its Hungarian plant.

Thirdly, Central European countries are close to the major markets of Western Europe. Therefore, it is possible to exploit the above advantages without incurring large transport costs or facing daunting logistics tasks. Fourthly, the Central European region can also be an important production base for speciality models, where volumes are low and demand might be cyclical, and therefore both assembly costs and flexibility are of vital significance.[10] Fifthly, Central European countries have offered attractive investment grants and tax holidays to foreign investors. Of course, there is an intense world-wide competition for the 'goodwill' of investors, and a number of recent cases indicate that EU countries can provide much more significant grants (for example, the VW–Ford van plant in Portugal or the Rover case in the UK). Finally, as some cases already indicate, the region can also act a source and/or 'test bed' for a number of technological, organisational, managerial and social innovations to improve products, processes and flexibility of automotive companies.

Investments in car production

Most foreign investors have introduced new models, upgraded and extended production facilities.[11] Volkswagen has introduced three new models since it took over Škoda in 1991, investing DM2.4 billion by the end of 1998. Output has been increased from 172 000 units in 1991 to 403 000 units in 1998 (see Table 10.1). VW intends to spend a further DM3.4 billion by 2003. That includes a new, DM1 billion engine and transmission plant with an annual capacity of 500 000 units, commencing production in 2001.

Daewoo, the ambitious Korean car maker, based its strategy on expanding its overseas capacities and entering new markets both in Western and Eastern Europe. Poland, with both its potentially large domestic market and its location in the middle of Europe, offered an attractive location to implement this strategy. Therefore Daewoo acquired controlling stakes in two formerly state-owned Polish automotive companies: a 61 per cent stake in FSC Lublin was acquired in June 1995 for $61 million,[12] and then in February 1996 Daewoo took a 70 per cent holding (later raised to 80 per cent) in FSO, the producer of the outdated Polonez saloon car.[13] Daewoo renewed the Polonez and added a number of new models developed in South Korea. It had invested $1 billion by the end of 1998, while further projects are underway. Daewoo–FSO's capacity was 190 000 units per year in 1998, to be increased to 500 000 by the year 2000.[14]

Fiat was not only a pioneer in the previous era, but also among the first movers in the transition period. It started to restructure its long-established partner, the state-owned Fabryka Samochodow Malolitrazowych (FSM) in September 1991, and by May 1992 it had acquired a 90 per cent stake in the firm. Subsequently, the subsidiary was renamed Fiat Auto Poland. The Italian parent company had invested some US$1.3 billion in Poland by 1998, and planned to spend a further US$500 million by 2002 on new cars and engines. Fiat Auto Poland increased its output every single year after 1992, reaching 336 665 units in 1998. GM Opel's bid to acquire FSO was rejected by the Polish government in favour of Daewoo in 1996, but the European subsidiary

Table 10.1 Major data for Škoda, 1990–98

	1990	1991	1992	1993	1994	1995	1996	1997	1998
Production (units)	187181	172074	200059	219612	173586	208279	263193	357170	403515
Sales (units)[a]	187181	171885	199682	227013	179208	224771	279363	373451	400269
Revenues (billion Kc)	n/a	14	30.3	34.6	31.0	44.0	59.9	90.1	105.8
Profits (billion Kc)	n/a	−0.9	1.1	−4.3	−2.4	−1.6	0.2	1.2	2.2
Employment	21000	16983	17000	17048	16153	16835	17992	22205	22768

Note: [a] Includes imported Audi, VW and Seat models.
Source: Sdruzeni Automobilového Prumyslu and Škoda annual reports.

Table 10.2 Major data for Magyar Suzuki, 1992–98

	1992	1993	1994	1995	1996	1997	1998
Production	992	13021	19412	36453	51777	63630	66351
Domestic sales (units)	929	12659	16065	12178	13594	16039	23788
Exports (units)	n/a	n/a	3309	23873	38183	47700	42001
Sales (Ft million)	1907	9338	15468	36831	56777	77035	87152
domestic sales (Ft million)	1903	9272	13098	13333	15652	19117	31867
exports (Ft million)	4	66	2370	23498	41125	57918	55285
Profits before tax (Ft million)	n/a	−6840	−2046	−351	887	1651	16.0
Employment (average)	279	487	652	1032	1417	1547	1528
Productivity (cars/employees)	3.6	26.7	29.8	35.3	36.5	41.1	43.4

Sources: Magyar Suzuki and press reports.

of the world's largest carmaker did not want to abandon the largest market in Central Europe. Therefore, it built a new factory, initially investing DM530 million in a greenfield, integrated car plant at Gliwice, near Katowice, to manufacture 72 000 Astra Classic cars a year. Production began in August 1998, and local content was expected reach 60 per cent in 2–3 years. Opel invested a further DM375 million to launch a new mini car, developed jointly with Suzuki on the latter's Wagon R+ platform. This will be produced in Hungary from the year 2000 by Magyar Suzuki (see below), and marketed under different badges. The Opel version, called the Agila, would both increase capacity at Gliwice to 150 000 units a year and raise employment to 3000 workers.

Magyar Suzuki, a Japanese–Hungarian joint venture located in Esztergom, some 50 km from Budapest, commenced commercial production of compact cars in October 1992. Investment had totalled $260 million by 1997. A further $146 million has been invested to produce the aforementioned new small car. As a result of this project Magyar Suzuki's output will reach 100 000 units a year.

Finally, having opened an engine plant in Győr in Hungary in 1994, Audi also started assembling its two brand new sport models, TT Coupé and Roadster in 1998. Some 14 000 cars were produced in the first year, and output is expected to reach 40 000–50 000 units a year at full capacity.

The growth of car sales

With steadily increasing local production and liberalised imports, the Central European car market has grown in every single year since 1994, almost doubling in size by 1998, in spite of temporary contraction in some countries in certain years (for example, the Czech Republic in 1998, Hungary in 1995, Slovakia and Slovenia in 1997). Poland is not only by far the largest car market in the region, accounting for 57 per cent of the aggregate sales in 5 Central European markets, but it is also among the fastest growing ones, with sales more than doubling in the past 5 years (see Table 10.3). A significant part of this demand is supplied from Western Europe, as is shown in Chapter 3 by Humphrey and Oeter, in this volume.

As car ownership is still way behind the Western European or North American level, and economic growth and rising disposable incomes are forecast for the coming years in Central Europe, car sales should continue to increase, at least in the medium term.[15]

Table 10.3 New light vehicle sales in five Central European countries, 1994–98 (units)

	1994	*1995*	*1996*	*1997*	*1998*	*1998/94 (%)*
Poland	275368	294032	428168	503987	565098	205.2
Czech Republic[a]	119549	131790	179563	192150	156813	131.2
Hungary	102737	81128	87734	96529	126588	123.2
Slovakia	n/a	28285	80275	68498	76394	270.1[b]
Slovenia	48246	60926	66825	65275	72607	150.5
Total	545900	596161	842565	926439	997500	182.7

Notes: Light vehicles are understood as cars and trucks not over 3.5 tonne gross weight.
[a] Includes Slovakia for 1994. [b] 1998/1995.
Source: RJT Information Services.

CENTRAL EUROPE'S ROLE IN THE EUROPEAN DIVISION OF LABOUR

Central Europe has been rapidly integrated into the traditional Western European car space, mainly through FDI. Three major forms of specialisation can be observed in Central Europe *vis-à-vis* the EU. The bulk of the car production is comprised of low-end, high volume models meant for the EU, the domestic markets as well as other Central and Eastern European ones. High-end, low volume models, however, are also produced in the region, to be marketed mainly in the EU countries. Finally, components manufacturing is organised in European-wide production networks into which Central European plants are integrated. These patterns are analysed in some detail below, together with two other forms of inter-regional co-operation. One is testing and experimentation with organisational and social innovations which can later be transplanted back to Western Europe, and the other one is Central Europe's role in facilitating the access of East Asian car manufacturers to the EU.

Low-end, high-volume models for multiple markets

As has been described above, small Fiat models have long been produced in Poland for all Fiat's markets. This tradition has been continued by Fiat Auto Poland: first with the Fiat 126P, then the Cinquecento and currently the Seicento model. Output was around 230 000–250 000 units at the end of the 1990s, with half being exported, mainly to Western Europe.

Daewoo intends to expand its sales in Europe – both to the East and West – through its newly acquired production facilities in Central and Eastern Europe. To this end, its Polish operations offer a number of advantages: low production costs, a strong presence in the domestic market, geographic proximity to Western Europe and a 'back door' to this market to overcome trade barriers.

Opel intends to serve only the Central and Eastern European markets from its Polish operations, where a low-cost version of the last-but-one version of the Opel Astra model is produced. Of total output 60–70 per cent is planned to be sold in Poland, and the remaining 30–40 per cent in other Central and Eastern European countries. The primary driving force is low production costs, which makes it possible to offer moderately priced, entry-level cars in the region.

VW pursues a somewhat more complex strategy with its Czech operation. It has not only replaced the former small Škoda models, but also diversified its product range by introducing a medium-sized car, the Octavia, to compete with new Asian entrants, especially with the Korean firms, on both price and technology. In effect, it offers European-styled cars based on the same platforms as those used by other brands in the VW range. This represents advanced technology at a price below that of less advanced Korean models. These models are sold throughout Europe. This strategy seems to have been successful so far. As can be seen in Table 10.4, output has significantly increased and a major shift has occurred in the sales structure of Škoda: while two-thirds of its cars were sold in the domestic market (including Slovakia at that time) in 1990, Western European sales have since increased significantly, from 21 per cent of total sales in 1990 to 47 per cent in 1998.

High-end, low-volume models for EU markets

VW also has operations in Slovakia and Hungary, where flexible labour regulations and low wages make it profitable to produce low-volume, niche models for export. Having acquired BAZ, the largest Slovak vehicle company, in December 1991, VW has gradually moved the production of its four-wheel-drive Golf Syncro and Bora models to Bratislava. The operation has become the only plant making these

Table 10.4 Distribution of Škoda sales by region, 1992–1998

	1992		1993		1994		1995		1996		1997		1998	
	units	share	units	share	units	share	units	shares	units	share	units	share	units	share
Czech Republic[a]	94 429	47.5	79 954	36.5	63 756	34.7	72 078	34.4	87 394	33.5	100 459	29.9	81 729	22.5
Central and Eastern Europe	25 971	13.1	44 652	20.4	29 138	15.9	39 504	18.8	58 122	22.3	85 502	25.4	92 841	25.5
Western Europe	59 603	30.0	60 830	27.8	65 537	35.7	70 316	33.5	88 530	33.9	125 388	37.3	172 058	47.3
Other	18 679	9.4	33 722	15.4	25 193	13.7	27 693	13.2	27 021	10.4	24 958	7.4	16 882	4.6
Total	198 682	100	219 158	100	183 624	100	209 591	100	261 067	100	336 334	100	363 500	100

Note: [a] Includes Slovakia for 1992.
Source: Škoda Auto.

sophisticated, top-of-the-range models for the world market. The new generation four-wheel-drive Golfs have also been assembled there since the Autumn of 1997. Car output increased from 3000 units in 1993 to around 30000 units by 1996, and doubled again by 1998. VW invested DM700 million in 1999 to expand the plant's capacity to 200000–250000 units a year. Some 90 per cent of the output will be destined for export.

As was already mentioned above, VW established its Hungarian greenfield plant in Győr, where the Audi TT Coupé and Roadster cars have been assembled since 1998. Given the very nature of these sports models, volumes are much lower than those of popular small or medium-sized cars, and demand is more volatile. Therefore both assembly costs and the high level of flexibility – which cannot be even dreamed of in Germany due to the rigid labour regulations and strong unions – are of vital significance for profits.

Components manufacturing for export

Practically all the major components firms have established subsidiaries – either through taking over local companies or through investment in greenfield plants – in at least one of the three Central European countries. They have done so because they are pressured to follow their clients wherever they set up new plants.[16] The other major reason is that component manufacturers also have to cut their costs[17] without compromising quality. Therefore, the Central European countries – with their low production costs, skilled and experienced labour and geographic proximity to the European assembly plants – are ideal locations for first-tier (T1) suppliers serving car makers all over Europe. These T1 suppliers, in turn, attract some of their subcontractors, the second-tier suppliers (T2), to set up operations in the region. Yet another – rather widely used – form of co-operation organised by a T1 (or T2) supplier is to place long-term supply contracts with indigenous firms, in most cases providing know-how and licences as well. Exports are significantly boosted by these agreements, although this form of co-operation might be less stable because there are no ownership ties.

There are no significant differences between the three countries in this respect. It worth mentioning, however, that Hungary's traditional specialisation in components manufacturing has been considerably reinforced by recent investment projects and long-term contracts with foreign suppliers.[18] Both technologically advanced, high value-added parts (for example, engines, gearboxes, brakes) and low-end, low value-added ones (wiring harnesses, plastic and rubber parts, interior fittings) are manufactured in large volumes.

To highlight some important aspects of these investments, the cases of the two engine plants are summarised below. Flexible labour regulations coupled with highly skilled workers are the key to these investments because it is more profitable to run the fairly expensive engine production equipment round the clock.

Audi AG invested in a new engine manufacturing plant at Gyor, in Hungary. Audi Hungaria Motor Kft (AHM) was opened in October 1994. It was the first engine plant in the world to commercially manufacture five-valve, four-cylinder engines. This new engine generation is built into Audi, Volkswagen Passat, SEAT and Škoda models. Audi had invested some DM1.2 billion by 1999, in several stages as output increased and various engine components were added to the product line. Production of six- and eight-cylinder petrol engines has also been re-located to Gyor. AHM assembled almost 1 million engines in 1998,[19] and it became Hungary's number one exporter.

GM Opel's Hungarian engine factory opened in 1992. It supplies various car assembly plants across Europe.[20] As a result of these secure markets Opel Hungary was making profits in the first full year of its operation, in 1993, and it was Hungary's fourth largest exporter. Opel also intends to build a new gearbox factory with a capacity of 250000 units a year. This is a new product, to be manufactured only in Hungary at first. Production is planned to commence in 2001 initially with 15 per cent local content, to be raised to 50 per cent. With this project GM Opel's investment in Hungary would total over DM900 million.

These two big engine plants, together with gearbox factories, in turn, attract suppliers to follow them. That is why German and French foundries, machining companies and clutch manufacturers are setting up their Hungarian operations (for example, ADA, Pre-cast, Le Belier, VAW, Erbslöh, Jung and LUK). It is a rather advantageous development from the point of view of the balance of payments, since less engine components are imported and more Hungarian value-added is created and exported. These cases deserve both analysts' and policy-makers' attention for another reason: they resemble the follow sourcing arrangement between car makers and their T1 suppliers, with its all complex corollaries.

Finally, it is also worth noting that the new market opportunities created by foreign automotive firms seeking Central European subcontractors has also facilitated the survival of some non-automotive firms whose former markets have shrunk or disappeared in the transition period. For instance, Videoton, previously only active in information technology and consumer and military electronics, has become a major automotive supplier by converting some of its established business units and building new ones. With declining demand for agricultural machinery, some commercial vehicle producers and their associated suppliers have also lost a significant chunk of their former markets, and some of these firms have found new sales opportunities thanks to the integration of Central Europe into the European automotive space.

A laboratory for organisational innovations

Foreign investors also use their Central European operations to test various managerial, organisational and social innovations. In greenfield plants employees and managers are not 'spoilt' by traditional Western European practices. Even when existing facilities are acquired, new plants are frequently built next to them, or only the former buildings are kept, and all the machinery is replaced in parallel with the introduction of new organisational arrangements. These new, or completely restructured, plants are usually smaller than their 'home' operations, and thus the risks involved in introducing new methods are correspondingly smaller. Unions are non-existent or much weaker, labour legislation is more flexible, and employees are more willing to learn. They are less protected by unions than, say, their German counterparts, less influenced by former practices, and more intensely motivated because of unemployment and the relatively high wages paid by foreign-owned companies. The introduction of these innovations is still far from a smooth, friction-free process, even in the new locations in Central Europe, and their results cannot be transplanted back to the 'home' plants without modification. However, even indirect, demonstration effects might have considerably impacts on the old production and management practices and unions agreements in the home plants.

The most notable experiment in the region is VW–Škoda's experiment with a JIT-type concept of cost cutting, called the supply integration scheme.[21] By 1999 seven firms had already been allocated special zones adjacent to the production line to pre-assemble parts into sub-systems, such as rear axles, seats, carpets, bumpers, instrument panels and exhaust systems. These are supplied directly to the assembly line for the new Octavia saloon, and Škoda is seeking to find further integrated suppliers. In this way Škoda can integrate them directly into the production process, cutting transportation costs and delivery times as well improving quality control and speeding up design and production changes. The current seven suppliers, each a joint venture with access to Western capital, have invested DM300 million in production facilities at the Škoda plant in return for long-term supply contracts. There are similar plans for allocating space to other suppliers in the press and paint shops.

Although this is a new factory, Škoda's century-long traditions do play a role. The unions were initially against the arrangement, and they eventually reached an agreement with the management that suppliers, who usually employ low-paid, non-unionised workers, cannot perform any jobs directly on the assembly line. Yet, they are still concerned that the presence of poorly paid workers, could influence the relatively good wages of unionized Škoda employees, which are some 40–50 per cent higher than the Czech average. As half of the workers at the Octavia plant are employed by the integrated suppliers, this fear is well founded.

Clearly, VW intends to test this new production regime in its smaller and more flexible Czech operation and then apply it in larger plants: 'Whether for VW or Opel, the aim is to transfer the experience back to Western Germany', says a manager who has worked for both companies (*FT*, 13 February 1997). Indeed, after the successful test with the new Octavia plant, including its supply integration scheme, the German engineer who designed it was given the even more demanding job of running the Wolfsburg facility in 1996.

Audi, the other branch of the VW group, is relying extensively on outsourcing to make its Hungarian operation even more flexible. A large chunk of logistics, cleaning, catering and data processing has been outsourced. In this way not only can employment contracts be replaced by supply contracts with service providers, reducing management costs, but it is also much easier to adjust to changes in the business environment, as there is no need to directly (re-)negotiate contracts with employees.

Tier one suppliers are also experimenting in Central Europe. ZF, the large German engineering firm, has taken over a relatively small gearbox plant in Hungary. Machinery has been replaced, and the whole production and management process has been re-arranged along the lines of the so-called manufacturing cell concept. The number of management layers has been cut drastically, and employees and the remaining middle managers have been given more responsibilities. Although it is not advertised as a new solution to be implemented at other ZF plants around the globe, most likely the experience gained from this experiment will also be utilised at other locations.

Asian firms: entry to EU markets through Central Europe

Central European countries offer an advantageous location for Asian firms seeking access to EU markets at least for two reasons. The most obvious one is their geographic proximity to the Western European market. But their political status is even more important. As they are associated members of the EU, local content immediately counts as EU content, and thus it is easier to reach the 60 per cent EU content required for duty-free access to EU markets. Magyar Suzuki exported almost 40000 cars to the EU in the late 1990s, roughly two-thirds of its output. This volume is likely to increase as its new model, produced from the beginning of the year 2000, is obviously meant for EU markets, too. Finally, Daewoo started exporting to the EU duty-free from Poland in July 1999 when the EU content of its Lanos model reached the 60 per cent threshold. Sales were projected to reach 8500–10000 units in the first year, gradually increasing to some 80000 units by 2007.

THE IMPACT OF AUTOMOTIVE FDI ON THE LOCAL SUPPLIER INDUSTRY

Automotive FDI projects are among the biggest new investments in Central Europe. In all three countries there are 2–3 automotive investments in the top ten FDI projects. These projects have a major direct impact on employment output and trade in Central Europe. Indirectly, through their demonstration effects, they also help to attract further investments, both automotive and non-automotive. These broad effects on the local economy cannot be discussed here. The more modest aim of this section is to analyse the impact of investments in the motor industry on the local supplier base.[22]

As car makers pursue different overall strategies in different regions and/or different periods of time when setting up assembly operations in foreign countries, diverse supply network strategies can be identified. As this is the case in Central Europe, too, it is useful to characterise these evolving new, local supplier networks in the form of a tentative taxonomy:

- *No local supply.* Car companies often set up so-called CKD operations, assembling imported kits. This gives access to otherwise protected markets, and can provide experience of local conditions that might be useful if production is localised at a later date.
- *In-house component manufacturing.* In some cases, especially in Central and Eastern Europe, a foreign investor takes over a vertically integrated indigenous car company. Thus the in-house component operations constitute a decisive element of local supply. However, more recently car companies are divesting even their organically developed in-house component divisions (for example, Delphi and Visteon in the cases of GM and Ford), and hence they have less interest in keeping inherited in-house manufacturing. In short, the current trend to vertical disintegration is undermining the significance of this type of supply strategy.
- *Long-established foreign suppliers.* Large car firms usually prefer to deal with their long-established, reliable suppliers when entering new markets. Therefore, the T1 suppliers are persuaded to follow – by setting up joint ventures with indigenous suppliers, acquiring local firms or investing in greenfield plants.
- *New foreign suppliers.* In other cases, a car company establishes contacts with new suppliers from a third country. This has been seen frequently in the case of Asian assemblers in Europe (for example, Japanese car plants in the UK purchase components from suppliers located in other European countries).
- *'Nurturing' a local supply base.* Strict local content regulations, including the 60 per cent EU content set by Brussels, or factors such as technological excellence in the host country's automotive sector, might motivate car assemblers to build a local supplier network. This might consist of indigenous suppliers or existing T1 suppliers, depending on the overall performance of the existing local suppliers.

Car makers have applied all the above strategies when devising and implementing their supply policies in Central Europe.

Negligible local supply

In addition to its Czech, Hungarian and Slovak operations, VW also has an assembly plant in Poland. In order to avoid prohibitive Polish tariffs, various models (in 1998 all Škoda models, three Seat models, five VW and one Audi model) were assembled from kits in Poznan. Not surprisingly these kits are, in fact, ready cars, shipped in just a few major parts. With the exception of Škoda Felicias and VW Transporters, these kits could be 're-assembled' in less than an hour.[23] The local content of Opel Astras assembled in Hungary until 1998 was also very low, at around 10 per cent.

These practices are a transitory. Opel has already consolidated its Central European car assembly operation by building its new Polish plant, and as automotive tariffs will be substantially reduced, VW also will have to reconsider its presence in Poland. Its Poznan plant will either be closed down, or developed into a genuine assembly operation. VW seems to be opting, having invested DM350 million to add a body welding plant, paint shop and assembly lines, initially for the VW Polo and Škoda Octavia models. It is still unlikely, however, that local suppliers will gain any business from this plant. They can only win orders if they ship parts for VW–Škoda, which probably means meeting the exacting demands of the entire VW group.

Local suppliers replaced or acquired by long-established foreign suppliers

When the Czech government and VW revised their original privatisation agreement in 1994, VW committed itself to develop further the Czech car components industry. Given that Czech and Slovakian parts accounted for some 80 per cent of Škoda's total purchase in the early 1990s, this commitment was of crucial importance, but not without conflicts: 'A lot of domestic suppliers have been unable to fulfil our orders so we have been searching for foreign companies willing to set up here', said a company spokesperson in 1998.[24] Thus VW strengthened the local supply base by attracting some 80 foreign components manufacturers to acquire indigenous suppliers or build greenfield sites by 1998. Therefore, the value of parts manufactured locally decreased only slightly after 1994, and still accounted for two-thirds of the total spending on components in 1998.[25] However, an increasing share of these locally made components have been supplied by foreign-owned firms.

Fiat acquired in-house component manufacturing facilities when it bought FSM. Since then, in line with current global trends, Fiat Auto Poland has been seeking to scale back these in-house activities in order to cut its costs and improve quality by transferring certain activi-

Table 10.5   Škoda's component purchases by country of origin

	1994		1998	
	Kc billion	*Share (%)*	*Kc billion*	*Share (%)*
Czech Republic	14.0	71.4	45.4	66.4
Slovak Republic	2.1	10.7	3.1	4.5
Other	3.5	17.9	19.9	29.1
Total	19.6	100.0	68.4	100.0

Source: Škoda Auto, annual reports.

Table 10.6   Fiat Auto Poland suppliers by ownership, 1992–96

	Dec. 1992	*Dec. 1993*	*Dec. 1994*	*Dec. 1995*	*Sept. 1996*
Polish	405	335	297	248	235
Foreign	215	211	193	188	177
Total	620	546	490	436	412

Source: Fiat Auto Poland.

ties to top-ranking international suppliers. In other words, it is reducing its level of vertical integration.[26] In the meantime, it has been restructuring its entire supply base by reducing the number of its direct suppliers and attracting foreign suppliers to set up businesses in Poland. As Table 10.6 clearly indicates, Polish suppliers are most likely to be axed as Fiat Auto Poland trims its supply base.

As in the case of VW in the Czech Republic, this does not mean that the share of locally produced components has been falling. On the contrary, the share of parts produced in Poland, rose from 55 per cent in 1993 to 74 per cent in 1997.[27] A declining number of Polish suppliers has been offset by a growing number of foreign suppliers operating in Poland.

Asian firms: strong incentives to promote local suppliers

Asian firms face a different situation. As they have to reach 60 per cent EU content if they want to enter EU markets without paying tariffs, they cannot simply import from their Asian supply bases. They are obliged to source more parts locally or from EU members or associate members. Daewoo's supply strategy in Poland is based on FSO's former in-house components divisions, which was included in the acquisition deal. These operations were quickly turned into joint ventures, with Daewoo–FSO retaining majority holdings. Altogether, some 20 joint ventures had been set up by 1999, and although most were with Korean partners, some were with US and German partners, such as with Dana and Henkel. In some cases, formerly independent local suppliers are also involved, but these are usually taken over by Korean firms. Formerly independent local suppliers are also teaming up with other foreign firms. Those that have had a long-established co-operation can act as more or less equal partners, but most indigenous firms are taken over by foreign suppliers. Leading components manufacturers have also set up their own Polish subsidiaries to supply Daewoo. In these cases, the plant will have other clients as well.

Magyar Suzuki also had to reach 60 per cent EU content in order to export its cars to the EU duty-free. It buys parts in relatively low volumes – it only produced some 60 000–65 000 cars a year in the late 1990s – but follows a single sourcing strategy. Therefore, it has very strong incentives to nurture a local supply base. Accordingly, it pays special attention to the viability of its suppliers. Together with its Japanese suppliers it conducts a thorough technological and financial audit, covering literally every single aspect of doing business from purchasing inputs through to production methods and machinery, accounting, sales and management. Joint efforts are made to improve the selected supplier's technical level and economic performance, as required.

Local content was only 25 per cent in October 1992, but it almost doubled to 48 per cent by the end of 1993 as a result of an extensive and rapid localisation programme. Since then localisation has continued at a much slower pace, reaching 53 per cent by 1997. Magyar Suzuki had 34 suppliers based in Hungary in 1995, and 45 in 1998. It has some 35–40 suppliers from EU countries, and three Central European ones, all partly or wholly foreign owned.

The impact of FDI on the indigenous components industry

Recent FDI projects have had controversial effects on the collaboration among Central European countries. FDI, together with some other developments in the transition process, have had significant impacts on the indigenous supply base. Sweeping changes can be witnessed both downstream and upstream. With the collapse of the CMEA and the advent of the new foreign players most former, long-established supplier relationships have been disrupted. Some local companies have clearly lost out in the process. For example some long-established Hungarian suppliers lost their former businesses when Fiat took over FSM in Poland.

Similarly, market volatility has affected suppliers. The Polish supplier, WSK, was to ship 20 000 radiators a year for a van produced by Daewoo Motor Polska. The assembler, however, after taking 6000 units, reduced the order to 50 units a quarter. WSK demands that Daewoo refunds the costs of the necessary tooling,[28] but this case shows how defenceless the local suppliers can be.

The foreign investors are organising their activities at a regional rather than national level. The most notable example is VW: engines produced by its Audi branch in Hungary are built into its Czech-made models, it also opened a diesel engine plant in Poland in 1999 to serve Škoda and other VW operations in Europe, and also started building a Polish seat plant. Opel Polska and Magyar Suzuki also co-operate to make sure that components for their jointly developed small vehicle – built both in Poland and Hungary – are produced in economical volumes. The timely entry of the foreign investors does mean that new opportunities are available. Some firms have been able to take these opportunities, and they have survived, often after a painful and radical restructuring process. Others, however, have failed and disappeared. The restructuring of the industry means, firstly, that indigenous suppliers cannot survive without a foreign partner, which either provides long-term contracts or assumes full control. Secondly, it means that in some parts of the industry, less sophisticated products are manufactured – for example, not engines or gearboxes but components for these products, or parts for dashboards rather than the complete system.

Some politicians would characterise this as 'colonisation', and even some observers might talk of downgraded suppliers and the destruction of skills and competences. However, one also has to ask if there is any other viable alternative to the current restructuring and integration process. History has proven that the planned economy system and the CMEA-type integration which created these local suppliers cannot be sustained. Some skills – especially technical ones – accumulated in that era might still be valuable, but obviously with some adjustment and upgrading. Others are no longer useful, and a fairly important set of skills and knowledge was simply missing, most notably marketing, finance and accounting. These need to be acquired, and foreign partners have been instrumental in facilitating this learning process. The introduction of new products, production processes and management techniques as well as access to new markets are, to a very large extent, due to these foreign partners. The real question is the future role of the local suppliers in European or global production networks. They can operate at a fairly low technical level, producing parts with low value-added, and hence pay low wages, or they can perform much higher value-added tasks by exploiting and continuously developing their skill base, as partners or subsidiaries of foreign-owned first- or second-tier suppliers. They might acquire some R&D functions, but again in co-operation with partners also integrated into the same network. Therefore, both governments and local managers should be aware of their significant responsibilities to choose and facilitate a given trajectory for the sector as a whole and for individual firms. Foreign investors, of course, do influence the strategic choices available for the Central European firms with their own decisions and actions. However, it is clear that it is no longer feasible to create or sustain 'national' first-tier suppliers.[29]

CONCLUSIONS

The history of the Central European motor industry clearly shows the importance of heritage, in the form of accumulated skills and specialisation patterns, as well as the vital corollaries of inter- and intra-regional structures, the wider socio-economic environment and industrial policies. These factors can be identified by analysing the radical changes that have occurred in the last 90 years. A detailed analysis of recent changes, however, leads to more direct policy conclusions.

Investment activities across borders have significantly intensified in the 1990s as firms attempt to cut costs via relocation of production, and to move closer to consumers in emerging markets. Central Europe is no exception to this: the region has moved again onto the global stage. Almost all the major automotive groups, with the exception of the leading Japanese car firms – Toyota, Nissan, Honda and Mitsubishi – have already set up operations in Central Europe.

These strategic moves have radically restructured the indigenous automotive industry, both assemblers and suppliers. In other words, the transition has been accomplished in this sector. Some local firms have been taken over by foreign firms, while others have been integrated into the global networks of major automotive groups as subcontractors. In both cases new products, processes and management techniques have been introduced rapidly.

Foreign investors have chosen Central European countries partly because skilled labour is relatively cheap – around one-seventh of the German wages. Yet, had wages alone been sufficient to improve competitiveness, Western car firms would have gone to the Ukraine and other parts of the Former Soviet Union, where labour is even cheaper. In fact, what really matters is that Czech, Hungarian and Polish workers are highly skilled as a result of a German-style vocational training system having been in place for many decades. As quality, reliability and productivity are all major concerns for car companies, there is no need to emphasise the importance of skills and experience. In short, the real advantage is the excellence of workers coupled with low wages. Further, foreign companies find flexible employment conditions in the region: shift work and overtime working is a commonplace, offering investors a production regime to suit their needs.

In sum, the successful restructuring of the Central European motor industry is not only due to 'push' factors such as fierce competition among automotive companies and the pursuit of cost cutting through production relocation, but also arises from 'pull' factors such as the attractions of the region's economic environment, broadly defined. However, some of the attractions – especially differences in wages and labour legislation – might vanish as early as the next 5 to 10 years. Therefore other 'pull' factors have to be strengthened, most notably skills, in order to find a mutually advantageous development path. In order to devise and implement such strategies, local managers and government officials should closely co-operate because both parties have their own responsibilities and tools. Their efforts can only be successful if they take into account the ever changing and global nature of the automotive industry, as well as the evolving strategies of the major multinational firms active in the region. In other words, no country can be complacent. On the contrary, continuously renewed, concerted efforts and well-devised policy measures are needed to achieve further results.

Notes

1. It should be noted that Yugoslavia never joined the CMEA.
2. When the current Škoda models, based to a large extent on VW technologies, are praised in the motoring press, it is always mentioned that former models became the butt of endless jokes, particularly in the UK.
3. Production was still 12350 and 11980 units in 1988 and 1989, respectively. The collapse of CMEA caused a dramatic drop in output to 7994 units in 1990, and almost every year since then has seen a further decline.
4. The single most important buyer was the (former) Soviet VAZ (Lada) factory. Other significant customers included the Polish FSO and FSM (Polski Fiat) companies, as well as Dacia in Romania. Although (the former) Yugoslavia never joined the CMEA, Hungarian parts were also shipped to its car producer, Zastava (now in Serbia), until the UN embargo.
5. This summary draws upon Volpato (1998).
6. Eventually Fiat 126P was produced until 1994 – in the last 2–3 years mainly for the domestic market – while output of Cinquecento reached 312000 units by 1997.
7. Layan, analysing the Spanish and Mexican car industries, calls a similar process 'as much a rational expectation as a self-fulfilling prophecy' (see Chapter 6 in this volume).
8. Opel Hungary stopped manufacturing cars in 1998 because of the opening of Opel Polska. Opel Hungary has concentrated on producing engines and cylinder heads, while gearboxes will be manufactured from 2001.
9. Note that Japanese investors have also opted for industrial 'deserts', or declining areas with no unions, when setting up their plants in the USA and UK. A similar pattern can be found in Mexico and Spain. (see Chapter 6 in this volume). Audi, however, has located its engine and car plant right in the heart of the Hungarian industry, in Györ, so as to get access to skilled labour, and also to take advantage of the developed infrastructure.
10. For example, see the cases of the Golf Syncro and the new Audi sports models discussed below.
11. From time to time, however, promised investments are postponed or cancelled. Obviously this causes tensions between the host country and the investor, see for example the VW-Skoda case in 1994 (Havas, 1997).
12. Daewoo also promised to invest a further US$340 million in upgrading production facilities.
13. The Polonez was launched in 1978, but its design dates back to the 1960s.
14. It should be stressed, however, that Daewoo's crisis in 1998–99 left many of these plans uncertain. Its subsidiaries in Central and Eastern Europe face an uncertain future.
15. Economic prospects are more gloomy in a number of Eastern European countries – for example, in Bulgaria and Romania.
16. The issue of follow sourcing is analysed in Chapter 7 by Humphrey and

Salerno, in this volume. The Central European case is discussed in the final section of this chapter.

17. It is a common practice to ask suppliers to slash their prices 5 per cent a year. Assemblers want to share the savings stemming from the so-called learning curve effect in return for their large, long-term orders.

18. Data analysed in Havas (forthcoming) clearly show that components manufacturing is much more important than car assembly in Hungary. Major components manufacturing operations serving European – or some cases even South American – assembly plants have been set up in Hungary by firms such as Delphi, Ford, Denso, Knorr-Bremse, ZF, United Brake Parts, BPW, Alcoa, Continental Teves, Lear, Leoni, Packard Electric, Delco Remi, Michels Kabel, Michelin, Keiper-Recaro, Superior Industries International Inc., Otto Fuchs Metallwerke, Happich, Hammerstein and VDO Car Communication.

19. The VW group produced 3.6 million engines in 1998, and thus AMH accounted for more than a quarter of total production (Economist Intelligence Unit).

20. Its original capacity has been doubled to 460000 units a year. This is around one quarter of Opel's total European engine production of 1.8 million units in 1998 (Economist Intelligence Unit).

21. VW introduced a similar but more radical scheme at its Resende truck plant in Brazil.

22. It is beyond the scope of this chapter to analyse the impact of 'automotive-related' investment and trade on employment and the balance of payments.

23. *Polish News Bulletin*, 13 January 1999, based on the 12 January issue of *Gazeta Wyborcza*, p. 18.

24. Cited in 'Selling to Skoda', *Business Central Europe*, July/August 1999, pp. 13–14.

25. It is not clear, however, if the value of the parts supplied directly by the VW group is included in this calculation. The answer is probably not, given that different sources put the 'German' content of the Octavia between 50 and 80 per cent.

26. Fiat Auto Poland is, in fact, following the strategy of its parent company. Fiat has recently sold a number of in-house components operations to independent suppliers. It should also be noted that Fiat was the most vertically integrated Western European car manufacturer.

27. Information supplied by Fiat Auto Poland.

28. *Polish News Bulletin*, 2 September 1998, based on the 2 September 1998 issue of *Reczpospolita*, No. 205, p. 11.

29. A similar conclusion for the cases of Brazil and India is reached by Humphrey and Salerno in Chapter 7, in this volume.

References

HAVAS, A. (1997) 'Foreign direct investment and intra-industry trade: the case of automotive industry in Central Europe'. In Dyker, D. (ed.), *The*

Technology of Transition. Budapest: Central European University Press, pp. 211–40.

HAVAS, A. (forthcoming) 'Local, regional and global production networks: re-integration of the Hungarian automotive industry'. In von Hirschhausen, C. and Bitzer, J. (eds), *The Globalization of Industry and Innovation in Eastern Europe – from Post-socialist Restructuring to International Competitiveness*. Cheltenham: Edward Elgar.

VOLPATO, G. (1998) 'Fiat Auto and Magneti Marelli: toward globalization'. *Actes du Gerpisa*, No. 22, pp. 69–97.

Index

·